In praise of *Amer*...

"Louise Esola has shed new light on a tragic chapter of the Vietnam War. She has dug deeply into an accident at sea that took the lives of 74 young American sailors and has told their stories brilliantly! *American Boys* is worth your attention."

—Joseph L. Galloway, Bronze Star recipient, Vietnam War combat journalist, and co-author of *We Were Soldiers Once...and Young*

"Louise Esola has done a remarkable job of research in putting together this forgotten story of 74 young men who lost their lives on the USS *Frank E. Evans* during the Vietnam War. Ms. Esola, writing with conviction and compassion, does a long-neglected service to the memories of those killed in the line of duty. As a Vietnam War veteran myself, I salute Louise Esola and all those who have given their time and energy to keep alive the memories of the fallen."

—Bestselling author and Vietnam veteran Nelson DeMille

"With Louise Esola's powerful storytelling, *American Boys* uncovers a lost chapter of history full of grace and determination. A compelling read."

—Gregory A. Freeman, bestselling author of *Sailors to the End: The Deadly Fire on the USS Forrestal and the Heroes Who Fought It*

"With stellar reporting and strong writing, Louise Esola has rescued a largely forgotten incident of the Vietnam War: the sinking of the destroyer *Frank E. Evans* in 1969. *American Boys* traces the sailors from hometowns across America to their service aboard the ill-fated ship, giving the sailors the respect that their country has denied them. *American Boys* could easily become a classic story of men and war."

—Tony Perry, *Los Angeles Times*

"*American Boys* is that rare offering, and deserves its own commendation as a piece of powerful research into a segment of Vietnam history that many have tried to bury over the decades...one that deserves to not be forgotten."

—*Midwest Book Review*

"This is the story of one of the greatest—still unresolved— tragedies of the Vietnam War, one the U.S. Navy has pretended had nothing to do with it. *American Boys* explores the realities of Vietnam naval operations and, in evocative prose and stunning detail, it reports the sinking of the American destroyer *Frank E. Evans*, along with the decades-long struggle of survivors and families to get the Navy to acknowledge the truth of the matter. This book should be read and those *Evans* sailors commemorated."

—John Prados, author of *Vietnam: The History of an Unwinnable War, 1945-1975*

"Louise Esola's finely-wrought account of a Vietnam-era disaster at sea and its unending impact on the drowned sailors' loved ones will echo in your mind long after you've put it down. This beautiful, heart-breaking book should be required reading at the Pentagon and the White House."

—Jack Cheevers, author of *Act of War: Lyndon Johnson, North Korea, and the Capture of the Spy Ship Pueblo.*

"*American Boys* is an important story, beautifully told. Long after you finish this book, you will remember the men of the USS *Frank E. Evans*, and understand why the fight to include the names of its 74 lost crew members continues."

—Kristen Graham, Pulitzer prize-winning journalist with the *Philadelphia Inquirer*

About the cover

Before he deployed for Vietnam 19-year-old Danny Clute bought a camera to document his adventures with the United States Navy. In May 1969 his ship, the USS Frank E. Evans, sat off the coast of Vietnam firing thousands of shells to support troops on the ground. Later that month Danny left the film in Subic Bay, Philippines to be developed. On June 3, 1969 he was killed. Kodak Eastman Company tracked down the Clute family in San Jose, California to give them Danny's slides. That, some letters, and a telegram were all that was left.

AMERICAN
BOYS

THE TRUE STORY OF THE
LOST 74 OF THE VIETNAM WAR

LOUISE ESOLA

For ordering information please visit www.louiseesola.com or write
louise.esola@yahoo.com.

PENNWAY BOOKS

ISBN-13: 978-0-9960574-0-0
LCCN: 2014913432

Cover Design by Jenni Wheeler
Cover photograph courtesy of the Clute family
Typeset by Sophie Chi

Printed in the United States of America

This book is dedicated to my children
Salvatore and Santiago,
who taught me the kind of love that made this possible.
To my husband David,
who supported me every step of the way.
And to those whose lives were forever changed that day,
lest we forget.

❤

"The definition of a modern approach to war is the acknowledgement of individual lives lost."

—*Maya Lin*

CONTENTS

would it help
the nightmares
I hear our ship breaking up
people calling for help
and they have people in the water
can't get to them
tried
help one
he was hit
steam
I caught his arms
I stayed with his skin
took him to sick bay but that was gone
people hanging from their dead
people calling for on the part that sank
no life jackets
just people walking around in shock
people in the water dying
this goes on 24/7/365 days a year

—Chester Moneaux,
USS *Frank E. Evans* survivor
Delcambre, Louisiana, 2013

PROLOGUE

NAMES

November 1982

In a city of white stone buildings and marble statues of great men long gone, they made an incision in the earth. From the fresh-laid grass rose a place to communicate with the dead. The leaves had turned gold, and there was a slight chill in the air. At dusk, as those in three-button suits who often decided the fate of the nation made for home under a purpling sky, workers polished the black granite, tracing the letters with their fingers. They, like the others, were taken aback by the immensity of it all: My God, the price in chiseled typeface. A terrible folly set forever in stone. Nearby, a long procession of monotone syllables echoed within the National Cathedral, like the reading at a holy day service: *John . . . Robert . . . Dale . . . James.* Each one a story.

The somber homecoming parade had begun.

Ann Armstrong Dailey was one of many on the way to Washington National Airport that second week in

November. The nation's capital seemed even busier than usual. Election day had just passed, and Thanksgiving was still to come, yet the hotels were booked solid. The incomers were less official, less touristy—no briefcases, no boxes of Kodak film. Some wore ragged U.S. Army fatigues, medals over denim, embroidered patches that told their stories. Some had beards and long hair. They looked like they'd been to hell and back—they wore it on their faces. A few carried signs: "Never Again" and "Never Forget." There were the old couples, too, the ones whose hair, and lives, had gone gray. They walked with canes, weighed down by grief. Brothers and sisters, much younger, pushed strollers, carried children on their shoulders, or dragged along teenagers, for whom this was all part of the legend, family lore, someone they'd once known but whose face they couldn't recall. These people, pouring into Washington that fall, had a bond. "It was as if they were all drawn by the same ghostly bugle," a newspaperman had typed. Their eyes still welled up if you asked them about that time—the day the telegram came, the moment they held a hand for the last time, the day they lost their youth, the time when they knew everything that was would never be again. A line between then and now. A barrier hard and cold as stone.

Ann was there, looking for her youngest sibling, thinking of another.

She remembers Alan in a black bow tie and suit at Patricia's wedding in Edmonds, Washington. It was May 1968, at an uncle's old farmhouse—Chubby Checker on the record player, buttercream frosting, the constant flash of the Kodachrome. There's one photograph in particular. It's a snapshot of two beautiful sisters, one in a red sleeveless number Jackie Kennedy might have worn around Camelot, the other in delicate lace, crowned with a swath of snow-white tulle. Their mother, wearing a thick, wavy-haired wig, faces them. The wedding was rushed. Their mother, ailing with cancer, would be dead within months. That they knew. Their brother Alan stands tall, to their right, gazing forward. A young, stoic patriarch, he's wearing dark-framed glasses, the kind his comrades would joke about as a sort of birth control—if an ineffective one; at twenty-six, Alan already had a wife and young son. *His whole life ahead of him.* It might be a cliché, but it was true nonetheless, and it's how his sisters remember him. So young.

Incredibly bright, Alan scored high on intelligence tests and was good with his hands. In high school he built a ham radio and gave himself the call sign W7JBG—"Jumping Beautiful Girls," to those uninitiated in the language of amateur radio. A university education seemed the obvious path. But despite his aptitude, Alan hated school, limping through his first go at college with Cs and Ds before calling it quits. After some talk with a family friend, a retired Army colonel, he enlisted in the U.S. Navy—the safest choice, he was assured, as war loomed on the horizon.

First he took on the life of a submariner. Not exactly safe, was his assessment after the Navy lost the USS *Thresher* and her crew of 129 men in the North Atlantic in 1963. That, and he saw firsthand the suffocating life of submariner. At the urging of some senior officers who were impressed with his intelligence, Alan applied to the United States Naval Academy, but was unable to secure a spot as a midshipman due to poor vision. In a story that made Ann chuckle, Alan intentionally left his eyeglasses home the day of his entrance exams so much that he squinted profusely during the tests, trying to mask the one inadequacy he couldn't help—nor hide, as a proctor would point it out immediately. But the Navy, likely keen on keeping him in the ranks, found him an alternative path to officer. On his second go, he finished a four-year college program in three, collecting a degree in engineering and a pretty young wife. He pinned ensign some time before his sister's wedding day.

The day the snapshot was taken. The last day they were all together.

Alan didn't have his assignment yet, but his sisters knew that their time with their brother would be brief. Eventually he'd do what sailors do: ship out. There was this war. A place no one could find on a map a decade before had become a hot zone—a dirty word on college campuses, a name intoned on almost every newscast. Vietnam.

A little over a year after the wedding, the war would take their Alan.

How fleeting their time with him would be, the young women in the photograph could never have imagined. It happened too fast, without warning. There was no peace about my brother's death, Patricia would say. "He was just gone, and that was it." In the years that followed, the thought of Alan would send this grieving sister to a mountain overlooking the ocean by her home, where memories and pain would roll fresh and raw. Life goes on, as they say. Yet years did nothing for Patricia and Ann. Alan was still young, would never grow old. They thought of him every day, but nothing could bring him back.

A decade drifted by; they woke to a new one. People were saying the war had been a waste, a mistake, a wrong turn in the fog. "Was there a point when the looming collision might have been averted?" one Vietnam War historian would ask. Rhetorically and with no answer.

And now two women found themselves woven into the droves of mothers and sisters, brothers and wives, children and fathers, descending upon Washington in the fall of 1982. All of them longing for meaning, for a chapter that would close the book. Something that memorialized their loss in a war nobody wanted to remember. Something that said: This all really happened.

There'd been nothing like that.

Nothing. Nowhere.

And then came the wall.

The idea of a memorial to the more than 58,000 Americans killed in the Vietnam War was born in March 1979, the child of Hollywood and a tortured combat veteran who couldn't sleep. As it did so many, the war haunted Jan Scruggs, who had spent a year in country with the U.S. Army 199th Light Infantry Brigade. The flashbacks were always the same. He's back in Xuan Loc, South Vietnam. It's the morning of May 28, 1969. He's a skinny kid, the son of a milkman and a waitress, and he's slogging along a trail in the hellfire heat. It was said the poor fought the war, those unfortunate sons. By the time the sun had burned the dew off the grass, the unseen enemy is at them again. Bullets graze him, a grenade goes off, and he's riddled with shrapnel. There's screaming and the sound of crushing leaves, crying and more screaming. It's deafening. People are scattering or down. He's alone. The thought is as unavoidable as the glaring sun: he's going to die. He says the Lord's Prayer and passes out. Another flashback takes him to base, a safe zone away from the fighting, where buddies are unloading an ammunition truck, and a crate full of mortars goes off. The sound is like nothing you want to remember, nothing you could forget. There are body parts everywhere, mangled flesh. They're all dead. Just like that. One year out of high school, most of them, just like him.

For many so fiercely wrung out by the war in Vietnam, especially around the crescendo that was 1969, the question became: Why were we even there?

By 3:00 a.m. Jan's in his kitchen. It's 1979, and the neck of his whiskey bottle rattles against his glass. That night he had gone to the theater with his wife to see *The Deer Hunter*, Hollywood's bloody depiction of blue-collar America's war, Jan's war, the one nobody cared about anymore. Vietnam veterans everywhere shared the darkness of these nights. Nobody will remember their names, he thought. They fought and died because their country told them to, sent them there, and no one will remember them.

"I'm going to build a memorial to all the guys who served in Vietnam," Scruggs told his wife the next morning over breakfast, the bright sun streaming through the window. "It'll have the name of everyone killed."

A t that time few Americans knew precisely how many had been lost in Vietnam. Nobody had a number to go with the nation's longest war. Yet it had touched every town and every city. *He used to live there. He went to school here. He played football here. I sat next to him in math class.* The personal stories could fill a thousand phone books. *He was coming home in two days. We left his room as is. I never remarried.* It became a page in American history few wanted to write, or even confront.

Long over and best forgotten, was the consensus. It's why Jan's idea first appeared pie-in-the-sky. After all, the war had just ended forty-eight months ago. The wounds were fresh on the American psyche, the term "baby killer" was in the vernacular of just how bad it all had been, and for what? But Jan didn't care whether America wanted to move on; he knew he couldn't, and neither could thousands like him. Within days, he had a plan. A few might have thought the dungaree-clad, shaggy-haired man naive, but many agreed that it was time. The donations were a mere trickle at first—a bitter former prisoner of war, a college student with nightmares that his country would send him to die in a place he didn't understand, a ten-year-old girl who wanted to remember her dad.

The memorial's design was as controversial as the war it commemorated: one prominent Vietnam veteran would call it a "black gash of shame," though it was also likened to the harsh listing of the dead in Homer's *Iliad*. A chevron in stone, it simply listed in chronological order the names of those killed in the Vietnam War. Rather than uplifting white, a massive headstone to trumpet a life lived, it was funeral black. Stone cold, dark and final as death, it made no attempt to glorify the loss.

The wall said only: This happened.

Some Americans didn't want to hear that. But Jan, now backed by a crew of veterans, persevered. By 1980 the Vietnam Veterans Memorial was unstoppable, a heavy iron ball rolling down a hill. In early 1982 workers broke ground in a coveted spot on the National Mall at the foot of the Lincoln Memorial, homage to a man who brought a divided country together, just as, eventually, this wall of granite would.

The lawmakers who fought ferociously for the memorial, the ordinary people who wrote letters to the papers, the journalists, the talk shows, they all, finally, said the same thing: the wall represented a decision, a peace, a consensus. Wholly funded by individual donations, the Vietnam Veterans Memorial belonged to the people. "They were ours," the guys who didn't come home, a newspaper columnist would write. It was that simple.

Months before the unveiling that November, an engraver at the Binswanger Glass Company in Memphis, Tennessee had just done her work. The woman took a cloth to the dark panel of granite, her eyes moist. She cleared the dust, and then polished enough to see her reflection and a name—her own brother's.

For Ann, who lived about ten minutes from the memorial site, it was something she needed to do with Patricia, then living on the opposite coast in Oregon. She couldn't see Alan's name alone, so finite and cruel. Brother and sister had had a special bond. When money and space were tight the pair shared a room. Their twin beds lined up next to each other, the tender voices of children in the dark, going on about the grown ups, the funny stories, their schoolwork, and peculiar places like the moon until one of them drifted off to sleep. Patricia was just a baby. Unbelievable as it sounds, both Ann and Alan were considered Pearl Harbor survivors. On December 7, 1941, Ann had been a toddler racing alongside her mother, the swollen-bellied wife of an Army officer stationed in Honolulu, dodging the fire from a Japanese Zero targeting military housing at the opening of the channel leading to Battleship Row. After a long and hazardous evacuation to the mainland United States on a not-so-luxurious cruise ship, the family moved to their grandparents' home in Utah. The Armstrong family's traumatic experience made headlines, and Ann's mother, still pregnant with Alan, gave speeches to small community groups, a celebrity in a small way for what she had survived. On May 22, 1942, Alan was born, and Patricia arrived a few years after that. The family had their stakes in American history. Two pages of a book. The lauded and the forgotten.

Ann followed closely the news about the memorial in the making. At the nudging of someone who knew well about her brother and through her connections in Washington, she volunteered to read a section of names of the Vietnam dead. The vigil was carefully coordinated, enlisting the help of hundreds to read all 57,939 names, nonstop, over the course of fifty-six hours. That Ann would read Alan's name would be ceremonious. An opening and a closing all the same. It was time. She wanted Patricia, her only living sibling, to be by her side.

The dedication of the Vietnam Veterans Memorial felt for many like a turning of the tide, a new beginning. People converged on the National Mall morning, noon, and night. As the *New York Times* put it eloquently, "Americans continued to arrive at the wall even after darkness fell. . . . They bore the slow grief of the Vietnam time and indulged in the simplest sort of human memorial, the act of touching stone, feeling the cold, stony texture of the engraved names of the dead that shows up by flashlight and in the wavering glow of matches struck in the dark."

The outpouring of emotions triggered by the wall would never be equaled in this town. Immediately, people began to leave offerings at the foot of the dark granite, and they would never stop: medals, packs of Marlboro Reds, black-and-white photos, teddy bears, letters, and flowers. A mother wrote to her son, "I am the one who rocked him as a baby. I am the one who kissed away the hurts." A widow left wedding photos, on which she wrote, "Our baby got married." Almost overnight the wall became a place where veterans embraced and wept. One pointed and said, there he is, that good lieutenant. A chum scribbled a note to a fellow he called 'Smitty: "Perhaps, now I can bury you...I won't again see you night after night when the war reappears and we are once more amidst the myriad hells..." Some stood a hundred yards away, unable to face coming closer. Years later a suffering old veteran would take his life under an oak tree near the memorial.

The wall had a poignance the likes of which Washington had never seen. It could take you back, lift you up, crush you back down again. And then you'd see someone else there, doing the same thing as you, and you'd embrace one another. You were strangers, but you had a common bond. What was first a memorial to the dead became a place of healing for the living, so powerful that within years half-size replicas would appear around the country, giving people the peace that could only come from seeing and touching a name. From day one, it seemed, the world stopped to see the names. And it would keep coming to see them, decades later.

It was about that time—sometime in the fall of 1982, before she drove to the airport to pick up Patricia—that Ann discovered that Alan's name was not on the list that she would have read aloud at a lectern in the National Cathedral. That it wouldn't be on the memorial. Surely there was a page missing. Someone had made a mistake—hadn't they? Patricia already had her plane ticket. If Ann told her over the phone she wouldn't come. And Ann needed her sister.

Ann told Patricia right away, in the car at the airport. She couldn't have hidden it if she'd wanted to. Patricia wanted to fight it. But it was lost in the parade; the whirlwind that came with the new memorial. Phone calls went unanswered. A television news interview faded after a few sound bytes. They dealt with it together—their anguish forgotten, their brother Alan, left behind. Something as simple as a name not on a wall. Something as devastating as a name left off that wall.

"It was like he was dead all over again," Patricia would say, remembering the days in Washington.

THE MESS

June 3, 1969
3:15 a.m.

The world as they knew it had gone sideways. Something had struck their back, their head, twisted their legs, tangled them in a mess of clothing, metal, and mattresses. In the middle of a deep, dark sea under a moonlit sky some would never live to see, the floor below them rose to become a wall, the wall became a floor. "It's called a bulkhead, son," they'd learned just weeks before while tying their first knots and chipping paint, "and that's not a floor, that's the deck." Everything was going, rolling, topsy-turvy. And fast. They tried to remember what their dog-eared Bluejackets' Manual had said. Were they supposed to wait for an "Abandon ship!" over some loudspeaker, the voice that would tell them what to do?

Roused from dreams that had carried them to storybook islands of white-sugar beaches, coconut palms, and sloe-eyed women, or home to Mom's cooking, to the cloud of dirt on a farm, they woke violently, and became bleary, confused. The sound was unlike anything they'd heard before. Steam and steel; something came apart. It paralyzed some of them. The racks were a jungle of mangled metal. There was crying and praying, shouting, blank *stares that seemed to say, What do we do now? And there was water. A man from Colorado knew this sound too well—the gush and gurgle of water, like river rapids, but infinitely more sinister.*

"Get out. Now!" one man would holler over the commotion, the praying, the crying. There was no time for pants. Shoes. The scene was the same one compartment over. "Fuck your pants and your shoes!" someone yelled to the men searching in spilled-out lockers for their dungarees. "GO!" Whatever was happening, it was happening fast.

No time to wait for a whistle or a call to general quarters. Was this just a test? They squinted to see who was in front of them. Where was the light? It was all the panic of an ambush minus the bullets. There was an explosion, and the floor tipped more sharply. More confusion and less light. Kaleidoscope vision. Dizzying. Some only saw auras, their eyeglasses now lost somewhere in a pile of mattresses, playing cards, dirty magazines, and boots. Small flickers of light only added to the confusion. They felt their way around the crowded space.

As the men tried to get out, their fingers grazed bulkheads, conduits, cold iron fastened by bolts, screws scraping the skin from their bones, tearing into bruised flesh as they pushed the man in front and the man in front pushed the one in front of him. Some had broken bones, their arms and legs shattered. The jolt had been like nothing they'd ever felt or could imagine. It's likely some had never even woken up at all.

Get low. Crouch. Move. Fast! Hurry! But wait. Where to? Here! Over here! The voices were getting more desperate. In some areas, it was black. The water had risen past the battle lanterns. What do we do? Other compartments were faint, lit as if by dying candlelight, flickering ominously, casting moving shadows, adding to the nightmare of where to go, what to do. What now? Stay calm, one of them said, and we'll get out of here. Half of them were new. Half of them couldn't grow a beard. Half of them were so homesick that in the nights if you listened, you heard their soft cries. Now they thought of home, they thought of their mothers. They were like lambs in a herd.

Some who got out were the strong types, the big brothers. But they said that they knew, right then, that half of them wouldn't make it. And that if you helped, you might not make it either. Those who did help didn't make it. Those who survived would be haunted by this fact, climbing out to a moonlit sky and a glassy calm sea, wondering, panicked, who was still inside? It would practically kill them, in the middle of the night, shake them loose, in another decade, in another lifetime, it would seem. "How the hell we even got out, I have no idea."

*O**ne of the men would recall, dimly, that he crawled up through a hatch. He knew that the compartment before him was the mess deck, where some miserable hours before weevils had been swimming in the watery, lumpy mess the cooks called mashed potatoes. There, days before, they'd sat in the dark on benches and wobbly stools, eyes riveted to a battered, dirty yellow screen as Elizabeth Taylor wailed and hissed, laughed her wicked laugh. They'd just been killing time, waiting out the war in this cafeteria no bigger than a classroom, on this ship. That was the irony; this was to be their lifeboat, their ticket away from the blood and hell on the shore miles away.*

The floor of the mess deck was a dingy, spotted crimson

linoleum tile, chipped along the edges, curled slightly up at the corners like burnt toast. He knew this surface well. Others were heading for another hatch, but he knew that this could be, just maybe, a way out—and that there was no other way. He called out to the others. By now the men's screams were growing more desperate as the inrushing water licked at their heels. They lined up like ants, each pushing the man in front of him, looking for something to grab onto, as the water rose up their bare legs and, in seconds, reached their torsos. They clambered barefoot over the side of tables and stanchions, hopped the four feet between them. It was an obstacle course. Some slipped and fell, never to be seen again, sucked in and swallowed by the roaring water. The screams drowned out the telltale banging, fists on metal— someone was stuck. Someone was trapped. They knew it was bad, that it was really going down fast. The ship creaked horribly as it continued to roll. It was nearly upside down now.

That the linoleum floor of the mess was crimson was no accident. The ship had been planned in another war many moons ago, when kamikazes would nosedive onto the decks of ships, or bullets from the sky mow down sailors at the guns. The designers had thought of everything. When all hell broke loose, on such a tiny ship this space would be the only open area, perhaps serving as a makeshift hospital. The deep red floor would disguise splattered blood, fool the eyes and the brain, ease the panic. Hide the blood of the wounded as their lives slipped away, keep them calm.

They were, after all, in a war machine.

And their war machine was sinking.

I

THE WAR

1

BLACK CLOUDS

April 1969

The thing you have to remember is that many of them didn't really want to be there. That they had other plans. That they didn't want to get killed. Those were the days of body counts on the Nightly News, of physicals that checked for good teeth and flat feet, of kids who prayed it would be all over before graduation. When the inevitable question arose—*What are your plans, son?*—they'd sit there, ceremoniously uncomfortable. Were they expected to go? They hoped they wouldn't get called up. One's brother already had died over there. Another had glimpsed a classmate's funeral procession from a bus window, his forehead to cold glass, his eyes watching the black-cloth procession while big wheels rolled, taking him away from some nowhere Texas town, passing through the panoramic blur of America the beautiful for that buzz cut and a starched new wardrobe, onward to the safer choice. Off to see the ocean for the very first time.

Of course, there was the excitement of it all. They whistled "Yankee Doodle" and did their pushups. Their dads had fought in World War II, and now this was their chance. As kids they'd played soldiers in their backyards, heads held high to keep Dad's old helmet from hitting the bridge of their nose, the Battle of the Bulge waged between supper in a pastel kitchen and catching fireflies before bedtime. *You can be Patton, I just want to be Dad.* G.I. Joe was a favorite toy. On rainy days it was Broadsides on Milton Bradley's pad and paper. Most every one of them had a gun—a fake one just for killing the Japs and Germans in the woods near home, or a real one hidden under the tinseled tree at Christmas. War was a boy's thing, a boy's dream.

But when the time came, they didn't really want to die—at least, not for this. By then it was turning to shit over there. Everybody said so. Even their fathers, their knees never quite the same after the winter of '45, were scratching their heads. This was a different war, the one that would break the mold. When nothing about their destiny seemed under their control, there was one thing they could do to grab the reins, turn the wheels of fate just a little the other way. There was just enough time to chase down some prim, polished United States Navy recruiter, just as he was closing shop for the Christmas holiday, or even, in one case, on an emerald green golf course, just before tee time.

When it happened for him, raven-haired Robert Hiltz, a knot in his stomach, was likely wearing a sloppy sweatshirt, his long legs in jeans. That's what he'd worn all through business school, much to the dismay of his professors, who wanted the future market leaders of America in shirts and ties. *Another nonconformist, have we?* By then disillusion was rampant. Despite the dread—he felt out of place here, it was all happening too fast, the consequences too permanent—the Californian didn't hesitate as he pledged himself to the U.S. Navy: "do solemnly swear that I will support and defend... against all enemies . . . that I will bear true faith . . ."

And that was that. The recruiter signed some form and resumed his game.

It was the very day before Hiltz's official U.S. Army induction as a draftee. At twenty-three, he'd been caught between college and a not-quite career, doing the books for a chain of lobster restaurants in the party hub that was Redondo Beach, California, in 1966. On paper, he was just another able American male between the ages of nineteen and twenty-six whose birthday fell on a certain day; whose academic deferment, a draft board had recently discovered, had run its course.

On April 4, 1969, Hiltz was on his second Western Pacific cruise out of Long Beach, California, daydreaming. It was an unfortunate interlude because he was also at that moment charged with steering the USS *Frank E. Evans* through the complicated narrow channel from the Pacific to Pearl Harbor. He stood on the open bridge of the pilothouse, a space you could move through in a couple of strides, looking out onto a spectacular panoramic view. The air was thick and tropical. The lush greenery swelled against the heavenly blue sky like something out of a postcard. Hiltz scanned the channel ahead and stopped, his eyes arrested by something in the distance. The quartermaster and helmsman watched Hiltz and waited for the next orders. The radio emitted a noisy chatter of coordinates and call signs from ships in the vicinity, but Hiltz, by now looking through his binoculars, remained silent. A smile was beginning to break across his chiseled, tanned face.

Through the round scope, there they were—in bikinis, waving and bouncing in all of their glorious, hair-tossing laughter, in a party boat off in the distance. Soft-skinned, sun-kissed and voluptuous, with the hair of a mermaid—a Raquel Welch in their midst. They were all that the men on the *Evans* weren't, and all that they wanted. Girls.

The *Evans* was only on the very first leg of her 1969 Western Pacific deployment, and already the nearly 250 men on board were restless. Since they left Long Beach eight days back, it already felt like a broken record, the humdrum shipboard life: a cacophony of paint-chipping, the boatswain mate's calming whistle, tedious department meetings in front of a patchy-bearded officer, some asshole sticking his finger in your stack of pancakes just for the hell of it, a wild laugh, a punch in the nose and a trip to the ship's doc. The very sight of land, lights, and girls was worthy of a melody. A Friday night in port beckoned—a long weekend, sunsets, candy-flavored lip gloss, miniskirts. Full steam ahead.

The captain arrived on the scene like a record scratch.

"Hiltz, you gonna drive this ship or watch those girls?"

Hiltz was a lieutenant junior grade, the second step in the hierarchy of naval officers. One step up from ensign, "jaygees" weren't exactly the best ship handlers. When Commander Albert Sydney McLemore showed up, Hiltz was supposed to be tracking the buoys that marked the waterway leading to the harbor, a channel carefully mapped out to avoid sandbars and other hazards. The task was this, mapped-out turns and maneuvers, all the while considering other ships in the destroyer squadron astern and ahead, and not to mention a carrier in the lineup somewhere.

"Yes sir."

Focus. Focus.

The young officer's heart was racing as he went mechanical.

It was under the watchful eye of the dead-eyed, jowly McLemore that Hiltz conned the ship like a sixteen-year-old at his driver's ed examination, knowing full well that it could be worse. The young officer dictated the orders to the helmsman as a quartermaster jotted down the ship's coordinates— the time at which it passed certain buoys—the weather and the hour into the ship's logs. He wouldn't screw this up. He wouldn't let McLemore, a busy skipper already onto checking into something else, down.

McLemore was a fair guy, a likable skipper who, a smoker himself, didn't allow the ship's supply officer to raise the $1 price of a pack of cigarettes by even a nickel. He was a few months shy of his fortieth birthday, yet a head of salt-and-pepper hair and a fatherly manner made him appear older. Known fondly as Captain Mac, he was the sort who would look into the barrel of a five-inch, 38-caliber gun to see if that baby was still loaded. He wouldn't leave it up to some peach-haired kid who didn't know a shell from a can of oil. Few could recall a time when he was hell-bent on anything much beyond which kind of wrenches were used for repairs in the engine room and that the Filipinos in the wardroom fix the curry the way he liked it. Many of his subordinates loved him. Superiors and peers thought he was a "nice guy," and left it at that.

McLemore wasn't the prototype for admiral—not that he cared. Given his way, he'd be a truck driver, piloting a big rig along the snaking highways of North America. It was a matter of love how he ended up in the Navy. In 1945, when he graduated from high school in Vallejo, California, his sweetheart told him she wouldn't marry someone who drove a rig for a living. He ought to enroll in that college they were expanding down the road, she urged, the one looking for young men to fill its brand-new dormitories. California Maritime Academy looked a little like a summer camp, with wooden walkways over patches of mud and a few brown buildings spread out among tall, bushy trees. Student housing, built low in a cold, dank, swampy hollow, earned the name "pneumonia gulch." Not exactly the marble halls, immaculate lawns, and refinement of the United States Naval Academy on the opposite coast, but nonetheless it was a world-class institution for anyone who wanted to make his life on the sea. It had its own training vessel, which took students on training cruises as far away as South America. The curriculum covered everything from navigation to engineering; every facet of ship handling. In this fraternity of fighting men, McLemore was a party man on campus, a man's man, the sort you loved and trusted. He was famous for the parties he threw in his parent's small wood-frame bungalow in Vallejo. Navy life was a brotherhood, and he took to it.

And that's how he wound up in charge of a U.S. Navy destroyer, on the last leg of an exhausting career path that had sent him off to war in 1950, and then again in 1965. It was a career that provided for his family of five boys, and gave his now-wife Alice, a woman who welcomed adventure, something to write home about. It was a career that took him everywhere, it seemed—and, eventually, a career that would leave him jaded.

McLemore had a long, serious face, with eyes that drooped slightly. Or perhaps he was just tired—sleep was a luxury for a ship captain in those days. It was restless endeavor, always something to do, something to sign off on, someone to watch, questions to ask. He didn't always do all the talking, like those captains who'd ramble on, complacent in their lower-ranking captive audience. That was Thor Hanson, the ship's previous commander. As an obituary decades later would confirm, Hanson loved to ramble on about his jade collection and his desire to sing. Young officers like Hiltz, who served for seven months under Hanson, found this tiresome. McLemore was the preferred variety, the approachable sort. He walked with a slight hunch, as if embarrassed by his height, or as if he'd spent too much time crouching in the cramped, dark engine rooms of the U.S. Navy's steam- and diesel-powered ships, his preferred station on board. McLemore was an engine-room man at heart. The hoity-toity, pedestal type he was not.

His hands were almost always dirty, covered with a layer or two of grease to wash off in the head before entering the wardroom to dine with his officers at a table spread with white linen and porcelain. No surprise, really, if his uniform was a little unkempt, a little less starched than those of others who boasted the token gold thread—the prestigious insignia known simply as "scrambled eggs"—on their caps. Not flashy in any way, he had neither the time nor the desire to put on airs.

It was the spring of 1968 when McLemore came to command the *Evans*. He asked a lot of questions on his arrival, almost all of them about the ship herself. The men came and went—turnover was at an all-time high when men did their time and skedaddled. She was in bad shape after the 1967-'68 deployment. They had spent weeks on the gunline off Vietnam, her brittle insides rattling with every blow of the guns. The new captain with his first command at sea had less than a year to get her up to speed. Originally scheduled to deploy in May 1969, she'd been rushed into service due to the war in Vietnam and the demand for naval gunfire support. Infantrymen relied on this swift-moving, mobile artillery force; it could cripple the enemy, taking out bunkers and other targets. The *Evans* was an old ship, and even the slightest problem could throw her off schedule. Almost everybody there knew she'd probably get delayed coming back. It was just the way it was.

McLemore was honest with the crew, and he let a lot of stuff slide—there was only so many problems before one had to prioritize. He gave his men second chances, third even. That's what men like Hiltz loved about their commander. If anyone could appreciate him as a breath of fresh air in a Navy of superfluous and increasingly backward regulations— no sideburns, no civilian attire on base—it was his junior officers. McLemore listened. He let his officers speak. He was different. Hiltz, the pedigree of jaygee McLemore would later call the "sleep with one eye open" type, knew this all too well. The young officer was smart, yet easily distracted. And Hiltz himself was the first to admit he didn't know everything. Had their been no war and no draft, he admitted he would have been doing something else.

Days earlier Hiltz called on a sailor to wake McLemore in the middle of the night because the ship's radarmen had discovered an unidentified contact in the formation of ships headed for Hawaii. The vessel could have been on a collision course with the *Evans* or that of some foreign foe, and the young officer was alarmed—perhaps overzealous. With binoculars, even, Hiltz couldn't tell. The captain slept just several feet from the pilothouse, and he was there in a few seconds—groggy and barely in uniform, maybe, but there. He asked Hiltz a few questions, helping the young officer figure out the scenario. It might not have played out so well on the previous voyage across the Pacific.

Hanson, an imposing hard-line United States Naval Academy type, might have grabbed the junior officer by the shoulder and thrown him against a bulkhead. Strict and well on the path to admiral, Hanson had done just that in 1967 when Hiltz almost ran the ship too close to an oiler while refueling. On that April day in 1969, the young officer in control of the ship was unsure of himself but was sure of McLemore. He would write home of the vast responsibilities of a junior officer, the politics of being in the Navy, and the headaches that wouldn't go away—in Hawaii he'd suffer one that stuck around for a week. He'd wake up in the early morning in his officer stateroom, steel-walled confines no larger than the bathroom of his parent's home in Santa Barbara, unable to sit up in his rack, his bed, due to low clearance. The ship rocking, he'd wonder what the day would bring. What challenge, what nuisance lie ahead. By then he was the weapons officer, a duty usually reserved for someone more senior, and likewise, the officer in charge of bringing her in and out of ports. "Terrible headache…," he'd write home.

The *Evans* would slice through Hawaii's welcoming, sparkling blue waters with all the expertise of the finest ship handlers. Hiltz, still working on autopilot, eyes where they needed to be, wouldn't even remember the scenery. He wouldn't recall the puffy clouds in the blue sky, the buzzing overhead, the black smoke above, and the magnificent horror at that very moment being captured by Hollywood.

Sailors who weren't on duty belowdecks or in the ship's navigational spaces were topside, watching vintage Japanese Zeros soar through the skies of paradise. Some caught the scuttlebutt early on: they were filming something about Pearl Harbor and the bombing of '41. The spectacle gave longtime islanders nightmares, and would eventually win filmmakers an Academy Award for special effects. But for many of the crew on the *Evans*, it was as though the war stories their uncles and dads told them about had gone Technicolor, three-dimensional. The same blue skies. A ship just like this. Planes just like theirs. Sailors just like us.

For some of them, the sideshow was just another reminder that this war, their war, was very different. By now, it had become a quagmire. Their fathers had the kamikazes, the torpedoes . . . the giant flag over Iwo Jima! For the boys of '69, on the other hand, there was a groundswell of people calling their war a farce, a ruse, the senseless slaughter of women and children. The previous winter, while the *Evans* was on a show-and-tell family-day cruise off the coast of Catalina Island, California war protesters in speedboats baptized her gray hull with rotten fruit.

Even Hiltz's two younger sisters, standing on a pier days earlier as families waved good-bye and babies wailed for fathers they'd never see again, had pleaded, "Bob, don't go. Make a stand. Stand here with us. We'll stand by you."

Hiltz just laughed. The reality was that by now the young officer had taken a liking to Navy life: the exotic ports; the friends he made; the power of the guns he was now in charge of; and yes, the girls. And he thought, *these kids have gone crazy.* Almost every California household, no matter how old-fashioned, housed one of those stringy-haired hippies by then. The state was a kind of ground zero for the buffoonery, as some would call it, that caused older generations to gasp. Yet even for servicemen, the thought crept in as a whisper and grew: *What are we doing here? Still?*

At the time, on that spring day in Oahu, the *Evans* was just another U.S. Navy ship on a pit stop. To those who knew her men well—their classmates, their mothers, their hometown newspapers, the men who ran their local Veterans of Foreign Wars post—and knew what it meant to wear the uniform in 1969, it was as clear as the blue sky. They were all going over there. Over there, to Vietnam. Yet these boys knew that their chances were good, that *they* wouldn't come home in a wooden box.

2

The Chiefs

The chiefs' mess on the *Evans* was a narrow space full of long tables, redolent of coffee and sweet tobacco, the kind you put in a pipe. The green leather upholstery was worn, and the brown drapes had seen better days. The chiefs were often served the same slop as the kids crammed into the crew's main eating compartment, one level below—but at least they had their own space. And space on a sardine-can destroyer was solid gold, even if the pipes groaned and clanked and the leather covering the benches was torn.

Chiefs were everything the lore said they were. Experienced and opinionated, they ran the show. They knew it all, had seen it all. Some were father figures, or the father of someone you might have felt sorry for. They drank their coffee black and, if supplies hadn't come in, stale and reheated. Or cold. They all smoked, even when they weren't supposed to. Their language tended to the profane. Some mechanical thing busted on this floating tin can was "broke-dick"; the "blue dick" was what you got when the U.S. Navy screwed you over, which happened all too often these days. At least two of the chiefs, on their last leg of their long Navy careers, had tried to avoid this cruise. They were among the first to notice that the Navy had taken a turn for the worse. Literally for one of the chiefs stationed on the *Evans* that spring; he had been involved in two minor collisions at sea on other ships and joked that he was bad luck. The chiefs could hardly help noticing; a lot of the problems fell into their laps.

True to their insignia—a tangled rope around an iron-cold anchor—the chiefs were the ones who fixed things. There was a lot to fix; in the 1960s, a whole lot was going wrong. Their crisp uniforms couldn't hide their leathery salt-and-sun-damaged skin, their tattooed arms. They were the go-to guys. And their mess, like the part of a church only the chosen can visit, was where they passed along the scuttlebutt, the news of the day, whether true or not.

Topping the social agenda in Hawaii was the induction of a new chief, by unofficial Navy custom a fabulously rowdy affair that involved plenty of drinking and shenanigans, a great distraction for a group charged with fixing every loose screw on board. And this induction would be like no other.

The new man's name was Willie King. A Georgia country boy born and raised, King had joined the Navy in 1956, and he'd been in charge of the ship's deck crew since early 1968. Becoming chief was a dream for him, the finish line on a long, tough road. The road had been tougher for him than for most: he was black. Navy life was difficult for anyone, but even more so for those who checked "colored" on official forms. True, the armed services experienced some of the same racial tensions that shadowed towns and cities across the United States. But that wasn't quite it. Well into the 1960s the U.S. Navy was riddled with an institutionalized racism that pushed certain races into specific roles on a ship. One look at the officers' dining facility workers on the *Evans* in 1967–'68 makes the point: every single steward was Filipino. Black enlistees, on the other hand, who were once thought to have night vision too poor for combat, tended to be mess cooks.

Working hard and earning the respect of many on board, King managed to break out of this stereotyping. In this he followed in the footsteps of Navy legends like Doris Miller, a cook on the USS *West Virginia* who was collecting laundry when the Japanese attacked his ship at Pearl Harbor. Upon hearing the call to general quarters, Miller spun into action, heading straight for the guns he had never been trained to operate, and managed to fire for fifteen minutes, downing at least one plane and earning himself a Navy Cross.

Just like Miller, King was a doer, not a complainer. A black chief was rare at the time; a black chief in charge of the all-important deck force, the crew responsible for handling the ship in and out of ports, was unheard of. King's accomplishment in being named a chief was, in the words of one naval historian, "exceptional." Within days the old chiefs would gather around to toast their new colleague at the Chiefs Club at Pearl Harbor, glasses raised, laughing and smiling. Why no racism on the *Evans*? "We didn't have time for that junk," one chief would say later.

But before the clinking of highball glasses, there were

others matters to attend to. Word had spread in the chiefs' mess that they'd need to tidy up extra special, make sure everyone was neat and clean. "What is this, Easter Sunday?" one might have jabbed, for chiefs were known for their amusing banter. And a smart-ass might reply, "That's actually in two days, sir." It was in fact the tail end of Holy Week as the ship pulled into Pearl Harbor. The wives and mothers had already packed Easter candy for their servicemen and the mess cooks usually did their best for holidays. Fancy menus, dolled up in calligraphy, listed Virginia baked ham, creamy snowflake potatoes, and fresh bread among the delicacies, with "cigarettes and cigars" as an accompaniment to the cake and ice cream, Baked Alaska if they were lucky. Holidays brought nothing but homesickness, even for the most crotchety pack on board. And nobody was daring enough to make a wise crack at a chief. No sir.

These chiefs likely had their own words for the request that all crewmen spruce themselves up extra special and don their squeaky clean, sandpaper-starched dress whites: "Mickey Mouse bullshit." The *Evans* sailors, along with every sailor with a Dixie cup cover in the vicinity, were slated to serve as extras in this film about Japan's Pearl Harbor attack (an American-Japanese production, it would be released as *Tora Tora Tora*). Things were maybe even more chaotic on the USS *Kearsarge*, the carrier in the *Evans*'s group. Her numbers painted over, she would star in the film as the renowned aircraft carrier the USS *Enterprise*, a symbol of American might in World War II, which sailed into Pearl Harbor after the 1941 bombing, just in time to witness the smoking, mangled wreckage that remained.

Finally scrapped in 1947, the old *Enterprise* remains the most highly decorated U.S. Navy ship of all time having participated in such notable naval campaigns as Midway and Guadalcanal. The *Kearsarge* sailors were proud to portray her that spring, although that didn't prevent the typical grumblings.

The Navy would catch hell for this sort of dog-and-pony operation—which it blithely categorized as "good publicity"— later in 1969, when the Pentagon discovered that the carrier USS *Yorktown* had also been used as a massive prop a few months prior. On her way to Vietnam, the *Yorktown* had starred as a Japanese carrier, launching planes for the cameras, her sailors pressed into service as actors. It didn't help matters that several *Yorktown* sailors were injured during the filming. "Here the Navy has suffered in the last two years very badly, I think, from some bad performances, winding up with the [USS] *Pueblo*," the *Yorktown* gunnery officer said in a United Press International article, referring to an embarrassing 1968 incident in which U.S. surveillance ship *Pueblo* was seized by the North Koreans. "In the *Pueblo* case, nobody apparently had any manpower or military power to rescue the ship. . . . The Navy had no carrier, they say, they had no planes. And yet it now appears while we're at war, we've got a carrier that they can turn over to Fox films."

Ironically, just as the *Evans* and *Kearsarge* were making their way to the harbor, the second U.S. Navy aircraft carrier to be named the *Enterprise*—and the world's first nuclear-powered aircraft carrier, commissioned in 1961—was docked nearby for repairs after a deadly fire off the coast of Hawaii that past January. The *Enterprise* was the third American aircraft carrier in as many years to suffer a major fire. The previous fires had both happened off the coast of Vietnam, on carriers preparing to launch fighters in a war just going from simmer to boil. In the first, on the USS *Oriskany* in 1966, 44 American sailors and airmen died. The second, on the USS *Forrestal* in 1967, was even deadlier, with 134 killed.

The U.S. Navy of yesteryear might have been covered with glory, but a quarter of a century later—between the accidental fires, the *Pueblo* affair, and what admirals in meetings called "leadership deficiencies" and "a collision situation"—it seemed more notable for its screw-ups. And with an antiwar press salivating over each new revelation, it had the headlines to prove it. By its own admission, in an analysis of where it ranked in the American armed services lineup against the Army, the Air Force, and the Coast Guard, the Navy came in dead last.

3

CHIEF DAD

In charge of discipline and getting every enlisted sailor squared away on the *Evans* was Master Chief Lawrence Reilly, a man who wore more medals than anyone on board, including a Bronze Star with a Combat "V" for helping to deter a kamikaze attacks on his ship during World War II. A straight shooter, he liked to say he had been in two entirely different navies: that of World War II and this one. Small but strong, at five-foot-eight Reilly had the look of a man who could throw you overboard without spilling his coffee, which he drank black—and if it was a day old, so be it. Forty-four years old, he smoked a pipe to soothe his nerves. When somebody complained about weevils in the food, he thought of '43, when his ship, dodging Japanese submarines while never seeming to come across a supply ship, went weeks without a sliver of bacon or powdered eggs. "Why complain? It's fresh meat!" A New Yorker with the accent to prove it, he didn't like funny business and could be brutally candid. He had a talent for dealing with the men, the ones he called "kids." When he found one of them asleep on watch, he'd take the slumbering sailor's shoes off, walk into the pilothouse, and hand them over to the officer in charge that evening, a young officer who'd tell the captain about the transgression. Captain McLemore, in turn, would let the poor kid off the hook. Reilly's reaction was one of slight shock. "In a time of war," he said, "you could get shot for sleeping on watch." But still, Reilly maintained, McLemore was good with the crew. He was tough only when he needed to be—and there were times when a heavy hand was necessary, Reilly would recall. Before the *Evans* left Long Beach, there had already been a handful of courts-martial. And being understaffed, well, you had to let some things go, Reilly would later say.

The chief's hair was receding, leaving a vertex of thin, combed-back hair where his forehead ended. With his stern brow and creased forehead, he had a serious, all-business look—the kind of look that might send someone who saw him coming down a passageway off the other way—as he headed out to deal with the latest trouble. "There were some good kids," he later recalled, "and then you had the other kind." You had the drug problems, the Cool Hand Luke wannabes with bad attitudes, the deserters or those who threatened to, the men who slept on watch, the complainers, and the drunks— actually, "the drunks, well, that was nothing new." The chief laughed when he told stories about his first Christmas in the Navy in 1942. As most of the men were enjoying a slice of roasted turkey or ham, he was sobering up in the brig, a military jail. It came with the territory. "Just don't get into any fights," he'd warn the guys setting out on liberty. After payday was the worst. All the chiefs had been there themselves, and they knew just what to say to the younger enlistees: stay out of trouble, and watch out for venereal disease.

In 1940s Reilly barely had a foot on the bottom rung, just another eighteen-year-old seaman on a ship tracking the Imperial Japanese Navy. Smaller and slimmer than most, he was charged with cleaning out the inside of the massive torpedo tubes, a job he hated. "I felt like a giant dishrag," he said, but he did it—no complaining, no sir. When the time came, he sheepishly asked to switch out of the torpedo dishrag job, and he was on his way to operating an antiaircraft gun. He knew what made the lowly sailor tick, knew he wouldn't always like what he had to do, but he'd do it anyway—" 'Cause we were fighting for something," he'd say. But not in this new Navy. This Navy was something else. Some people would outright refuse to work, or not show up at all. "Never before," his stories would begin. And they'd end, rightfully so, with the old chief getting someone squared away, or else.

Born in Brooklyn in 1924, and raised in Queens, Reilly saw the Great Depression from the eyes of a city kid. The 1939–40 New York World's Fair—built on Queens's Corona Ash Dumps, the vast trash-burning field that F. Scott Fitzgerald fictionalized as the "valley of ashes" in Great Gatsby—transformed his neighborhood. The fair's "world of tomorrow" brought the green glow of television sets and silky smooth nylons to the American people, but the shining new era that the fair ushered in had a darker side. Ominous clouds were already rolling in, as the increasing tensions between world superpowers threatened peace.

Perhaps eager to see more of the world he'd glimpsed in the vast New York fairgrounds—more than sixty countries participated in the fair, building pavilions in which displays celebrated their culture and achievements—and kill Japs at the same time, Reilly walked to the nearest recruiting station as soon as the date on his birth certificate allowed. (He would have gone earlier, but his mother refused.) As though he or she had a choice; there was an Army draft then as there was in 1969—except nobody was really complaining about it after Pearl Harbor. The country went to war and that's the way it was, Reilly would go on to say, coolly. Within a year of the first Pearl Harbor anniversary, he was in. His first ship was the USS *Oakland*, a brand-new light cruiser, both fast and roomy at 6,000 tons. The *Oakland* was a lucky ship; she suffered only three casualties during the entire war, even weathering the infamous Typhoon Cobra (also called Halsey's Typhoon), which sank three ships and exacted a death toll of more than a thousand men. Reilly's ship was one of those charged with picking up survivors once the storm had passed, leaving behind miles of eerie, calm ocean, a discouraging task.

Reilly had actually been on watch the night of the typhoon, certainly among the war's most frightening moments for him. As he told the younger crewmen on the *Evans*, "those were some scary times." The men Reilly called friends back then were a tough bunch. One was among the ten men to survive the spectacularly horrific sinking of the USS *Juneau* in 1942; the survivors fending for themselves in open water for eight days before they were rescued. "Frank Holgrem," he'd recall the name. "Didn't want to sleep belowdecks again, but he went. We had to."

On the street Reilly grew up on, the windows displayed ninety-six stars—a blue star for each family member away on service, a gold star for each family member killed. Droves of New York City boys never came home. It was the price of freedom, the tribute given to a country worth fighting and dying for. Reilly's sentiments about life in the service during World War II read like a recruiting poster: "We were all in it together." By the time of the Japanese surrender in 1945, the *Oakland* had collected nine battle stars. By the time he turned twenty-one, Reilly had his medals and ribbons, and much more.

Just before the war, a neighborhood girl named Marion Louise Thomas had caught Reilly's eye. Marion was petite, with movie-star looks—a twinkle in her blue eyes, full red lips, high cheekbones. She dressed fashionably and wore her hair in rockabilly bangs, her ivory face framed by loose curls. She was a funny gal and could handle herself well, the kind of character that comes naturally, growing up in a city like New York. Their courtship was brief, as they were in those days. They married on a chilly Wednesday in January 1945, while Reilly was home on a much-delayed leave. Marion wore a long white wedding gown and veil; Reilly, his sailor blues. A honeymoon at the famous Roosevelt Hotel in Manhattan followed before the young couple ventured west, renting a small, one-windowed room in a quaint building along Forest Avenue in Burlingame, California, just south of San Francisco. The *Oakland*, undergoing maintenance and preparations, was moored nearby at Treasure Island. Within a few weeks Reilly's warship would pass under the Golden Gate Bridge, outward bound for the great Pacific war zone once again.

Marion and Reilly's romance was whirlwind and productive; by November of that same year a son was born. Reilly sat in the radio shack on the *Oakland* among the other expectant, nail-biting fathers, waiting for a signal that never came. He wouldn't get the news until he got home, months later. With the Japanese submarines tracking American ships in the Pacific, radio was a luxury. He'd meet blond, plump James while on leave, sometime in the spring of 1946. It was the same story told a million times over, resulting in the generation sociologists would later dub the "baby boomers"—a whole generation of babies borne by war brides, babies who wouldn't meet their fathers until long after they'd left the hospital, or even, in some cases, after they'd started walking.

The *Oakland* returned to the United States for good about a year after the Japanese surrender. In 1948 Marion gave birth to a second son in a very crowded maternity ward in Balboa Naval Hospital in San Diego, California. It was a scene out of a comedy sketch: another slippery baby born every half hour or so, and only one doctor on duty, a hurried, nervous fellow whose name, spoken in a rush because there simply was no time to do otherwise, sounded like "Padamajerski." Back then fathers couldn't be in the delivery room but they could smoke in the waiting area, leaping to their feet at the sound of hurried footsteps. The hospital corridor that night was a hundred-yard football field, the players white-capped nurses, the rubber soles of their white shoes squeaking at every turn and shuffle. *Here, hold this one. Take this one. Did you get that one?* Fifteen babies had been born that night alone, but Reilly knew his right away. James, by then a curious, toddling two-year-old, took after his father, but little Lawrence John Jr., wrapped tightly in a blanket, had a head of feathery soft, dark hair, and his mother's face and eyes. One look at him . . . *Beautiful Marion.*

Reilly put the Navy behind him, taking his growing family back to New York to settle down. Another boy, Gerald, arrived in 1952. In no time, it seemed, two girls followed, Luanne and Suzanne. Reilly's sister Dorothy Reilly, a nun in Queens, once joked: "my brother's big family made up for my not having children." The industrious type for which his generation was known, the chief spent much of the 1950s helping to build out the high-ranch and colonial homes of suburban Long Island, New York. Lindenhurst, like the more famous Levittown, was an iconic place in postwar America at the time, a utopia of growing families, living rooms with fireplaces, backyards with grills. There were strip malls and burger joints, dime stores and A&P supermarkets. With the help of savings and a mortgage people could only dream of today, Reilly bought a two-story house with a spacious lawn. He built the fireplace himself, framed the windows, helped install the banister, making all the finishing touches on his wonderful life with Marion.

It was the America of soft-hued kitchens with shiny appliances and flashy muscle cars, of jukeboxes that played happy-go-lucky songs like "Blue Suede Shoes" and dreamy doo-wop ballads like "Earth Angel." The couple's three boys went by the endearing nicknames Jimmy, Larry, and Jerry, and were typical of the era, spending their weekends and afternoons outside playing baseball or football, or war in the backyard and eventually, trading guns and helmets for makeshift spacesuits, pretending the nearby swamp was the moon, or Mars.

Their childhood stories read like adventure tales. While playing in the woods near their house, they once found what they thought was a rocket. They and a dozen other neighborhood boys put the metal cylinder on a red wagon and pulled it back to the house, bumping the wagon along the sidewalk and grassy knolls. The real excitement came when they got their trophy home. Their father was the first to announce that it really was likely a live round, left over from the U.S. Army's nearby World War II ammunition range. They called a bomb squad, as the senior Reilly—by then a member of the local volunteer firefighting force—counted his blessings.

It was always something with the boys, never dull— fights, fires, booby traps. When the boys didn't have school, they'd leave after breakfast and not return 'til dinner, doing God knows what in between—"being boys," the youngest of the trio Jerry would say. And when, much later on, someone discovered that the Reilly childhood home on Kansas Street in Lindenhurst sat only a few towns away from an infamously haunted one in Amityville, New York, Marion would quip, "Honey, my house was the Amityville horror."

The girls, on the other hand, stayed close to home, playing house with their dollies and a miniature kitchen table they'd pined over in some catalog—though in the end their handy father made theirs for them. "He could build anything," Luanne said once. "Mom would say, 'There, I want that,' and he would build it." Although money was tight, the kids never knew it. There was always food, always something fun. It has been said that poor is a state of mind. In the Reilly household, a noisy domicile where there was love in every embrace, every bedtime story, and every chicken pot pie or beef stew, *poor* just wasn't the right word.

When the kids got a little older, Marion worked part-time at a Howard Johnson's, the orange-roofed restaurant known as a "landmark for hungry Americans," with a sprawling menu and twenty-eight ice cream flavors Marion likely knew by heart. The middle son, Larry Jr. was her right hand at home, helping with grocery shopping, ironing, cooking, and cleaning up. Larry's close relationship with his mother started out of necessity; as a toddler, he'd been infamous among the Reilly clan for never leaving her side. Marion struggled to take even a step with that small child clinging to her waist. Not until Larry enrolled in school did teachers discover the real reason: not a terrible case of separation anxiety but nearsightedness, the kind that requires glasses with those lenses that look as if they're cut off the bottoms of a couple of Coca-Cola bottles.

To help make ends meet and because he missed the Navy, Reilly reenlisted in the reserves. In 1961, well into the Cold War and in the midst of the Berlin Crisis, the Navy called him into active duty. Reilly received orders for a West Coast ship, and within a few years the family had sold their Lindenhurst home and moved to Costa Mesa, California. According to family lore, they were able to buy their small townhouse in California on a ten-year mortgage with a down payment of just 16 cents—old coins from Reilly's coin collection, which were worth a whole lot more when he took them down to the pawnshop. Coincidentally, his new assignment was the carrier USS *Kearsarge*.

Thus began Reilly's second life in the Navy, in what was shaping up to be an exciting era. Once Reilly even found himself sitting across from John Wayne, the rugged actor on a naval education stint in preparation for his role in *In Harm's Way*. In the background, a muffled drumbeat was gradually gathering strength, as the nation braced against the possibility of nuclear war with Communist Russia and its red allies.

Jimmy Reilly wouldn't follow the family to California; his educational path took the handsome overachiever, both bookish and athletic, up the Hudson River to West Point Academy instead. (Poor vision kept him out of the Naval Academy.) Meanwhile, the rest of the family got situated in Costa Mesa. Larry Jr., who by then looked a little like Buddy Holly, liked to dress in a style his father proudly called "sharp": shirts ironed and buttoned to the top, fitted slacks, and shoes buffed to a high shine. At Garden Grove High School, where the huarache sandals and loose clothing of the 1960s were de rigueur, his iconoclastic style made waves. As family lore goes, a teacher once called the senior Reilly at home, asking that his son not distinguish himself with such eccentrically formal dress. The request unleashed a tirade from a shocked father who couldn't understand why a school could actually prefer a student to dress like, as he put it, a nothing-going-nowhere-looking "hobo."

By the time California's summer of love was in full swing, Larry Jr. had left high school to enlist in the Navy. He liked the idea of naval tradition, of discipline and neatness, of a clean, tidy place to sleep and eat. His deep admiration for his father also played a part. Little did he know that his high scores on Navy assessments, indicating a mechanical inclination, would destine him for one of the Navy's dirtiest jobs, working in the muggy, greasy crevices of the ship's engineering spaces. The job of boiler tender was a filthy one. It made the chief laugh to think of his son, a guy who'd been shining his shoes since kindergarten, climbing down into the ship's grimy belly.

In 1967, when the chief took on his new assignment on the *Evans*, he requested that his son come along with him. The young Reilly had taken to the rough-and-tumble life of a sailor like a duck to water, and he'd been getting in trouble frequently. It would be best, the argument went, if Reilly Sr. could keep a sharp eye on his son. And it worked. True to form, the young Reilly arrived on the *Evans* already in trouble for a drunken fight. "Straight to captain's mast he went," his father remembered, regarding the ship's court where a ship's commander could dole out punishment as he saw fit. Reilly Sr. just watched, knowing his son had done what most do.

By 1969 the young Larry was married to his high school sweetheart, a petite girl named Joyce, and the pair had a child. Lawrence John Reilly III, barely a year old, watched from his mother's arms as his father and grandfather's ship pulled out of Long Beach Harbor. It would be father and son's second cruise together to Vietnam. The chief's tedious job would be to keep all the enlisted in order, with a special eye on his son. On board some affectionately called him "Chief Dad," calling for the chief to throw down a loaf of fresh bread, into the hole where his son was working, likely polishing up some rusted piece of machinery older than he was—the junior Reilly could never escape his need for refinement. Truth was, despite the way the chief swore when things went wrong and the aura of intimidation that surrounded him, the sailors loved him. They could ask him anything, and he'd tell them the truth. And grab a coveted delight from the cooling rack in the galley when nobody else could, or would, and pass it along.

The old chief wasn't too impressed with the Zeros buzzing across the blue Hawaiian sky above him in the spring of 1969. Frankly, this get-cleaned-up business was just one more thing to worry about. By now one of the five-inch guns on the *Evans* was malfunctioning. And from the looks of the young sailors hanging eagerly over the railings as the ship slid over the aqua waters, a liberty port could only mean trouble. The ship was already undermanned. Some sailors had gone absent without leave as the growing public antiwar sentiment trickled into the minds of those in uniform. Some had refused to go to Vietnam once more. Some had been pulled off altogether because of drug use, some were already slated for a captain's mast, and others—well, you could just tell that something was about to go wrong. One guy had been caught smoking a joint on the fantail about a month before. Another one had a cigarette "in a gun mount, if you can believe it." Another crawled into a cranny and fell asleep on watch. Stupid young kids. Just kids, was Reilly's assessment, stuck on a boat.

When it came down to it, when things went sideways, it was always this damned war.

4

"SHOOTING ON WHALES"

The Vietnam War was at first referred to as "a police action" and stationed on the *Kearsarge* in 1964, his first active-duty assignment since World War II, Chief Reilly had a hunch early on that it would be a very different animal. Funny how it all worked out, he'd later recall. The same ship gearing up to star in *Tora Tora Tora* as the first carrier on the scene at Pearl Harbor in 1941 would be one of the first carriers to respond to a controversial event in the choppy waters off the coast of North Vietnam, in a place that was soon to be a household name: the Gulf of Tonkin.

On August 2, 1964, enemy torpedo boats attacked the USS *Maddox* while the American destroyer was on surveillance patrols. The ship was so close to the enemy coastline that even her captain had deemed the maneuvers provocative—a dangerous game, history would later write. At that same time South Vietnamese commandos were landing on nearby beaches, aided by American "advisors" in Vietnam. The number of Americans in country hovered around 20,000, and climbing. Unable to catch up with the craft closer to the coast, the North Vietnamese torpedo boats were ordered to fire on the much slower American destroyers nearby. The *Maddox*, in turn, fired over 280 three- and five-inch shells, sinking two of the three enemy vessels, while the last one reportedly fled. Two days later the *Maddox*, accompanied by the destroyer USS *Turner Joy*, patrolled the same waters. The two ships zigzagged through the gulf's dark eight-foot swells like a pair of drunken tortoises on an erratic, evasive course, searching for enemy craft.

It was on this night, August 4, 1964, that America blundered clumsily into a deepening commitment to war with Vietnam, a war that would define the nation's next decade.

It started in the sonar shack of the *Turner Joy*, and then in its gun director's chamber—strange specks on a green-tinged screen in the dead of night, and the sounds . . . the sounds of what? "Torpedoes in the water! Torpedoes in the water!" The radio went alive; a young sailor manning the main gun director on the *Maddox* prepared to press a button and then waited, refusing to fire until he had confirmation. The *Maddox* had not located anything. The minutes drifted into the darkened sky. Then the *Turner Joy*'s guns threw flashes of orange into the black velvet night sky, flashes that turned to silver smoke as they rose. That it was firing furiously at something was enough to identify it as an aggressive vessel, but what was it firing at? The *Turner Joy* was reporting ranges of targets. The *Maddox*, meanwhile, couldn't find the enemy;

the *Maddox* couldn't even find its American escort *Turner Joy*. Finally the command team on the *Maddox* reported a target, a big one, fifteen hundred yards off the side, "a nice, fat blip."

For men trained for war and little else, the sighting fueled a surge of adrenaline. Seconds felt like hours.

Goddammit. You see it? You see it?

The sailor in the gun director on the *Maddox*, meanwhile, refused to fire until the *Turner Joy* was located, even though command had ordered him to engage.

Goddammit.

Finally, over the radio, another order went out.

"Turn on your lights, *Turner Joy*."

A few seconds passed, and there she was. That "nice, fat blip" the *Maddox* crew had seen on radar moments ago, the vessel they'd almost blown to smithereens, was one of their own. There was no other aggressive vessel.

The sun rose on a clear, calm day on the gulf, not an enemy in sight.

Thousands of miles away, Washington went wild, in a hysteria mirroring the tension on the *Maddox*, and, as hindsight would have it, just as unprovoked. This time, it was the suited gentlemen in Washington who would pull the trigger.

For America, and especially for its media, the alleged unprovoked "attack on the high seas," as President Lyndon Johnson called it, was a direct threat to American interests, and those of our anti-Communist allies. Meanwhile, the U.S. Navy, unsure itself what had really happened, was just finalizing its report on the incident. By end of business on

August 4, the captain of the *Turner Joy* sent this memo to the naval command in Honolulu: "Review of action makes many reported contacts and torpedoes fired appear doubtful. Freak weather effects on radar and overeager sonarmen may have accounted for many reports. No actual visual sightings by MADDOX. Suggest complete evaluation before any further action taken."

Washington didn't get the memo—or, rather, it didn't wait for it. An estimated 90 percent of the reports that threw doubt on the idea of an enemy engagement on August 4 never reached Washington in the days that followed.

In a state of confusion and panic, the hangover of a generation who'd grown up in the shadow of World War II and the devastating blow that was Pearl Harbor, the bureaucrats rushed to act. Communism and the Cold War were very scary monsters; the music on the newsreels played at movie theaters gave the impression that Godzilla, even, was nothing compared to the threat of our red enemies. Thus, armed with Southeast Asia Treaty Organization rhetoric that "aggression unchallenged is aggression unleashed," Johnson argued that the United States must intervene on behalf of the South Vietnamese democracy. America, once again, had been attacked.

The ink was not yet dry on the Tonkin Gulf Resolution— which coasted through Congress with only two passionate naysayers—before carriers were steaming into the Tonkin Gulf, ready to unleash their lightning-fast jets on bombing raids in North Vietnam. The resolution, as history would paint it, was a blank check, giving the president the power to go to war with nothing more than a wave of his hand. That same president would later admit that the second "attack" had not happened at all.

The sailors in the Tonkin Gulf that night could have been "shooting on whales," for all they knew, Johnson said in his rapid-fire Texas twang.

The scene the *Kearsarge* arrived at was one of choppy blue waters, a clear blue sky, and not much else. The Americans on board ships steaming to the gulf were eager for action—finally, in the military term, they'd "get some." But Chief Reilly couldn't help recalling the real scares in the Pacific just two decades prior, the call to general quarters in the middle of the night, the threat of Japanese submarines lurking, the painstaking searches for survivors, wondering whether you'll ever see your mother again.

Of the Gulf of Tonkin in August 1964, he had only this to say: "It was a whole lotta nothing." Certainly it was no Pearl Harbor. But nearly every media outlet at the time had taken Washington's ball and run with it. In large font, it was in every newsstand in America, on every television newscast. On every street corner, in every country church, and in every high school classroom, the talk was of the evils of communism.

But still, the administration promised they were not seeking to escalate to war. In a campaign speech that same year, Johnson himself said, "We are not about to send American boys nine or ten thousand miles away to do a job that Asian boys ought to be doing for themselves."

Yet within a year of the Gulf of Tonkin Incident, Johnson

doubled his draft calls. And off they went, American boys marching nine or ten thousand miles away.

Once the war got started, it was like a massive ship, unable to change course—a wrong course that historians and journalists will dissect for decades to come. That those in charge felt it couldn't be stopped, that hotheaded war planners believed there was no other choice was a tragedy in itself.

5

AMERICAN BOYS

The farmhouse on the hill was the largest the Sages had ever lived in. It was five winding miles from town. A car going that way would have to cross a narrow bridge over the Niobrara River, catching its lazy, jagged confluence with the Mighty Missouri in the rearview mirror, a beautiful haze of powder-blue sky and tall emerald grass. There would be a sharp left and then a long, bumpy road with only one curve, a trail of dust in their wake, way out to a place the people of Niobrara referred to as simply "the country." The dirt road to the farm was narrow, sleepy acres on either side, lined in some places with tall elms, cedars, and yellow ash trees, while in others only green pastures rolled by.

The 160-acre farm was rented, a step down for the family, who'd owned one nearly twice that size along the silt-lined Niobrara. But the sandy, moist bottomland soil there had been no good for growing corn, or anything else, for that matter, and it had flooded often. Plus, the tall, lanky Sage boys had outgrown the intimate confines of the much smaller house there. When Ernest Sage heard that a farm on a hill, with a bigger house, was for rent about two miles away, he wasted little time.

This house would be another venture for Ernest, who knew little else than fishing, hunting, and farming. It would be cows and corn on the green hills, lush with promise, a short drive to Lazy River Acres for fishing or rangeland for quail hunting on a rare day off. Ernest was the roll-up-your-sleeves type, the kind who wore flannel shirts even in summer, and dungarees with dirt caked on the knees. He could handle a larger farm; his boys were strong and capable, raised on Nebraska corn and beef.

It was well into the era of the supermarket, superhighways, and superheroes. But outside cities like Omaha and Lincoln, insulated by their acreage, folks in much of rural Nebraska still deemed telephones a luxury. Electricity had only made its way up these hills barely 30 years ago. A trip to town still meant trading milk and eggs for potatoes and onions, with indulgences like perfumed talcum and nylons laid in only once in six months. The butcher still brought the carcass in the back door in the morning, and by suppertime the lucky family would sit down for hamburgers or pork chops. This simple life, uncomplicated by the outside world, still thrived across rural Nebraska in those years, when 80 percent of Nebraskans were still making their living as farmers.

Trees clustered around the Sage farmhouse. Its clapboard siding was painted a faded, peeling white, and it was topped with the moss-colored gable roof of a child's drawing. In all likelihood the house had been ordered kit-style from a homebuilder's catalog in the early part of the century. A four-columned porch with splintered-wood floor led to a creaky storm door, with a rusted screen that still managed to keep the home cool at night and free of bugs in the daytime. Four front windows looked out on a long dirt road and endless greenery. Behind the house sat a windmill, a large A-framed white barn, and a few small, ramshackle outbuildings; dirt pathways led to a hilly pasture where the dairy cows grazed. A rickety outhouse nearby stood as testament to a time before indoor plumbing; by the time the Sages moved in, though, there was a small washroom with a toilet inside.

The house was one and a half stories, with one bedroom on the first floor; a staircase led to three more, with slanted ceilings, upstairs. Dark woodwork paneled the walls and crowned the doorways. The plaster was cracked, wallpapered over in some places, painted in others. The kitchen was cozy, with a small old-fashioned stove and just enough space for a little Formica table pushed against the wall, with chairs to match and a few extra in folding metal.

Eunice warmed the house with mostly secondhand furniture—things that had come from other farms, the long-gone homes of long-gone country folks who had lived this same life. There were some wooden chairs, a floral sofa in hues of marigold and beige, a small credenza on which sat an antiquated model of a tall ship and framed photographs of the boys. A yellowing linoleum patterned with pretty English-garden flowers covered the hardwood floor, all ice-cold in the winter months. The drapes were a faded off-white, but pretty all the same. The living room was bright and inviting. In the mornings the house smelled of cinnamon and bacon, sausage and eggs; later on in the day, of fresh-baked bread, out of the oven just in time for the boys to get home from school, when they'd polish off a loaf of fresh bread in a matter of minutes.

Perhaps as a final touch after moving in, Ernest took a fine paintbrush and some dark paint. With some letters big, some small, each one sloppy, he worked the brush along the side of the weathered white mailbox at the end of the long dirt driveway, so passersby would know who toiled the land there: ERNEST SAGE.

Genteel poverty, it was called.

Eunice Cornish was born in 1923, the seventh of the ten children of Howard and Dorothy Cornish, farmers on the low-lying land along the Missouri River between Niobrara and Crofton. Most Nebraskan villages were the same back then, founded by fur traders and made famous by the likes of Lewis and Clark, with wide main streets and false-fronted buildings. In town, as they called it, there wasn't much to buy. Not that anybody had any money, anyway—the Great Depression was well under way during Eunice's formative years. She knew never to ask for much, a restraint she carried well into adulthood. The Cornish family grew their own food, and few remember anything heartier than a pheasant or goose along with some boiled potatoes or carrots, whichever crop had done well that year. When the drought came, there was not much to go around. Typical farm kids, they were, skinny yet capable. The girls each had one dress they called nice—not beautiful nor frilly, just nice. The boys each had one button-up shirt and a pair of dusty dungarees. One pair of shoes a year. The children would reach eighth grade in the country schoolhouse and then, their course already set from the moment their mothers first swaddled them, hit the farm as laborers. An adaptable generation, perhaps the last of their kind the country would see, they were worthy descendants of the brave pioneers who had stopped and unloaded their wagons less than a century before. Doing the best with what you have was in their blood.

The Sages were the Cornishes' neighbors, another large family that by the 1930 Census would list eight children under one roof. With few others around and not much else to do other than farm work and dreaming, the two families did what surprised no one: they started pairing off. First Betty and Harry, in a country church. Eunice was just a scrawny child at the time, Ernest a teenager, already broad-shouldered and growing handsome. There were six years separating them, to quell any wild notion that they might also join hands in holy matrimony.

World War II helped pave the way. Within a year of America fighting both Germany and Japan on fronts that went beyond the most adventurous notions of a middle-America farm boy, several Sage men, along with other town boys, would pose bravely before the concrete steps of a municipal building three towns away, a building that housed the county's draft board. It was off to U.S. Army basic training and then duty, fighting in faraway corners of the world, saving the land from tyranny. To these boys, the land they loved wasn't just a line from song; they'd worked it from the time they took their first steps.

Ernie came home early, sometime in 1944, after suffering bouts of pneumonia during training in California, the cough severe enough for the U.S. government to keep him out of Europe or off a ship headed for an island in the Pacific. It's unclear when he again noticed Eunice, by then twenty-one years old, a lustrous-haired, ivory-skinned beauty, but without the delicacy of the city girls he'd seen elsewhere in his brief travels. Eunice, this woman he'd once known as a frail girl, was home to him. She was both tough and tender. She loved, and she cussed. She had a pretty nose and wonderful smile, and blue eyes that could light up a drab room. She loved children—watched over several of them as work—and knew her way around the fields and barns that likely sat on her vocational horizon. She was, in all, the perfect wife for a farmer.

Ernest, tall with gentle eyes, won Eunice's heart immediately. In January of 1946, with just a few dollars in his pocket and in all likelihood the same suit he'd worn for his Army induction, Ernest placed a tin-thin band of gold on Eunice's finger in a bell-towered courthouse in nearby Hartington, Nebraska.

And so their life together began.

By the early 1950s, Eunice was chasing after three barefoot and blue-eyed children in a two-room farmhouse along the Missouri River. They'd arrived one after the other, products of cold winter nights, quiet summer sunsets, and no television set. And certainly there was passion. Eunice wore a youthful happiness in her smile, one that made her look like a girl playing house with new dolls on Christmas morning. It was the glow of motherhood that Ernest provided. That they were all boys made Ernest the happiest man around.

Gary Loren Sage was born just ten months after the wedding in an aunt's house in nearby Bloomfield, in the middle of a skin-biting cold snap, an eight-pound blue-eyed baby. The winds roared outside, piling drifts of snow against the side of the clapboard house, kept warm with heat from a stove and a love such as Eunice had never before known. Fourteen months later came Greg Allan Sage, a ten-pound baby who within two years was nearly the same size as his older brother. Two years later Kelly Jo Sage arrived, joining his two brothers and a dog on the farm.

Relatives would visit Eunice and Ernest often. In some form or another, they all leaned on each other. Ernest went into business with his brother, earning enough money to buy a 260-acre farm along the Niobrara River. Eunice's sister helped her with the children while she toiled in the vegetable garden. They made out okay—or at least no better and no worse than anybody else.

Back then almost everybody was poor. The thing was, nobody knew it. There were no Joneses next door, flaunting something you had to have but couldn't. Maybe someone might be lucky enough to have a color television set, but that was it. The Sage boys attended country schools, the primitive one-room wood-frame schoolhouses that had disappeared by then in other places. They dotted the rural landscape, half a dozen of them within a few miles of downtown Niobrara— simple, picturesque buildings with potbellied stoves and long tables. Usually the children shared books, and there was likely little paper. Children practiced arithmetic and penmanship on small chalkboards. They went home for supper when the weather permitted it, stayed to feast on warm bread and beans when the snow was up to their waists.

On Saturdays Eunice, as most country mothers did, bathed the boys one after another in a tub made warm with hot water boiled by teakettle over fire. It was a life unseen in dream-filled afternoons poring over a glossy Sears & Roebuck catalog, but one that brought Eunice joy. There were simple pleasures; never-ending embraces and soft little hands that clung to her arm as she walked the grocery-store aisles in town once a week, wondering how much butter or flour or potatoes she could barter for the good she had in the truck. She picked up the useful skills of canning and bread-making through a local extension club, a sorority of farmers' wives who exchanged know-how and recipes, women who posed for pictures, bellies prominent under a curtain of fabric—always, it seemed, at least one was pregnant.

Most farms in Nebraska raised corn, hay, and sorghum, feeding their own families with the harvest from vegetable gardens and fruit orchards. Livestock meant pigs, chickens, and an average of five milk cows. When trade fell short, a little extra could be made by selling eggs and dairy products on a rural milk route. It wasn't always enough, but most families made out okay. Niobrara's two grocery stores brought in outside goods, colorful cans of Dole peaches and bottles of Heinz ketchup, the accompanying cartoon advertisements telling you how yum-yum good it all was. The town grocer, who promoted generous discounts in the *Niobrara Tribune*, wouldn't hassle a family too much about an unpaid bill. When one grocer went out of business some years later, a shoebox full of crumpled unpaid tabs helped explain what might have gone awry.

If kids wanted to get away—dream of an afternoon escape in a red-hot convertible, the larger-than-life glow of a Hollywood starlet, or even a jungle adventure with Godzilla at their heels—there was the movie theater. The Niobrara Theater, one of the oldest buildings in town, had a roof that could give you the weather report. Buckets would fill some of the seats on rainy days. But the theater never charged more than a dime, at a time when cinemas elsewhere asked 75 cents. Green's Café served soda pops and milkshakes for a nickel, when everywhere else it was 30 cents. Nobody really got rich in Niobrara, but nobody really minded. They didn't call this the heartland for nothing.

Ernest watched his boys grow like stalks of corn in a good season. They were taller than Eunice by the time they hit high school. Ernest taught them how to hunt and fish, how to milk cows and bale hay, how to raise livestock, and what to do with eggs that don't look so good. Ornery and mischievous at times, they'd throw the eggs at one another until Eunice came in, hollering. Probably would have been okay with just two boys, but three made for a noisy house—always some sort of ruckus going on, Eunice would say. The boys were bigger than she was, but she knew how to get them in line, the same way a farm girl knows how to herd livestock.

And the cooking never ended. One loaf of bread was never enough, Eunice found. She knew the corned beef would go much further if she put some potatoes in the pot and stir-fried everything together in a hash. Breakfast was oatmeal or eggs, bacon if it was around. Cookies were a special treat; sometimes sugar was hard to come by. The younger always wore hand-me-downs until the three had morphed into the same size, more or less. Safety pins worked their magic. Sometimes, for special holidays or reunions, Eunice would head to a department store in Yankton, South Dakota, or straight down to Omaha for matching shirts and trousers. Eventually everything would come apart; holes in the elbows, threadbare in the knees. Sewing was next to cooking when it came to raising boys.

The 1960s brought in a new era for the Sages: a television set that took several minutes to warm up, and a new baby. Doug Sage, born in the summer of 1962, was a bundle in a knitted white blanket in Kelly Jo's arms, with Gary and Greg alongside, all three squinting in the summer sun as a proud Eunice snapped a photo. The family spent their days on farm chores, schoolwork, and, a true Nebraskan pastime, televised University of Nebraska football games in the fall. By the time the boys hit their teen years, little Doug had become a tyrant on a tricycle, charging about the living room floor while the older boys chased him, hollering for the little pest to get away from the television. Blond and freckle-faced, he was the little rascal of the household, adored and loathed at the same time. Spoiled by his parents, teased by his brothers, Doug could get away with a lot. His brothers would toss him over their shoulder and throw him down softly, tickle him or wrestle him. Whichever it was, Doug loved the attention. And they loved him.

Gentle Gary, with his blond hair and freckles, was a typical older brother, a little on the silent side, with a sense that he was somehow responsible for his younger brothers. He took to the farm chores the best, rising early to milk cows and make sure the livestock was fed. He aspired to be a veterinarian one day, but wasn't all that studious. At school he sang in the choir and performed in class plays. And when home, he enjoyed cooking alongside his mother.

Greg, a dark-haired athlete who charged at life the way he charged down a football field, was the most passionate of the brothers. He had the hot temper, the fire in his belly. In almost simultaneous milestones, he'd be the only one to ever get suspended from school—for cussing at a teacher—and, out in the open for all to see, fall in love. Greg met Linda Angel at the Knox County Fair the summer of '64, somewhere between a ride on a Ferris wheel and a cloud of cotton candy, and was instantly smitten. Her last name was perfect for her. A bopping band played doo-wop as he eagerly jotted down her address—telephones were luxuries. Linda, with dark hair and a wide, pretty smile, was from a neighboring town and went to a rival high school. Equally smitten, she sat on the Niobrara side when her Lynch High School played Niobrara High School that fall. The two wrote mushy love letters; Eunice teased that she would steam one open and read it, while Gary promised he'd find the stash of letters and hand them over to the *Niobrara Tribune* one day.

Kelly Jo, who resembled Gary in looks, with thick blond hair and freckles, could always be found with his brothers. He followed Greg onto the Niobrara High School football team, yet had a quieter hobby, drawing sketches of bears and other wildlife from a how-to book he'd gotten as a gift. His love was an old Honda motorcycle, one he famously tore around town in, revving at every stop. While the boys had their fancies, family life was work, school, and church. They were a strong Lutheran family—the three eldest brothers had been baptized on the same day, in June of 1954. And of course there were the minor boyhood vices—cussing, smoking, or playing pranks.

Outside Niobrara, the world was changing just as fast as the boys were growing. Ernest followed the news on television and in the *Omaha World Herald*; the *Niobrara Tribune* devoted its front page to livestock auctions, wedding and military service announcements, and advertisements for farm help and supplies. In the 1950s, as the Cold War became a fact of life in America, the nation was growing preoccupied with the foreign evil of communism, the cornerstone of dangerous regimes thousands of miles away. First there was the Cuban Missile Crisis, and then a popular president assassinated by a Communist sympathizer—like all others, Eunice and Ernest remembered that dark day.

The world wasn't what it used to be. The year Gary entered his senior year in high school, the Tonkin Gulf crisis was all people talked of. War was on the horizon, as was manhood for Ernest's three boys. One after another, they would face the same decision. It was like a storm front creeping in, dark clouds in tornado season, a powerful wind that would change everything.

When the U.S. Marines first landed on South Vietnam in 1965, in the first amphibious landing since Korea, Gary watched on the black-and-white television that sat in the corner of the farmhouse living room. When he finished high school in two months, his thought was, he'd join the Marines. Ernest grimaced at this, recalling his days in Army training, the dirty holes he'd learned to dig and sleep in, the days without food—his brother, who'd fought as a grunt in the Pacific, could attest to this, and just how dangerous it could be. The fact that war was nothing glorious hadn't been a subject for dinnertime conversation in the years since World War II. But when the men who'd fought then saw war looming as their own sons came of age, they couldn't help feeling dread. And this war, they were already saying, was going to be different. Already the rumblings were ominous.

"Gary, go in the Navy," Ernest urged. Eunice kept her eyes fixed on the table—on something to clean, something to cook, anything to keep her mind off the notion that her three eldest boys had grown up, and too fast.

At kitchen tables and in living rooms everywhere in America, the same quiet family drama played out: the glare of the television, the background ripple of machine-gun fire, precious boys becoming men, Uncle Sam calling.

6

ALL THREE

In 1965 things picked up steam. There'd be no going back.
President Johnson, speaking at a press conference at
about the same time Gary and scores of other young men
across the nation were tossing their four-cornered caps in
the air, didn't sugarcoat. General William C. Westmoreland
wanted more troops on the ground in Vietnam, he told
America. The general in charge of U.S. operations had
warned the administration of a growing threat, a sinister
army lurking in hidden corners, one that had to be stopped.
That summer he'd raise troop levels exponentially and double
draft calls, from 17,000 a month to 35,000.

By the end of 1965 nearly 200,000 Americans were
serving in Vietnam. That number jumped year after year—
385,000 in 1966, 486,000 in 1967, 536,000 in 1968. Hidden
in those numbers is that for the first three years of the
war, Johnson refused to call up the National Guard or the
reserves, bucking two hundred years of custom in American

warfare. The thought of doing so made him nervous; it would mean admitting that it had become the wider war he'd promised to avoid.

As troops in country increased, so did the death toll, as many as 16,000 in one deadly year. By 1969 there were upward of 30,000 dead, with no letting up; roughly two hundred American families received telegrams every week. And that wasn't counting the thousands of Vietnamese deaths.

It was an ugly scenario. The reality was, a U.S. Army induction notice felt like a death sentence. Meanwhile, the antiwar movement spread like wildfire on campuses everywhere, as young men worried that their academic deferments would be up before graduation. Many who weren't in college—either because they hadn't been strong enough academically, or because they were too poor—were looking for a way out as well. Those with sense and money hired fancy lawyers and became "conscientious objectors," people who thought it was wrong to kill. They'd embraced religions that preached pacifism, stroke another man's buttocks while standing in line at the induction center, wear a bra and say they liked it dirty—anything to get out of going. They burned their draft cards, said Fuck you, Uncle Sam. Some left the country altogether. Some never came back.

Anything to get out of it.

Anything not to die.

Middle America, however, was different. The three eldest Sage boys were in the Navy by 1969, serving their country with pride. That's just what American boys do, Eunice supposed. Gary had joined in late 1965 and spent a few years on the USS *Merrick*, a cargo ship ferrying supplies to South Vietnam, before joining Greg on the *Evans*. Gary and Greg weren't the only set of brothers on board; the ship also carried the three Jones brothers, from Sioux Falls, South Dakota. This fact may have helped lessen any resistance of allowing brothers to serve together—it was just a matter of paperwork.

At the time there was a rumor that the Navy wouldn't allow brothers to serve together on the same vessel. And in fact, the Navy had at one time put in place a ban on sons serving together, after five brothers—the Sullivans, of Waterloo, Iowa—were all lost at sea in 1942, when the light cruiser *Juneau* was torpedoed in the battle of Guadalcanal. The ban was almost impossible to enforce in the first place, however—to gather all the Smiths or Joneses among more than a thousand men assigned to an aircraft carrier and make sure they were not related was a personnel nightmare, and then there was the difficulty of reassigning them if they were. It was lifted altogether following the war.

In 1945 a Japanese submarine torpedoed the cruiser USS *Indianapolis*, taking the lives of nearly nine hundred men on board, many killed by sharks after the ship went down, in the largest such attack in history. It was a major black eye for the U.S. Navy, both because of its failure to respond to distress signals from the sinking ship and because of the controversial court-martialing of the ship's skipper. Perhaps overshadowed by this public relations disaster was the fact that among the *Indianapolis*'s dead were nineteen-year-old twin brothers: the Koeglers of Cincinnati, Ohio, who'd still been in high school when the Sullivans had perished on the *Juneau*.

The famed battleship *Arizona* had thirty-eight sets of brothers on board when she was sunk at Pearl Harbor, and twenty-three sets of them perished there, as well as a father-and-son pair. "Simply put, brothers want to be with brothers," reads an information card at the USS *Arizona* Memorial.

By the time Gary came aboard the *Evans*, the ship had already collected a sizable amount of battle stars and commendations for firing off the coast of Vietnam, and was slated to return. Within his first months of serving with his brother, Gary received orders for a brown-water navy vessel in Vietnam—a scary assignment. The *Evans*'s executive officer managed to pull strings to have the order changed, the boys would write in a letter home to Eunice. The brothers would stay together.

Greg by then had done what everybody knew he was going to do when, in the middle of a polka-blaring, bustling county fair, the world around him seemed to pause, and all he could see was Linda Angel. On September 19, 1966, he gathered his savings, money earned selling farming equipment in Omaha just after high school graduation, and bought a $125 ring at Malashock's Jewelry. He gave it to her just before boot camp. They kept the engagement a secret for a while—but everybody, it seemed, knew. And they couldn't wait to be married, together. It was an era when, in their world, at least, people waited. They were nineteen and head over heels in love, their letters filled with the tenderness and yearning of a lost, more innocent time.

At Niobrara Lutheran Church on July 1, 1967, while Greg

was home on leave between radarman school and his first deployment to Vietnam, the couple married. They celebrated in the church basement with a crepe-paper-and-buttercream-cake reception. A newspaper announcement called it a "dance," and invited everyone in town to celebrate. In 1968, while Greg was on his first Western Pacific deployment on the *Evans*, their first son was born. Greg Allan Sage Jr., a cherubic blond, met his father when he was three months old.

As the *Evans* geared up for its 1969 Western Pacific deployment, Greg, Linda, and Gary shared a one-bedroom apartment in San Pedro, California. Greg, Linda, and baby Allan—who went by his middle name so as not to cause any confusion, at Greg's suggestion— slept in the bedroom. Uncle Gary took to a twin bed in the living room. Linda set up a modest home, complete with the pastel-striped towels and stainless steel dinnerware the new couple had received as wedding gifts. She thought it was fun to have Gary—an excellent babysitter and cook, and an overall nice guy—around. One day, she dreamed, he'd marry one of her sisters. And Kelly Jo, just finishing high school, could marry another sister. And they could all be together always.

It was a tender time for the couple. Linda enjoyed watching Greg lie down next to Allan, feeding his son bottles of milk. The couple wanted more children; they saw a future as farmers in Niobrara, with a litter of children. But such things had to wait. Even with Linda working at the telephone company, money was tight. They'd buy cheap loaves of ground beef, cans of spaghetti sauce, and noodles for no-frills meals. Just before payday, when times were especially tough, Greg and Gary would go back on board the *Evans* to dine with the unmarried crew, while Linda and the other wives from the *Evans* chipped in together and made do, mostly just getting food together for their little children. By then, many of these young Navy wives had a baby on one hip, or one on the way.

Kelly Jo Sage, the last in this set of Russian dolls in dungarees, followed in his brothers' footsteps, enlisting right out of high school. After a buzz cut that made him look like Dumbo, his brothers joked, and eight weeks of boot camp in San Diego, he naturally jotted down a confident "USS Frank E. Evans, DD 754" when a form asked for his preferred assignment.

Ernest, as always, was following the news of the day closely. As a reporter in some never-before-heard-of place like Khe Sanh or Xuan Loc talked about a new offensive, a counteroffensive, or a body count, he could see young men in drab green running for their lives in the background on the television screen. Ernest was relieved he wouldn't have to look for his boys in the horror that was America's first televised war. That's why, when Gary and Greg wanted to serve together on the same ship, he signed the paper, giving them his blessing; and when Kelly Jo applied for a job on the *Evans* in early 1969, he was no less agreeable. For the most part, the U.S. Navy fought in Vietnam unopposed. The boys would be safe, and together.

Meanwhile, Eunice was growing uneasy. Maybe it was the bad news she watched on the television day after day, the fact that her sons were out there in that hard world, not too far from that mess in the jungle. Certainly they were a long way from the farm, the emerald acres that had sheltered them from the terrible things beyond. They were far from the warm kitchen where she could watch over them, setting before them sustaining meals of potatoes and corned beef. The Navy was safer, Ernest and others kept reminding her. Yet she had trouble sleeping in that big—too big, now, for the few people it still held—farmhouse. She spent nights pacing the creaky floors, hoping not to wake up six-year-old Doug, who was having a hard time without his brothers. "He cries every day," she wrote to Kelly Jo the winter of 1969, as her middle child finished boot camp.

March 1969 brought a great joy to the Sage household. It would be the first time since Gary had enlisted that all the boys would be home at the same time. Gary and Greg would be driving in from California on a two-week leave before their next West Pac. Of course Greg would bring Linda and baby Allan. Linda was going to stay in Nebraska while the boys shipped out, the plan went; California was a wild and unfriendly place for a farm girl like Linda, and she thought she'd miss Greg even more if she waited for him in their $60-a-month tenement on noisy Santa Cruz Street in San Pedro. Besides, they'd save money if she went home. And within a few days of their arrival in Niobrara, Kelly Jo would arrive in Omaha by airplane.

Niobrara looked more like the polar ice cap, more than three feet of snow blanketing its hills and thoroughfares, the naked trees and tangled thickets glistening with ice. Eunice wondered how the boys would make it off Highway 12, which had already been plowed. She worried how they'd negotiate the rural road home, snowbanks heaped along it like mountains against the backdrop of sugarcoated plains, all the way around the bend to the farmhouse that sat warm and huddled, practically hidden in the white that surrounded them. Into Nebraska, along unnamed die-straight roads, the boys could only tell where to turn off by the trees and the colors of the houses strung out along the road, miles apart.

Eunice had her worries, but she knew they didn't help, so she just watched the clock and kept herself busy, baking loaf after loaf of bread. God willing, she'd have her boys home once again.

As always, there were plenty of things to do around the farm. Ernest, at only fifty-two, still had his strength, but there were just some things that you needed your boys for. Plus, while he wouldn't say it too much, he missed them terribly. One wouldn't know it by looking at him, as his hands were rough as sandpaper, Ernest was a sensitive man on the inside. Everything around him reminded him of the boys. Without the thunder of three tall boys rushing up and down the narrow wooden staircase, the silence in the house weighed on him.

Once the boys were all home, the short winter days were kept full. There were plenty of visiting family members; the boys had more aunts and uncles than they could count on baby Allan's fat fingers and toes. Oblivious to the harsh weather outside, Eunice kept warm in her housedresses and aprons, once again feeding her boys those hearty breakfasts, meals of meat and potatoes, pies and coffee. They chewed over town gossip, who was marrying who, who was shipping out, like them, and who was already gone. They watched television and played cards, all the things you do when you're snowed in and, just this once, you don't mind. Little Doug liked following baby Allen around, grabbing the chubby baby with both arms and leaning back to carry him as if to say, *Look at me, look what I can do.*

Then came the photograph. The one that invoked waves of pride, first—and later, pain and the questioning of God the Almighty, if anyone dared. It was Linda's idea. At first, grinning goofily, poking fun at one another as brothers often do, the boys just went along, dressed up in their "crackerjack" dress uniforms and white caps. Seeing Eunice with her sons earlier that week made Linda, now a mother herself, think of it as the perfect Mother's Day gift for Eunice, who missed her grown-up-and-gone sons, Linda could tell, with a fervor the older woman could barely hide. Not from another mother at least. The portrait photographer in Omaha took several shots, one in order of age and size, yet another with the younger Kelly Jo in the middle. Winding up the film, he said they'd be ready in a few weeks. Linda's job with the telephone company transferred her to Omaha, where she would rent a small apartment near her sister Gretchen. She could pick the photos up in April. Perfect.

It was a bittersweet scene, even more so later on, looking back. The long, sweet week in Nebraska had come to an end. In the little Omaha airport, rows of plastic chairs faced panel windows. The fields beyond the runway were covered in patchy snow. The Sage brothers left their home state in uniform, their sea bags slung over their shoulders. The prairie hills rolled past outside the airplane window. The moon chased them through the night sky's clouds, and a bright California sun burned orange ahead.

7

SAILORS

The Sage brothers went by taxi from the bustling city airport in Los Angeles to Long Beach Naval Station, where the *Evans* was moored alongside a small armada, all gray, all anchored in water that looked green, all gearing up for another trip to Vietnam. There were just a few days left to go before the ship pulled out, and still much to do. It came as no surprise that several had already gone AWOL, or failed to come back from leave. The paperwork piled up. Desertion had become a major problem, as had drug use and the fellows who did their jobs poorly because they simply didn't want to go. With less than a week before castoff, the ship was shorthanded and in need of parts, among a litany of other problems.

Greg slept in OI Division, a compartment just under the mess deck. In a classic navy-life story, Greg had once gotten into a fistfight with another sailor in that same compartment. In the middle of his last deployment, out of boredom, perhaps, the two had begun to argue over whose state university had the better football team, Nebraska or Texas, and eventually the argument got physical. Greg wrote to Linda about the fight, saying he'd won. The other sailor didn't remember it so. Later the two would become so close that they were like brothers, lending one another clean underwear if the laundry were late. Just forward of OI Division was the First Division compartment, home of the deck apes, where Gary, a senior first class boatswain's mate, slept. Kelly Jo would start out there; all boots started out as boatswain's mates.

An iron ladder led down to the First Division berthing quarters, where forty racks (the navy term for bunks), most stacked in sets of three, were fastened to the wall with nuts, bolts, and chains. These were World War II-era furnishings, from a time when comfort took second place to the more pressing needs of navigation, guns, and ammunition. Each rack was of canvas stretched across a metal pipe framework and wire springs, topped with four-inch-thick mattress. Clearance once you got into your rack was zilch—new men unfamiliar with this sleeping arrangement would wake, try to sit up, and immediately bang their heads, then cuss like the sailors they had become. Each man was assigned a footlocker, into which he could cram a few essentials: soap, paper, pens, uniforms, skivvies, a few paperbacks, and—there was no denying it—dirty magazines.

The space between the racks was narrower than the racks themselves. There was room for only one man at a time to stand between the racks to dress; the rest would have to stay in theirs and wait their turn. The entrance to every compartment was a dangerous bottleneck. Even the U.S. Navy admitted that it was hardly a workable arrangement, estimating that there was roughly 11.5 square feet of space for each man serving on an American destroyer. About fifteen years earlier they had petitioned lawmakers for more money to improve living conditions on these same, now-geriatric destroyers. "Human dignity is at stake," as the narrator of a video created in 1952 to document everyday life on tin cans like the *Evans* put it. But in the end, a paint job and the addition of antisubmarine capabilities was deemed enough "modernization" to last another five years or so. Then came Vietnam, and these aging destroyers were called back into service. Living standards, meanwhile, continued to nosedive.

The entire ship stank of fuel. It was an odor you couldn't shake, something that crawled up your nostrils and stayed there. If you woke up in the morning darkness before reveille and forgot where you were, the scent was the first thing to remind you—and after that, the noise. Being in a naval vessel on the move was like living in a factory, with its whistles and bells, a machine in constant motion. And even those mechanical sounds couldn't compete with those of the men on board, the laughing, hooting, hollering, whispering, yelling, slamming—name it—of nearly forty men crammed into a space no larger than their living room at home. When she was anchored or moored and went cold iron—her engines cooled to a dead silence—it was like living in a Dumpster. It could make you crazy.

The deck apes were charged with taking the ship out and bringing her into port; they worked as helmsmen in the pilothouse, as lookouts, and, when there wasn't much else to do, as menial laborers, mopping, cleaning, chipping away old paint and repainting. They were the heavy lifters, charged with loading both ammunition and cartons of powdered eggs. For that reason First Division was where you went when you didn't know a hatch from a bulkhead, or you'd hit your head so many times on the low doorways that you couldn't be relied on for serious duty anymore. It was where you got shitcanned when you couldn't make it anywhere else. It was a compartment full of dreamers, Motown singers, troublemakers, zealous seamen, brawlers, drunkards, and the wide-eyed weeping type. There were the Don Juans, the ones who knew where to go in foreign ports and how much you needed; the ones who prayed and said they were waiting for marriage; the ones who wouldn't let them live that down. Ever.

You ain't never had no one love you?

I'll love you, baby.

Messing with the wary new guys was something all navy men excelled at.

A lot of them were clowns—it helped the time go faster. They were characters, like Snow White's Seven Dwarfs. There was always that grumpy guy who wished everybody would shut the fuck up, and the one who threatened to throw someone overboard if he ever heard another twangy, hang-yourself-from-a-pipe Hank Williams ballad. There were the readers and the quiet types, the ones who sat in their racks and wrote letters home to their mothers and their sweethearts, drawing pictures of a boat with two smokestacks like chimneys on a house, with an arrow pointing to the bow: "This is where I sleep." Then, of course, there were the ones who'd do anything to get out of work—*Go see the doc, he'll get you squared*—and the ones who said, "Screw it, I got to be here," and just did their jobs.

Everybody cussed. It might be nothing those farm and town kids had ever heard, but the rough-and-tumble city kids, the ones from the concrete jungles of Philadelphia, New York, and Chicago, it was nothing they hadn't. It started at boot camp, your swearing in. "Welcome to the Navy!" Suddenly, in a symphony of profanity, they'd gone from all-American boys to maggots, faggots, sissies, and ladies. *America's at war, you sons of bitches!*

In the spring of 1969 the *Evans* was just another ship getting ready to go to Vietnam, and it seemed as if they all had the same story. One who'd just turned nineteen summed it up: "I was going to get drafted. I knew my number. So I went in the Navy, 'cause fuck the Army."

Amid these deck apes, it's likely Kelly Jo looked to Gary. That's what new guys did; they searched for one of their own, someone who reminded them of home, or of someone they'd met in boot camp, someone they didn't know but might have grown up in a neighboring town, or someone they'd shared a bed with as a child. In less than one year the younger Sage brother had gone from the boyhood innocence of life on the farm—Eunice in an apron, scrambling eggs for breakfast, fresh bread already in the oven, a breezy ride on his motorcycle along the lazy river, bronze fall leaves on the trees—to this. Racks and racks of young men cussing, smoking, hooting, hollering, shaking their fists in the air.

And it's likely that Gary, the big brother who'd already

been living this navy life for nearly four years, looked at his younger brother as if to say, *You'll be okay, kid.*

That would be just like Gary.

Men of war. Boys really. Stacked like kindling, ready for a fire.

8

THE INCENDIARY

On the night of his inauguration, on January 20, 1969, President Richard Nixon and his wife Pat were relieved to finally call the White House home. In 1960 Nixon had lost to the more popular John F. Kennedy, but so much had changed since then. A lone rifleman, a Communist kook, had taken out Kennedy in 1963. Jacqueline Kennedy's pristine pink suit splattered with blood, Camelot was gone. It was the beginning of the end of America as they knew it, so the old-timers would later say. In 1968 it was a very different race: Nixon ran against Hubert Humphrey, who, as vice president under Lyndon Johnson, was seen as an artifact of an administration that had sunk America deeper into a ground war on the other side of the planet, a war to which no end was in sight. It was a different race and a much different country.

As the death toll from Vietnam mounted, even the fatherly Walter Cronkite had told his loyal television audience that it was time for the nation to withdraw. As Lyndon Johnson himself mournfully put it, "If I've lost Cronkite, I've lost America." Less gentle was the chant of youthful militants in protests on college campuses across the nation: "L-B-J, how many kids have you killed today?" The sentiment percolated into the music of the day, with the political anthems that spoke of a disenchantment creeping slowly, rhythmically, like vines devouring a pristine palace, like short hair growing long and stringy. Authority and mores abandoned, giving voice to the ones who had been silent, consenting. There was an unwavering pulse of change. Finally, it said. Pay attention, the music said. It shouted lucidity. It crowed cool. It cooed and flowed. Listen, it said. The ground is shifting. Can't you see? They said, follow us.

It was clear in 1969, at the closing of a turbulent decade, that America was ready for something new. People were angry with Washington, with the direction of the nation. The raw noise was everywhere. It was on the street and in front of news cameras, painted in scribbles blood-red on wooden signs. It was unavoidable for the new president making his way, motorcade fashion, to the big house on Pennsylvania Avenue.

Broad-shouldered at five-foot-eleven, always dressed in conservative dark suits, Nixon kept to hazy generalities when he spoke of Vietnam. His dark eyes, under heavy brows, were serious as he intimated that America couldn't afford more of the same old thing, and that he could turn it around. "There isn't a place in the world where the United States isn't worse off than it was eight years ago," he said in a 1968 campaign speech. As president, he promised, he would "defuse trouble spots and negotiate where we need to. We shall have peace."

What America didn't know at the time was that just before the election, Nixon had gone through secret channels to sabotage his predecessor's peace talks, promising the North Vietnamese better conditions if he won the presidency. (In fact, the compromise Nixon hammered out in 1973 essentially mirrored what Johnson had on the table in late 1968.) "This will be an open administration," Nixon trumpeted on November 6, 1968." We want to bring the American people together." He'd just turned fifty-six in January 1969, and he welcomed his presidency as almost all do, with the firm handshake and wave that promised a new era, that things would be different. In fact, as it turned out, his administration would just be more of the same.

Angry people lined the streets along Nixon's route to the White House, with their cruel signs and chanting. Never before had a new president been welcomed in such a way. The political cartoonists were having a field day: Nixon made for the perfect caricature, with that wide, confident smile and that ski-slope nose. This new president had his work cut out for him, a mess to clean up. The nation he was to lead wanted something done—and now.

The new commander-in-chief, seeking refuge that evening, sat down at the grand piano in the quiet family quarters of his new home and played Norwegian composer Christian Sinding's "Rustle of Spring," a popular piece, showy, seemingly a bit complicated, but repetitive, meant to symbolize the excited restlessness of spring. It was a calculated choice. Nixon called himself a peace president, and there was so much to do.

Promises to be kept. On his first night in the White House, Nixon slept just four hours. While shaving just before 7:00 a.m., he recalled a hidden safe Johnson had showed him during a visit in November, which contained what was to be his first order of business. The safe looked empty when he opened it, but upon closer inspection there was a thin folder on the top shelf. He pulled it out and opened it. It was the president's daily "Vietnam Situation Report" from the intelligence services for the previous day, Johnson's last day in office.

Nixon flipped through the report. One page contained casualty figures. During the week ending January 18, 185 Americans had been killed and 1,237 wounded. The yearlong toll was staggering for a war that was going nowhere: between January 1, 1968, and January 18, 1969, 14,958 men had been killed and 95,798 wounded. Nixon closed the folder, put it back in the safe, and left it there until the war was over. It was "a constant reminder of [the war's] tragic cost," he would later write. Vietnam was the root cause of the sagging national morale that Nixon would struggle to lift, and the war's death toll would haunt him in the first few months of his presidency. That, and that the times were changing. A general was dying.

Like the slow closing of a curtain, Dwight D. Eisenhower was in his last months. Nixon had served as President Eisenhower's vice president throughout the 1950s, and while they shared the distinction of being the only two Republicans elected into office since 1933, the pair couldn't have been more different. Eisenhower, the revered general and supreme Allied commander who'd led forces into Normandy during World War II, selected Nixon as his running mate in 1952 for reasons of strategy, not necessarily of personal preference.

Eisenhower and Nixon disagreed on politics, and were known to squabble, often and bitterly. Nixon was younger, a hawkish anti-Communist, popular in his home state of California—his name on the ballot alone won the pair the Golden State. When Viet Minh revolutionaries drove the French out of Indochina in 1954, Nixon pressured Eisenhower to intervene on behalf of French forces at Dien Bien Phu, even publicly advocating boots-on-the-ground U.S. involvement—a position he would later distance himself from—but Eisenhower adamantly refused. Nixon had sharp words for the dovish defense policies Eisenhower supported, like the formation (also in 1954) of the Southeast Asian Treaty Organization, which attempted to contain communism with regional alliances. "This togetherness bullshit," Nixon called it. "I don't believe in that. I think the time will come when we'll look back at this era and ask ourselves whether we were crazy or something."

Still, the looming death of Eisenhower, who had spent much of 1968 in Walter Reed Hospital in Bethesda, Maryland, weighed heavy on Nixon. He may have disagreed with some of Eisenhower's foreign policy decisions, especially, but the new president was distraught at seeing his predecessor so ill, noting that "he looked like a corpse—waxen face."

In the last days of March 1969, the two posed for press photos, the old president and the new, like bookends: Nixon in a suit, legs crossed and looking on at the old general beside him, Eisenhower in a gentleman's red robe over loose white pajamas, pale and gaunt yet smiling, his feet in slippers lined with wool. One couldn't help remembering where they'd been, how far things had come and gone. Nearly 15 years ago to the date Nixon had looked on as Eisenhower held the historic press conference at which he first mentioned the infamous " 'falling domino' principle," which held that if one small country fell to communism, all the others would follow. It was this theory that made the fate of a small country like Vietnam, only slightly larger than Texas, loom so large, embroiling America in a bloody undeclared ground war. Nixon, smiling alongside his former running mate and beloved friend in the spring of 1969, wanted desperately to get out of Vietnam, yet he found that he could not. It was that massive ship again, unable to change course. What was it? This jam in the wheel?

As much as 70 percent of the reason America did not pull out of Vietnam in 1968 and 1969—when it was clear the war needed to end—polls later revealed, was simply put, national pride. In 1968 Nixon had run on the promise of peace, and he would spend his first few months looking for ways out of the war—or at least ways to make the American people think its boys would be coming home. Yet soon after his swearing-in he would initiate a secret bombing campaign in Cambodia known as Operation Breakfast, actually widening the combat zone. Such was the "schizophrenic nature," it would much later be penned in a book chronicling the landmark year of 1969, of Nixon's first hundred days. The jets were actually incinerating targets just as Nixon posed for the press alongside his dying, war-famous predecessor. The press before him had no idea of the secret bombing.

That's not the only secret weighing on Nixon at the time. A two-year task initiated by former secretary of defense Robert McNamara had just been completed, with only fifteen copies released. The top-secret Pentagon Papers found that virtually every administration, even that of the now-fading Eisenhower, had systematically lied about America's involvement in the Southeast Asian peninsula. The study gave credibility to every single hippie protester causing an eyesore in the nation's capital. But even though the war couldn't go on, even as America shouted, tore its way through barricades, prayed silent prayers for peace, the war would go on. Just as they sat there, friendly smiles and plush chairs.

The troops would march on.

The warships would set sail.

Eisenhower's death made every front page on March 29, 1969. Few believed in the domino theory that he'd made famous anymore. Those dominoes had all come tumbling down, kindling style, right up to the steps of the White House, an administration now charged with ending this war in Vietnam. The *Long Beach Telegram*, a steely-eyed Ike pictured on the front, sat folded sloppily on the wardroom table the day the *Evans* left for Vietnam, barely prepared for what lay ahead. The *Evans* was leaving a few months earlier than anticipated; in the fall of 1968 the crew had been told they'd deploy in May 1969. Strong words from the U.S. Navy headquarters trickled down in official memos and harsh conversations: Get the hell over there.

The *Evans* sliced through the waters of the mighty Pacific, water splashing on her bow with every dip into a wave, a trail of white froth behind her. From afar she was a vision—agile and sleek, her mighty whale-gray sides glistening in the sun.

Premonitions are a tricky thing. Some prove eerily apt; some are just imaginings born of dread, that foreboding that's inseparable from warfare. By March of 1969, several men had had premonitions about the "Fighting Frank." A man who had come on board the *Evans* in January to tour his twin brother's new digs, the narrow bunk bed and cramped desk that welcomed a junior officer, had a vision of something terrible, of something crashing, exploding, of fire. He tucked the vision away and forgot about it—that is, until two months later when he watched the *Evans* steam out of Long Beach Harbor. He waved to the brother with who he'd shared a womb and knew somehow that it would be the last time.

One sailor on board that winter wrote his father wildly descriptive letters about his visions and nightmares, telling him how he'd dreamed of an explosion and hell-hot steam, of trying to get away from the fire. "Everybody's trying to get off this thing," he wrote his father, a former Navy man himself. "The Navy... it's not like when you were in." He fought hard to get reassigned, making a total of thirty-one transfer requests. Nothing worked, until this young sailor admitted to drug use and mental problems, mentioning that he could hear Aretha Franklin's powerful vocals in the hum of the engine rooms. That earned him a Section 8, the discharge given to the mentally unfit—just another crazy bastard. Relieved, he helped cast the line from the dock at Long Beach and watched his friends leave, sailors in white, waving back, becoming smaller and smaller, just specks against a vast crystal sea. His own heart sank. He had an empty, lost feeling, a feeling that something was going to go terribly wrong, he wrote in a letter to his father some time after that. He apologized for any shame he had caused his family, he wrote, but he simply "could not go."

The most official of premonitions came from the highest of places. The psychic Jeanne Dixon was a sort of pope when it came to visions of the future; she was said to have predicted the John F. Kennedy assassination and the mysterious loss of the USS *Scorpion* submarine in 1968. Her annual syndicated column for 1969 predicted "great danger around our defense set up . . . there seems to be a healthy death toll around the middle of the year . . . caused perhaps by human carelessness or sabotage." Perhaps somewhere, somehow, a more specific rumor had trickled down to the *Evans* crew. The scuttlebutt made its way from the wardroom to the mess deck, and into several letters home. "I forgot to tell ma and dad a big rumor. See if you can find a book or something of Jeannie Dickins predictions! She was supposed to have said the Frank E. ain't going to make it back...," wrote one sailor to his sister. Another wrote to his parents saying he saw an article about it in *Stars and Stripes*, yet no such article existed.

By spring of 1969 the latest figures had come out in news reports: some 24,000 men had been lost in Vietnam, with scores of others injured. An impatient public wanted to know: When will Nixon stop it? The U.S. government was about to reach its halfway mark in American blood without ceasing. The *Evans* was just another ship, another cog in the machine, a stream of froth behind her, heading for Southeast Asia.

She passed clusters of other gray ships on her way out of Long Beach Harbor. Off in the distance crept the long shadow of the 1,000-foot-long, 81,000-ton ocean liner the RMS *Queen Mary*, which the City of Long Beach had just purchased as a tourist attraction. Bigger than the doomed *Titanic*, the *Queen Mary* had a macabre story all her own. During World War II, her career as a passenger and pleasure ship put on hold, she was painted battleship gray and pressed into service as a troop transport. En route to England to deliver twelve thousand soldiers for the European invasion in late 1942, while performing antisubmarine maneuvers that called for a course that zigzagged every few minutes to confuse and evade German U-boats, she rammed into the 4,000-ton British cruiser HMS *Curacoa*. The collision—caused by confusion among officers on both ships—cut the smaller ship in half, sinking the vessel in minutes and sending more than three hundred sailors to their death in the icy waters of the north Atlantic off Ireland. The *Queen Mary* was ordered to keep steaming; a rescue attempt could jeopardize the massive ship in the dangerous waters west of Europe. The loss of the *Curacoa* was not reported until the war was over, and not until 1945 were families of those who died in the collision told the truth about their sons and husbands. Legend has it that she is haunted; that even today, in the midnight hours, a banging on her steel hull can be heard.

The *Evans* sailors watched her with wide, curious eyes, her smokestacks visible from a distance. They watched the coastline disappear. And then, there was nothing but blue and the rattling, apprehensive hum from the engines below.

9

THE GRAYING GHOST

That the USS *Frank E. Evans* was heralded as a "super destroyer" when she glided through the shadow of the New York City skyline on October 3, 1944, would have the sailors of the 1960s rolling in their faded dungarees. Now the twenty-five-year-old vessel's frail, rusty innards were virtually patched together with baling wire and globs of the sticky adhesive known around the fleet as "monkey shit." A chief might have wisecracked, seeing an eager-to-please seaman apprentice scraping away at paint on a bulkhead, "Not too much, son, the paint's what's holding this thing together." In 1969 it was hard to believe the *Evans* was still serving her country.

Just as every old lady had once been a lovely lassie, the *Evans* had had her heyday. In 1944, when she rolled off the World War II assembly line in New York Harbor, the number 754 stamped in muted white letters on her glistening hull, she was intended to incinerate what was left of the Imperial Japanese Navy. With her sleek dagger-nosed lines and proud superstructure, she was an inspiring sight for a country three years into a world war, a country searching for heroes. The newspapermen called her a "Jap buster," with the speed and agility to outmaneuver Japan's fleet of heavy armed cruisers.

The *Evans* belonged to the *Allen M. Sumner* class of destroyers. Fifty-eight of these sleek new destroyers were built, coming off the line beginning in 1943. *Sumner*-class ships were among the first to boast of an operations room, or combat information center. Just big enough for a small team of radarmen to work around an antisubmarine plotting table, the combat information center was the ship's nerve center. Sailors called it "the CIC." Here information was collected, processed, evaluated, disseminated, both internally and externally. With its eye-friendly dim red lighting, scopes, telephone radio handsets, arteries of silver conduits, wired headsets, and round screens, the combat information center looked like something out of a spaceship—and in fact, Rear Admiral Cal Laning, who helped develop the first combat information centers, acknowledged that he was inspired "specifically, consciously, and deliberately" by E. E. "Doc" Smith's Lensman sci-fi space opera, which first appeared as a serial in 1937.

Such operations rooms grew out of the desperate need for ships in World War II to better coordinate with friendly vessels. It had become all too apparent during the Pacific theater's Guadalcanal Campaign of 1942–43, which cost the U.S. Navy twenty-nine ships in all. Many of those losses were due not so much to the enemy's strength as to confusion and lack of coordination between U.S. vessels—in short, in some cases, to friendly fire. It was so bad that one late-night battle was dubbed a "drunken bar fight in the night." Learning from its mistakes, the U.S. Navy included a combat information center in all of its plans for new ships. Combat, another name for this brain of the ship, was a layer of protection against mishaps.

The *Sumners* were also a step up from earlier, much simpler destroyers in their armaments: three sets of five-inch, 38-caliber guns in pairs—a total of six!-- that could fire full salvo (all at once), causing an earthquake-like rattling on board but incinerating any target within a nine-mile firepower range. Light antiaircraft armament was also increased by almost 50 percent, in response to the desperate Japanese tactic of ordering kamikaze pilots to fly into enemy ships. Agile and deadly, with a top speed of 33 knots, the new *Sumner*-class destroyers turned heads when they showed up at Okinawa and Normandy.

The *Evans* was the thirty-second ship built at Bethlehem Steel's Staten Island yard after the attack on Pearl Harbor. She and her like were considered World War II latecomers. Many bore the names of men who had perished earlier in the war: the USS *Hyman* was named after the commander of a ship that continued to fire its guns as it sank in the Battle of the Coral Sea, the USS *Blue* after another commander who perished at Guadalcanal. The *Evans* herself was named after Marine Corps brigadier general Frank E. Evans, a hero in both the Spanish-American War and World War I, who earned a Navy Cross in France in the infamous Battle of Belleau Wood.

Evans died in a veteran's hospital in Pearl Harbor only twelve days before the Japanese decimated the U.S. Navy's

Pacific Fleet in 1941. Within three years his widow, a pretty and polite southerner named Alleen Fisk Evans, sent a champagne bottle crashing against the hull of her husband's namesake, while a band played and flags waved in the cool autumn breeze. It was both a celebration and a promise, embodied in steel: the United States would prevail, the war would be won. Patton's Third Army was already well into France or beyond. Nearby, a woman held an infant child on her hip so that he might marvel at the thing his daddy had helped to build. That infant would grow up, join the Navy, and go down with this same ship. In another wild coincidence, the ship's namesake had served at Marine Corps headquarters in the early part of the century alongside another Marine officer named Albert Sydney McLemore—the grandfather of the man who'd be skipper of the *Evans* on her final cruise.

During World War II, however, the *Evans*'s scorecard was subdued at best. She'd arrive on the scene in Okinawa just in time for one last dance with some eighty-eight desperate Japanese planes, which she survived unscathed, her maneuverability standing her in good stead against the dreaded kamikaze attacks. Within a year after her commissioning, ticker-tape parades would celebrate the end of the world's second great war. A few years after that the *Evans* was decommissioned, mothballed alongside her sister ships until the need for her arose again. The country at the time could hardly even imagine another dreadful war—yet it was, as most are, already on the horizon.

By the time things heated up in Korea five years later, the

Evans was back on the line, stationed off the coast of North Korea to support U.S. Marines on the ground. She earned the nickname "Gray Ghost" for her dead-on accuracy, followed by her smooth disappearance into the low-lying coastal fog off the Korean peninsula. The recognition that eluded her in World War II would come in plenty in Korea, where she would earn seven awards and commendations for her participation in such events as the Siege of Wonsan of 1951–53.

As the guns cooled on the *Evans* once again, talk of war went cold—though *hotheaded* might be the better word. During the Cold War, Soviet Russia built up its submarine fleet to a staggering degree, and the U.S. Navy countered, in part, with the Fleet Rehabilitation and Modernization (FRAM) program. Under FRAM, the Navy's aging destroyers were given a new lease of life as submarine hunter-killers, supplied with improved radar, sonar, and weapons systems. By 1962 the *Evans* herself was polished up and ready for Hollywood, starring as the fictional USS *Appleby* in the television hit *Ensign O'Toole*, a military comedy that examined the trials and tribulations of a wide-eyed ensign who fumbled his way through navy life on a ship full of cantankerous men one character would call simply "depressed." The show, which starred the handsome Dean Jones, would air for thirty-two episodes at 7:00 p.m. on Sunday nights. In this slot it was unlucky enough to face off against the vehicle for a much bigger name—the dog America would come to know simply as "Lassie."

When *Ensign O'Toole* was canceled in May of 1963, the

stage lights dimmed for the *Evans*, but within two years Vietnam had put her to work as a fire-breathing warship once again. In 1965, just as boots were hitting the ground in South Vietnam, the *Evans* joined others in the Seventh Fleet off the long and dangerous coast of South Vietnam and into the Gulf of Tonkin. Naval destroyers have long been considered the greyhounds of any navy; small, swift, and yet mighty. These smaller warships juggled multiple roles in the Vietnam War like workhorses: naval gunfire, then surveillance of enemy vessels transporting supplies to the Vietcong in South Vietnam, back to naval gunfire, then off to support aircraft carriers in their bombing missions, with bouts of liberty at U.S. Naval Base Subic Bay in the Philippines for repairs, upkeep, and replenishment.

Ironically, though the *Evans* and her ilk were now equipped with the new technology needed for tracking and targeting Russian submarines, it was her old, overworked five-inch guns—supplied with a stockpile of antiquated ammunition shells, some with anti-Japanese rhetoric still scribbled on them in thick globs of black paint—that got the real workout in Vietnam. One of the Seventh Fleet's greatest challenges was how to meet the demands of this new war with a fleet of aging warships. In 1966, with the war in Vietnam in full swing, the Seventh Fleet decided to reactivate parts of its mothballed fleet and keep older ships on station. The U.S. Navy also attempted to pull some destroyers from the Atlantic Fleet and send them to the Western Pacific—fast becoming unofficial code for "Vietnam"—instead. Another ship would make headlines in 1969 when its sailors contacted a U.S. senator to report that the

Navy was forcing it to leave for Vietnam, even though it was two boilers down and there were no repairs in sight.

Meanwhile, the Navy was tagging ships that needed to go, ships not worth keeping around. By the spring of 1969 it had targeted nineteen old ships for decommissioning, among them several *Fletcher*-class destroyers, predecessors of the *Evans* that were still fighting in Vietnam. In congressional testimony in the spring of 1969, Admiral Thomas H. Moorer, chief of naval operations, would reveal that 58 percent of the Navy's nine hundred ships were at least twenty years old; in his opinion, he testified, fifteen years was a warship's maximum useful shelf life. In discussions over the matter of what one *Stars and Stripes* headline would reveal as a "fleet in trouble," a congressional subcommittee reported that many of the 475 ships in the Pacific Fleet did not "meet combat standards of readiness. They are either not ready or in a reduced state . . . caused primarily by age." It was a grim picture, as the congressional committee findings made clear:

> *There are frequent breakdowns in aging ships as a result of the pace that must be maintained because of the tempo of operations in Vietnam. . . . On occasion it has been necessary to tow an old ship home because of the failure of her ancient main propulsion machine. . . .*
>
> *The maintenance of ships would be impossible without the splendid devotion to duty of Navy crew members, many of whom work as much as 80 hours a week. . . . In addition many crews are required to put in long work hours of maintenance while in port.*

As for manpower, as well as calling attention to low

reenlistment rates, the committee noted that "because of the Vietnam War demands the experience level of the men who man the fleet has been diluted and today, about half of those at sea have been on their ships less than one year."

That spring the *Evans* was just another old girl in the lineup, with too many inexperienced hands on deck, struggling to meet the demands of the Vietnam War, with its pressures and morale problems. On the outside she sliced cleanly through the water as though she had just come off the assembly line. On the inside, though, she creaked a little at higher speeds. Flank speed might rip her to shreds. She rocked and rolled, shook at times. In the hell-hot engine rooms she clanked and roared when she was under way. Those who kept her furious boilers, gauges, steel wheels, and lava-hot pipes repaired with God-knows-what were just waiting and watching for something to go *ping*, a spring to go flying, a valve to blow, an eerie hissing to emanate louder, stronger than usual. Inside her belly sailors fussed and fought, in some cases cheated and stole, all to keep this "floating paint bucket" up to speed and ready for anything.

Vietnam was the reason.

10

A SINKING SHIP

When it came to getting an old steam-powered ship up and running, the unsung heroes were those who spent their days and nights crawling into the manholes that led to her engineering spaces. In World War II this lively bunch earned the name "black gang" for their resemblance to coal miners, their clothes, hands, and faces streaked with soot and coal until they looked more like minstrel performers than seamen. By the 1960s they'd become known as "snipes," though they remained just as grimy as their predecessors. They were subjects of a litany of modern-day naval folklore: a true snipe, it was said, couldn't tolerate direct sunlight or fresh air; he got nosebleeds at altitudes higher than the waterline, and he never drank coffee without a swig of engine oil. Given the 120-degree temperature and the poor ventilation in the places where these men worked, it did seem they'd almost have to have a few screws loose to do the job. It was like working in hell. It *was* hell. Who the hell would work there? On board, they called it "the hole."

Snipes of that era were a special breed. On paper, they were listed as machinist mates and boiler tenders. Those who ended up in the job often did so by accident, or by scoring high on assessments that found them to be "mechanically inclined." There were some who actually chose the position, though. In the *Bluejacket's Manual* chapter that described the job of machinist mate, an eager seaman-in-training might stumble upon a picture of a smiling gentleman in full dungaree uniform—starched shirt, pressed pants, and crisp white cap tipped jauntily just over his brow—standing in front of a panel, a fascinating and powerful array of gauges, dials, and wheels. He might think: What an interesting job! Only later would he find out that rarely does a snipe wear a shirt at all on the job, much less a starched one. Ditto for his white Dixie cup cover, which would eventually be stained with a bleeding halo of yellow or smothered in grease or oil. And rarely would he beam like the young man in the manual, though he might snicker or smirk. If he was smiling, you'd better watch out; either he'd just played a prank on you, or, on liberty, he was drunk.

Sunlight, they swore, would burn the snipe's eyes. They were the vampires of the ship, the midnight bandits who stole the breakfast cinnamon rolls. Tricksters, they almost always targeted the new guys. They might send some wide-eyed kid off hunting for "relative bearing grease"—which didn't exist— or a "bucket of steam." Within a few months the new guys would be initiated, their brains scrambled in the oven that was belowdecks. Eventually they too would come to see the rate as a proud, higher calling—a pride they'd carry into old age.

A new snipe learned quickly not even to imagine he might stay clean. Sweat was a constant, and the thick, hot air could make breathing difficult. It was a catch-22: you had to be crazy to do the job, but if you went crazy, you couldn't. (That sailor who believed he heard Aretha Franklin somewhere in the roar and hiss of the engines was a snipe—or trying to be.) In the mess decks, snipes sat together; as filthy as they were, with soot on their faces and engine grease under their fingernails, nobody else would sit near them. They took a certain pleasure in that involuntary exclusivity.

The men would grumble at the snipes when streaks of grease and oil sludge appeared on a deck that had just been swabbed or a railing freshly polished. The manhole-like scuttle to the engine room might be just barely closed when a deck ape would swing it open and holler for someone to go rot in hell. "Animals," a seaman would mutter, going for the locker of cleaning rags yet again. Laughter would ring out from below, as if from the demons of the underground.

On the *Evans*, one-third of the crew worked belowdecks. They were Captain McLemore's favorite bunch, for reasons that went beyond their miraculous ability to get a twenty-five-year-old ship from cold-iron dead to 23 knots. The sound of it was intoxicating. As far back as his college days at the California Maritime Academy, the captain had preferred the grimy, hot, dark compartments below to any other place on a sea-going vessel. After all, he was the man who'd just wanted to drive a truck for a living. His last assignment—as the head engineering officer, climbing into the rotting, noisy belly of the USS *Bonhomme Richard*, affectionately known as the Bonnie

Dick, to keep the old ship up and running—had been a dream for him. And his job had been vital, enabling everyone above decks—from the navigators to the pilots—to do their own. She, also, was a relic kept on the line to fight in Vietnam.

So at home was McLemore in the ship's low-ceilinged, dirty engine compartments that some thought he must be a mustang, a naval officer who'd first served as an enlisted sailor. Surely, they thought, perhaps noticing the moon-shaped grime under his fingernails, he'd started out just where they had. It was true enough that the captain knew the engine rooms inside and out, and he knew, as one *Evans* snipe put it candidly, that you can't get shit done if you can't get there first. McLemore understood these men. And on a ship like the *Evans*, whose duties could outstrip her capacity in the time it took for one bolt to loosen or one steam pipe to break, he knew how important they were. The engineering department made fighting a war possible, even if they were the dirtiest, cruddiest band of hooligans on board.

On navy ships, redundancy was a key engineering principle. There were two of everything: two engine rooms, and two fire rooms, where tenders worked the boilers that heated the water that created the steam that set the turbines—manned by engine room operators, who took orders from the bridge on how much and how fast—in motion. It was a matter of survival. If one area was hit with a torpedo, the other would still function to get the ship moving. If she couldn't get moving, she was dead in the water. Snipes fought their own war.

This redundancy came in handy later in the geriatric years;

when something went wrong on one side, the other could limp the ship over to a repair station and get her fixed. But by 1969 there weren't a lot of spare parts around to fix a fading ship, and often parts had to be cannibalized from other old ships. The irony was that the *Evans* had just come off a massive overhaul. Following her last stint in Vietnam she had been lifted out of the water into what's called dry dock, so the vast colonies of barnacles could be scraped off her hull, and she could undergo repairs and routine upkeep, amidst a skeletal cage of scaffolding

In reality, the U.S. Navy was as broke as a sailor two days before payday. There wasn't much that could—or would—be done. There was talk of decommissioning these old girls, putting ships like the *Evans* out of their misery. But she was needed for Vietnam, the counterargument went; they'd stick her back together with chewing gum if they had to. Some of the chiefs proclaimed her the worst piece of shit they'd ever served on. One *Evans* sailor had the misfortune of seeing her in dry dock the day he was to check in to his new assignment, her hull mottled with thick patches of orange base paint, her once-sleek body obscured by the scaffolding. They were planning to take *that* to sea?

"Conely! Conely!"

No answer. The dapper officer stood at the bottom rung of the ladder, not wanting to step farther into the hole. The lighting was dim. The heat unbearable. The engineering crewmen didn't move. Nobody said anything. It frustrated James Hopson, by now a lieutenant junior grade, a former enlisted sailor who'd worked as a corpsman before earning a commission, a pin and a piece of paper that qualified him to lead on board a navy ship. Many thought Hopson, who'd landed the title of main propulsion assistant by default, a duck out of water—even the captain would later say so. He was known for strutting about the engineering spaces with an old *Sumner*-class ship's manual in hand, looking for gauges and buttons. His demeanor might be a little officious, the captain thought, but he was eager to do a good job. Hopson questioned some repair jobs, and he'd demand that operators submit official paperwork for parts and supplies, a pointless task—it would have made about as much sense to send them to Santa Claus at the North Pole. There was the U.S. Navy way, and then there was the way it went.

"Conely? Dammit! Where's Conely?"

This scene had played out more than once in the ship's engineering compartments—the scene where someone was in trouble, and somehow no one could ever seem to locate him, even though they were all on a ship, a ship that often times felt no bigger than a school bus, where no one could possibly disappear unless he jumped overboard.

And if he had, Hopson likely thought, good riddance.

"Conely!"

More silence. The snipes were desperate to get the junior officer in his starched khakis off their backs so they could go on talking about whatever the hell they happened to be talking about—girls, liberty, who owed who how many "beer tickets," slang for foreign currency. All the while they were listening for bells from topside, signals that told them how fast the ship needed to go, how much horsepower they'd need to get it wherever it was they were going. The scuttlebutt was, they'd be in Vietnam in a few days.

Someone would have to throw Hopson a bone, just to get rid of him.

Butterball? Haven't seen him.

Of course they had seen him. There weren't many places to hide on a tin can no longer than a football field and no wider than a locker room. Hopson probably knew he was being taken for a ride. Knew it just like he knew, when they told him there was a fire in the hole, that there really wasn't, but he had to go down there and check just because, well, you never know. A fire on a ship was a treacherous thing. Sailors loved to screw with junior officers like Hopson. Like when they told one of these recent college graduates to watch out for the mail buoy, floating somewhere on the wide, deep ocean, which ensured they would receive letters from loved ones. *If we miss the mail buoy, we won't see the mail for weeks.*

It was Hopson's eleventh year in the Navy, but he'd spent most of those years in reserves and in college. The *Evans* was his first ship assignment, his first rendezvous on board a destroyer where you were the entertainment, the butt of countless pranks, if you were new, or just because you didn't fit in. Shoved into a position he wasn't comfortable with, Hopson focused his pent-up frustration on this ghost, this man who went by the name Conely—on the official paperwork and embroidered on his uniform, at least, if nowhere else.

Five-foot-five, with thick-framed glasses over a minute nose, twenty-two-year-old machinist mate Duane S. Conely was hardly invisible, though nobody called him by his real name. A little potbelly and a comic demeanor had earned him the nickname Butterball, and it stuck. A little off-kilter like all the rest, Butterball was a sort of top banana. He'd already been in the Navy for a few years when he was assigned to the *Evans,* and upon arriving he was quick to tell anyone who would listen that he wasn't the spit-and-shine type. "I don't care what it looks like," he'd say. Comfortable with rash dares and quirky, borderline criminal activity, he could walk into a navy parts shop with $50 and walk back out with $200 worth of items. How? "It's a secret." His biggest heist was a 150-pound engine part from another *Sumner*-class vessel docked down the line at Long Beach. "I just walked on there like I belong there, got myself a cart and wheeled it right off."

McLemore loved Conely the minute he laid eyes on this pudgy sailor, demonstrating how he'd managed to fix something with some doohickey he'd found somewhere, he couldn't exactly recall. Perhaps the captain had a hunch, but he found it prudent not to probe too hard. There was a job to do, and Butterball got it done.

One of three hundred or so people who lived in Warren, Minnesota, in the 1950s, Conely'd joined the U.S. Navy at the stern instructions of his father, who told his son he'd break both of his legs if he joined the Army. And he meant it. Dennie Conely had a military record that read like a condensed history of the European theater in World War II: Sicily, Rome, Rhineland, Ardennes, Central Europe. A paratrooper, he spoke little of his war experience. There were signs that it haunted him. Once Butterball came home from a friend's house with a Mohawk haircut, "because they were bored." It wasn't a hit. "My father shaved my head when he saw that. Didn't say a word." Later on it became apparent that his son's haircut had reminded the old veteran of his 101st Airborne compatriots, famous for the Mohawks they wore to intimidate the enemy. The unit lost many. The memory had hit him hard. War was hell, and he didn't want his firstborn son to see any of it.

Butterball was always a fun kid, his mother would say, with a penchant for surprises. One such surprise came when he was working at an uncle's farm, hauling truckloads of beets. The truck's engine seized, and after a brief inspection, Butterball was able to get it running again with a few makeshift repairs. He was the sort who could look at a machine, no matter how complicated or hopeless the problem, and figure out some way to jury-rig it and get it going again.

McLemore recognized this quality right away. "What else can you do?"

The captain had hit the jackpot: there was a pirate in his midst. Just the sort he needed.

"I can do everything but electrical."

That "everything" went beyond gears and fans. At first, Butterball never mentioned his ability to sweet-talk his way into getting things, when all else failed slipping things onto the cart in the naval supply shop without drawing anyone's attention. After all, his paunchy look didn't say sly. But those who did things by the books didn't like him. And Hopson— who didn't share the captain's tolerance for the out-of-the-box thinking often needed to keep a shitcan like the *Evans* running—was determined to clip the young sailor's wings.

Whenever Hopson showed up, it meant trouble. The men could tell by the way he roamed about the engine room, peering into every nook and cranny, every pipe and gauge. He was like a premed student studying for an anatomy exam, only this body was Frankenstein's monster, banged-up and bandaged, dead and brought back to life over and over again. Things that were supposed to be somewhere weren't, and things were there that weren't supposed to be. Hopson blamed people like Conely. The machinist made for an easy target at first glance—short, stout, bespectacled, the sort you almost felt sorry for—but first appearances are only half the story.

In the spring of 1969 Hopson was trying to get Butterball to admit he was on drugs. Butterball's dead-eye stare let Hopson know he wasn't budging; he wouldn't admit to something that wasn't true. At last Hopson turned away, and in a minute he was up the ladder and out of sight. And then it came: "I'm no druggie. But I am a drunk." Butterball's laugh was infectious. No one knew for sure whether he meant it. Some said privately they'd heard that signature *clink* of a bottle, but wouldn't dare accuse him out loud. Sure he was loopy, but then again, *aren't we all?*

Butterball walked a fine line between being candid and being comical, a squiggly line that kept you guessing. He made one thing clear enough, though: he despised young officers, the ones like Hopson. The enlisted called a lot of them "ninety-day wonders." They were college guys who came into the fleet to command after three months of officer candidate school. More often than not the enlisted men knew much more than these young officers did. It was a familiar dynamic in almost every military unit, on land and out to sea. For Butterball, it was never a matter of jealousy; he just scorned the officers for their lack of street smarts and savvy. He also despised, in his own words, "the goddamn need to do everything by the book."

Butterball already had a sea bag of stories. His first assignment, in 1966, was on the USS *Sperry*, a submarine tender charged with escorting and repairing the Navy's growing fleet of submarines. One Friday, while they were steaming across San Diego Bay, a junior officer ordered Butterball to release the ship's liquid nitrogen stores into the bay, a body of water practically surrounded by military installations, hotels, and fancy homes. The officer perhaps didn't know this would create a dramatic freezing chemical reaction. "There we had an iceberg, right in the middle of San Diego Bay," Butterball would later recall, chuckling. He'd known what would happen, but said nothing. "Just following orders."

Some months later, with Butterball already gone on to his next assignment on the *Evans*, the *Sperry* would make headlines, running aground in the Columbia River in the state of Washington, taking out a road along a muddy bank near the charming little town of Stella.

If there was one group that kept McLemore up at night, it wasn't the engineering crew; it was his officers. It wasn't anything personal. Of the sixteen officers McLemore dined with in the wardroom on the night the *Evans* left Long Beach, thirteen had been commissioned less than twenty months before. Most of them were ensigns, with four slated to make lieutenant junior grade within a month of the Hawaii port visit. He had one full lieutenant and one lieutenant commander, his second-in-command executive officer, a man who handled most of the ship's administrative duties. Altogether, only five including himself could command the ship's pilothouse in fleet operations, a man-in-charge position known as officer of the deck. There were some shining stars and polished academy types who had it in their blood. Some, he knew he couldn't trust. (He'd later put young Hopson in this category.) Some, he knew, were led to the Navy by the threat of the Army draft. Some were so quiet and introverted, he didn't know what to make of them, but he suspected they might not be ready for greater responsibilities.

Still, as the old navy rule goes, the captain is in charge of his ship; whatever happens there is ultimately his own fault. As one old ship captain of the era put it frankly, "Even if a rogue sailor decides to jump into the pilothouse, kill everyone and drive the ship into a rocky sea cliff, it's still the captain's fault 'cause he should have known he had a rogue sailor on board."

The U.S. Navy has in place a laundry list of skills the officer of the deck, the man in charge of the ship's operations, needs; things he should know. Unfortunately, as was all too common in those times, McLemore had lost many of his experienced officers of the deck just before deploying. The wife of one was said to have gone crazy. Some had been sent on to the Navy's new Naval Destroyer School, the brass's answer to the force's inadequate training and the abundance of recent accidents and near misses involving American ships. Some had gone on to other assignments, or gotten out of the Navy altogether.

It was no secret that the U.S. Navy had trouble retaining officers. Even the ones who swore they'd be lifers were out in less than four years. One overwhelming reason: it wasn't their father's navy anymore.

It was an era of naval surface warfare one expert would later call "the doldrums." Surface vessels were staffed at 81 percent, while aviation and submarine billets were staffed at a healthy 110 percent. Ensigns were being pressed into service as officers of the deck prematurely, many believed. Noncommissioned chiefs were called to serve as officer of the deck when there weren't enough officers around to fill the time slots for various watches. With much attention on submarines and aviation, surface warfare had become the "red-headed stepchild" of the Navy.

That spring, McLemore was on the hook to train more officers and get them on the line. It was a tough job, on a ship that had spent much of the past year in dry dock for upkeep and repairs—when the ship wasn't steaming, there was no on-the-job training—and in a Navy that had to do more with less. "You had to work with what you had," the ship's executive officer, George McMichael, would say, praising McLemore for working with the young officers, getting them up to speed on what to do and when, how to solve problems, and how not to run the ship onto an island, which had been happening frequently for other, similar vessels.

From the difficulties inherent in keeping a superannuated ship functioning to officers so young they had to cheat with grease pencils in beard-growing contests, new problems seemed to emerge with every new dawn on the big blue sea.

11

THE BIG GUNS

The dominant feeling in 1969 for any man in the service, from the top to the bottom, was pressure. Every man, from commander-in-chief Nixon down the chain to lowly captains like McLemore and to the ones who merely followed orders, was struggling to work with what he'd been dealt. And what McLemore had been dealt, in Pearl Harbor in April 1969, was one fresh ensign coming aboard to pile into junior officers quarters. Ensign Gregory Ogawa was a likeable, funny guy—a Japanese American from the San Francisco Bay Area, smart and quick. Within two months he'd surely be up to speed as a junior officer of the deck. But right now that wouldn't solve McLemore's problem: he didn't have enough experienced ship handlers. Not only that, but the ship was understaffed in enlisted rates by at least, rumor had it, a third. Word was, McLemore had put in for more men. His request wouldn't have far to travel up the chain, geographically speaking; the Pacific Fleet commander's office was within eyesight of the *Evans,* which was moored in Pearl Harbor now, as McLemore's men struggled to get one of her guns to work properly. But that didn't mean much—dare we mention Santa Claus again? The Pacific Command had its own set of problems: manpower, morale, money . . . the list went on. The problem that stood out right then was this: there were a lot of ships like the *Evans* on the line.

By April 1969 Admiral John Sidney McCain Jr. was back on the job as commander in chief of the Pacific Command, or CINCPAC, after suffering a stroke just after the New Year. Though McCain was headquartered in Hawaii, he traveled between the island and Washington, D.C.. A fair-haired man, he was the son of a famous World War II admiral and by then, the unfortunate father of a downed Navy pilot at that moment rotting in the infamous North Vietnamese Hoa Lo Prison, known as the Hanoi Hilton. The younger John McCain had been shot down in October 1967, beaten, given marginal medical treatment, and tortured. After his captors discovered that he was naval royalty, they offered him the chance to go home. He refused, because others had been in captivity longer. (This young man would later become a U.S. senator and run for president.) The admiral was short and thin, smoked cigars, and was known to spend Christmases as close to the North Vietnamese border as possible, to be near his son.

Admiral McCain, his eyes like stones, was shattered by his son's imprisonment, but he hid it well—he and his wife Roberta were said to have attended a dinner party in London upon hearing that their son had been shot down near Hanoi.

His new commander in chief wanted to end the war; McCain, a believer in the floundering "domino theory," knew some things could not wait and that he had to be on task. Already, since his month-long hospitalization in Bethesda Naval Hospital, he had met with Nixon, who took a liking to the Pacific Fleet commander's calm, confidence-inspiring demeanor. The admiral also flew to Vietnam to discuss the latest efforts in and around country with General Creighton Abrams, who followed General William Westmoreland as head of Military Assistance Command Vietnam, and himself had two sons serving in country as Army officers.

Standing side by side, Abrams and McCain seemed an odd couple. In one press photo they posed on a well-guarded tarmac at Tan Son Nhut Air Base, one in crisp khaki, a tucked-in shirt, and fancy, gold-threaded cover, the other in olive-drab Army fatigues. They met frequently inside the low, undistinguished white building known as Pentagon East, the U.S. command center in Vietnam. Appearances aside, the two had much in common. Both had their own blood in the war; one's son was a prisoner of war, the other's in the field. Both were fairly new to the job, both were impatient for victory, and both knew time would be running out sooner rather than later.

Among Abrams's concerns that spring was that the USS *New Jersey* was gearing up to return home after a year parked off the coast of Vietnam. In April 1968, when the *New Jersey* first made her appearance in Southeast Asia, air losses were at a maximum, and she was eagerly awaited. Ground troops had pleaded for 56,000-ton battleships and their big guns as early as 1966, though at the time it had been decided that destroyers would suffice as naval gunfire support. Eventually the U.S. Navy put in for two battleships, and the Pentagon gave them one. The Navy had four battleships left, mothballed but not forgotten from the heydays of World War II and Korea.

In April 1968 the *New Jersey* was a lifesaver; just her presence gave the beleaguered troops shivers. The headlines over the course of her stint in Vietnam trumpeted BATTLESHIP NEW JERSEY BLEW PART OF ISLAND OFF MAP and FIREPOWER FOR FREEDOM. Massive and mighty, she could fire from thirty miles away; her 2,700-pound projectiles could do the work of sixty bombers, without risking the lives of pilots who could get shot down. (Decades later the Marine Corps would calculate that 80 percent of the 1,067 U.S. planes lost in Vietnam could have been saved had battleships been used throughout the war.) Several thousand yards from the green Vietnam coastline, the *New Jersey* patrolled unopposed; the North Vietnamese junks, as they were known, were no threat to her. But by the spring of 1969, she was old and in poor repair, long overdue to head home.

Nobody in Washington was happy to see her go. In February of that year the Nixon administration was circulating a memorandum with the subject heading "A Scenario of Possible Military Actions Related to South Vietnam" in preparation for a major spring or summer offensive. Tactics outlined included

> ...a combination of background maneuvers involving assets not currently tied 100 percent to the war in South Vietnam. This would involve an effort to orchestrate the impression that we were really plotting something

big in South Vietnam. On the commo side, it might involve the establishment of a phone net suggesting an intent to move more forces into South Vietnam. The assembly of ships in the far east, including naval and civil craft could be phased in. A series of commanders' conferences could be held to give the impression of planning for big new initiatives. On the covert side, to get the enemy edgy, agents could spread the word that something big was coming.

This show of force was perhaps one reason commanders wanted to keep the *New Jersey* in place: she was a symbol of American determination and might. A heated meeting at Pentagon East in March 1969 between Abrams, a handful of other generals, and Vice Admiral Elmo Zumwalt, then chief of the Naval Advisory Group for Military Assistance Command Vietnam and head of the Navy's brown-water riverine forces, made clear Abram's frustration with what he saw as a great mishandling of the war. McCain, who had earned the nickname "Mr. Seapower" in congressional circles for his fondness for strong naval presence, was not present. Abrams, who'd just met with the admiral a few days prior, was a spitfire—"The reaction's got to be quick. You can't wait around studying the goddamn thing." He started with the battlefield and went on to criticize the fleet anchored off and on along the coast, questioning the reliability of such a "fair weather thing that floats in and out of the theater occasionally." Another Army staffer present would add that an extension for the *New Jersey's* crew had been requested. In response, Zumwalt lamented that the decision was out of their hands; the battleship would carry on a rotation, "like cruisers," deploying for a year at a time and then returning home. He continued: "Now it could be kept out here by rotating personnel. At the eleventh hour, now would be a real mess to try to do it. When we raised this a couple of weeks ago, general, you thought you'd prefer to wait for Admiral McCain to take it up. And I understand he asked a question or two but we haven't seen any action yet. . . . This thing has a tremendous payoff."

"It's hard to figure it into your plans," Abrams replied; it was "sort of a fringe benefit that comes and goes. You're lucky when you've got it."

What the U.S. Navy did have was its carriers, a few cruisers with guided missile capabilities useless in the sort of war they were fighting in Vietnam, and a flexible force of destroyers, all-around workhorses that could perform a multitude of functions. In 1966, when infantry commanders begged for the big guns of the battleships, which at the time sat in mothballs, they were told they'd have to rely on the smaller, more agile warships. Ships like the *Evans*.

The word for McLemore and his ilk that spring: *Hurry up and get there. The military doesn't like excuses.*

Make them think we're planning something big.

12

Presents for Charlie

Within a month of their Hawaiian pit stop the *Evans* and her crew were there.

Vietnam was a seek-and-destroy war, its planners relying on the notion that if you found the enemy and killed enough of them, eventually they would call it a day, pack up, and go home. It was the brainchild of the best and brightest, a team that tried to tame warfare with numbers and statistics. It was war as business. Rather than plant flags, watch enemies retreat, and inch forward toward victory, you counted dead bodies. Eventually there would be no more fighters. Early on, one prominent war proponent said the United States could pave North Vietnam into a parking lot, paint stripes, and be home for Christmas. This country of caves and barefoot fighters was no match for America, it was thought.

By 1969 the death toll had mounted to hundreds of thousands dead, yet nothing had really changed. The Tet Offensive of 1968 was a massive defeat for the Vietcong and the

North Vietnamese regulars, yet even that made no difference; a year later American war planners found themselves bracing for another major offensive in the summer of 1969. In February of that year the president's men studied what could be done to prepare. Tet, while a win on the battlefield, had been a public relations mess back home, crippling public support for the war. The lesson: a major offensive was best avoided.

For troops, the principle was much the same. Seek and destroy. Kill them before they kill you.

The *Evans* arrived on station on May 4 with enough fifty-pound shells on her main decks and in her magazines to blast a town back to the Stone Age. *Welcome to the gunline*, those who had been there before would say to those staring at the calm terrain in the distance. *A war, there?* The sailors, by then coated in a sticky film of sweat, were entranced by the pristine South Vietnam coastline, with its lush greenery of every shade, fat, leathery leaves standing out against beaches that made it hard to think that they'd come to fight in a war. From a mile away, all looked peaceful, rural, primitive. "Like something Hilton would want to confiscate and build a resort on," ran the constant joke on board.

Many *Evans* sailors knew that gunfire support meant a lot of work, and sleepless nights. Those who didn't—those giddy, helmet-clad young men posing for photographs before the shells stacked liked firewood on the deck—learned quickly. The *Evans* spent the latter part of 1967 and early 1968 off the coast of Vietnam, supporting the Army's First Cavalry Division, among other infantry troops, in such operations as the Tet Counteroffensive. At times they fired around the clock, and ammunition had to be replenished daily. Many sailors had sewn the Battle Efficiency " E" patch onto their uniforms, a boast that the *Evans* had done her duty before and was a tip-top ship, ready to serve as needed. In 1968 her return home had been delayed, and already the scuttlebutt around ship was that she would be delayed a month or so this time around, though at least it seemed that everybody would be home by Christmas still. But first, it was this. Barely six weeks into their West Pac deployment, sweaty and bored, the guys were ready to get some. The latest operation had a hard-hitting name, something that practically breathed resolve, bravery, and victory: Daring Rebel.

Barrier Island, twenty miles south of Danang, was known as a Vietcong staging area, forty square miles of rest and relaxation, untouched by the hell of warfare—until now. Operation Daring Rebel would be the first major offensive along that five-mile coastline, a typical seek-and-destroy mission. The plan was simple: First Battalion, Twenty-Sixth Marines would arrive on the beaches via helicopters, after naval gunfire had neutralized the area. When spotters found ammunitions depots and bunkers, they'd call in for fire support from either howitzers or ships parked offshore. The engagement began before dawn on May 5, and the first wave of infantry Marines landed unopposed. Flying between the USS *Okinawa* and combat landing zones, four thousand Marines were put into action, along with more than 11.4 tons of cargo for logistical buildup. Across rice paddies and open fields, villages and other hamlets, Marines were instructed to seek out Vietcong combatants and sympathizers for capture or kill.

Naval gunfire, from ships already stationed along the coast, was an essential part of the plan.

The *Evans* stood by, ready to fire at a moment's notice. An estimated 80 percent of the fighting took place at night. Sailors would be roused from slumber or called from other activities to general quarters, then sent to stations scattered about the vessel, each sailor helping to load magazines and fire rounds. Within moments the pitch-black sky would be lit up like the Fourth of July. Mortar rounds inshore looked like lightning in the distance. Tracers arced across the night sky like meteor showers. And then all would go quiet again—until the next call, the next unleashing of the tiger in the deep, dark night.

The twin barrels of the *Evans*'s three gun mounts sprayed out fifty-pound shells at a rate of fifteen per minute on a good day, as many as twenty-two per minute if they pushed it. Depending on the task at hand, a crew of nearly two dozen men were needed for each mount—a few men working topside and the rest below, loading the magazines and more. Shells had a range of nine miles, and the work was done with so much gusto and so swiftly that the men had no time to survey the damage, even if they could see it. In the sticky heat, if the smoke from the guns didn't blind you, the sweat running into your eyes would. If one didn't flinch, all he could see was the fiery red halo in front of each gun after a director pulled the powerful trigger, the ship rattling with each blow. They'd find out what they'd done later, in official reports and thank-you memos from the troops on the ground. In true navy tradition, the *Evans* crew started painting the number of decimated targets on the side of the pilothouse.

The gunline could be a boring place or an exciting one, depending on how you looked at it. There was a lot of waiting around, waiting for something to heat up, watching a jungle that seemed as peaceful as Eden from afar. The anticipation made the men restless. There were small diversions—a card game or a movie. The interruptions were so constant that it took them days to watch *Who's Afraid of Virginia Wolf?* This close to shore, they could pick up the Armed Forces Vietnam Network on the radio, getting a taste of home in the music, the banter, and the public service announcements that made the young guys chuckle: "No venereal disease is worth it . . . stupidity, that's all"; "Anything you ever wanted to know about drugs but were afraid to ask." Inside the mess decks a sailor could hear "Wooly Bully" or Bob Dylan's lyrics and not care that his breakfast toast was going limp in the thick, humid air, which always smelled of coffee, engine oil, and phosphorus. Outside they could look at the calm, bluer sky and clouds like they had never seen and watch the warm, flat water below, a sampan or little Vietnamese fishing boat in the distance and think of how far they really are from home.

And then a call to general quarters would break in, interrupting a dream, a meal, or a card game, aces and kings scattered onto the deck of the berthing compartment as sailors rushed for helmets and ladders. After minutes, hours, or a night of firing, finally the ship would return to its slumber.

There were, of course, the mishaps. Usually it was the old

ship and her war-fatigued guns that put a frightening pause on matters. In one heart-stopping incident on May 12 one shell got stuck in the hell-hot barrel just as a cluster of sweat-soaked undershirt-clad and sunburned sailors were getting ready to fire. It was like an unpinned grenade on a patch of grass with no place to run. There were wide eyes all around as they worked the water hoses. Steve Espinosa, a gunner's mate from California, saw that the prompt efforts to cool the gun barrel had been ineffective, with steam engulfing those on deck, some running away already. "With complete disregard for his personal safety," a Navy Commendation Medal citation would later read, "and fully realizing that the round could explode at any moment, (he) entered the (gun) mount and succeeded in cooling the gun barrel sufficiently to allow the round to be safely removed." Similar accidents had proved fatal on other gunline warships. And Espinosa, when his family would discover this heroic act a month later, would be long gone.

At night on the *Evans*, an eerie quiet fell. The ship usually went dark, lights-out on the main deck. "You couldn't see the guy in front of you," one sailor would write home. Between calls for gunfire support, some sailors stood watch on the main decks from the rear fantail and forward to the forecastle, armed with rifles, eyes peeled for the seven-foot poisonous snakes that lived in these waters, or for the junks or small craft that might hold enemy combatants aiming to take out the ship's gunfire capabilities. Ships just like the *Evans* received enemy fire on several occasions, although the incidents were usually mild compared to the carnage ashore.

Enemy shore batteries weren't a major concern during

Daring Rebel, but that wasn't much comfort to the sailors on board. (Other ships, in other engagements were not so lucky.) A head cracked on a ladder or a shin scraped on the bottom of a hatch were the only injuries, but still, the men worked with purpose, energized by the idea that there was a war going on, right over in that jungle. They were going to do their part—"Even if it saves just one American life," as Lieutenant Junior Grade Jon Stever, on his first tour in Vietnam, would write home.

Stever stood in the combat information center, concentrating on keeping the ship steady for accurate fire. The *Evans* was typically anchored some five thousand yards offshore, where tiny swells could shift her position slightly, affecting the guns' firing trajectory. Older than the average sailor at twenty-five, Stever had enlisted in the U.S. Navy after an unpromising visit to the Los Angeles County Draft Board, where he and his twin confronted a scene not unlike that portrayed in the cult film *Alice's Restaurant*. Long-haired hippies lined up, claiming diseases with long Latin names as reasons they couldn't go to war. Ron Stever was off the hook due to a childhood accident having marred up his insides: his twin had accidentally shot him with their father's hunting rifle while the two were rummaging through a closet, and mangled his insides. The accident, which made headlines in Altadena, California, haunted Jon Stever, and going into the service was something he felt he needed to do, both for his country and for his brother. He might not have had a choice in the matter, anyway; his mother's desperate, long-winded letter to the draft board, in which she pleaded that Jon Stever needed to stick around as possible spare parts for his brother, did little to sway officials, who saw handsome Jon Stever as just the red-blooded, all-American type they could use in the armed forces.

On first glance, Stever looked a little like Elvis Presley. He was tall, clean-cut, and strong, with intense blue eyes and the kind of face that won him a girl in every port. He had a sense of humor that pushed the envelope. In one of his last tapes home to his mother, he told her about a date with a girl in Japan, describing a visit to her apartment, a massage, and then . . . a pause and an abrupt closing: "Will tell you more tomorrow, Mom." But he never did. Ron Stever could see his mother listening to that tape, going, *Oh, don't tell me that!*

At one time engaged to be married, Stever was indifferent to navy life at first. And then, sometime into his officer training, he began to feel that it made him wiser, more grown up. His letters became deep, philosophical, almost. Responsible now for younger men, he felt like a part of something larger than himself. In one particularly poignant letter home, he wrote,

> I am still trying to discover myself and my place in the world. . . . Being in the Navy I have learned to live life more intensely. . . . Living a protected life at home somehow does not allow one to develop a full appreciation of what riches one has there until he gets away from them. Perhaps that is why so many have forgotten the treasures of freedom our republic provides.

Just two months into his first overseas deployment, Stever longed for home. He hoped Nixon could do something about the war he'd heard so much about as a student at California State in Los Angeles, this war he now watched from a distance, firing away with a combination of excitement and dread, past the flickering lights of the compartment and the shouting of coordinates over the noisy radios, at targets he couldn't see or hear.

Stever's roommate, Ensign John Norton, was in charge of public relations on the ship, keeping tally of what the *Evans* did and how much hell she delivered to the Vietcong. His job was to boost morale, to let everybody know the *Evans* was a part of something larger. In the May family gram he'd inform parents and wives at home that the *Evans* had hit seventy-five targets, of which fifty-seven involved "harassment of enemy positions." The *Evans* had incinerated seven bunkers, fourteen other structures, and a fortified gun emplacement, and had partially destroyed nine more bunkers, he wrote: "The ship's company worked hard, either shooting or loading ammunition almost continuously during the gunline period." In all, the *Evans* fired more than two thousand rounds in ten days, nearly a quarter of what it had done during its entire last West Pac deployment. For Daring Rebel alone the ship answered eighty-six calls for gunfire support, firing on bunkers, trails, and supply centers.

The results prompted Marine officers on the ground to praise the *Evans*, in one particular memorandum, for its "accurate, intensive and deadly fire second to none," calling it a "key role in the success of the operation."

Norton wrote home that his first trip to the gunline was

eye-opening, making the war he'd heard so much about on the Columbia University campus in the years up to his graduation more real. In the typical sarcastic manner common in young fighting men, he wrote to his mother than he was now "a professional killer, a maimer and burner of women and children," something that didn't make him happy. He couldn't wait to be home again, he wrote.

A New York City kid born and raised, Norton had excelled academically. He had a special interest in science, everything from the mountains to the moon race. He'd almost missed the ship leaving port in Oregon once, not because he was drunk or had met a girl, as happened with so many navy men, but because he'd been searching for a rock to add to his collection. He grew up watching the documentary television series *Victory at Sea*, and he'd always known, if and when the time came, that he would go into the U.S. Navy. But Vietnam and the student protests on campus had made him think again. He tried to delay his Naval Reserve Officer Training Corps commitment so that he could teach geology as a graduate student, but the Navy said no.

Norton was never political; he just wanted to get in, do what he had to do, and then come home and study rocks. There was peace in studying the beauty of nature. When Columbia University erupted in student protest in 1968, Norton bought a potted flowering plant for his dorm room. Something pretty to stare at, he told his mother, because they were tearing this place apart.

The word in the wardroom was, expect at least four more trips to the gunline. These stints left the men drained and the ship in need of repairs. Every salvo caused the vessel to shake; anything not bolted in place shook loose in the constant rattling. A stint on the gunline beat the hell out of rickety old ships like the *Evans*. After gunfire support, there was maintenance and engine checks, making sure the ship would be in tip-top shape for its next rendezvous off the coast of Vietnam. By late May the Navy reported a 100 percent increase in naval gunfire support missions and a 50 percent increase in round expenditures, a pattern that would continue throughout the summer.

Operation Daring Rebel was deemed a success, although the victory was a more modest one than war planners had envisioned. The Barrier Island affair went on for a week after the *Evans* left for Subic Bay. Security leaks may have given the fleeing Vietcong a head start, the press reported, allowing them to leave behind booby traps as they had done in other, similarly clandestine operations. Four out of 4,000 Marines were killed; for the Vietcong, the toll was much larger, with 400 dead and 328 captured. In a sweep of the area, the Americans seized 118 weapons total.

Once the Marines had gone, though, the Vietcong returned. A second seek-and-destroy operation along the same island stretch would take place in September. Such was the nature of this war: a tactical sweep of the area, followed by a retreat, and later on a return to the same spot to sweep again. For war planners, it was all about the body count: how many dead enemy combatants?

The people at home would catch wind of such a tactic, played time and again throughout the war, only after details from another engagement surfaced later that month. Operation Daring Rebel would make headlines, but another bloody frontal assault starting to take shape just as the *Evans* sailed for Subic Bay would quickly take center stage.

The battle for Ap Bia—a 3,000-foot-high mountain near the Laotian border, riddled with sophisticated tunnels that made perfect hiding places for enemy combatants—began on May 10, 1969. Operation Apache Snow called for three battalions from the famed 101st Airborne Division to clear the mountain of the enemy—on the face of it a simple task, just another seek-and-destroy mission, if on a larger scale. American and South Vietnamese troops encountered fierce resistance, however, and an enemy well entrenched. Air firepower was severely limited, and in some cases American leadership called for troops to engage in repeated frontal assaults, orders that their men questioned, their comments— "That damn Blackjack [the soldier's battalion commander] won't stop unless he kills every damn one of us," said one wounded paratrooper—making headlines in the *New York Times* and the *Washington Post*. The battle became a flashpoint not only between the enemy and foot soldiers, but also between the administration, its generals, and the antiwar set.

After nearly a dozen attempts to seize Ap Bia, on May 20, finally, the stronghold fell. The cost was seventy-two dead Americans; considerably less than the six hundred reported enemy fatalities tallied by the U.S. Command. Yet more than five hundred Americans were injured, many horribly. One soldier cut out the bottom of a C-rations box, nailed it to a tree, and printed on it the words "Hamburger Hill."

This all-too-catchy name for a battle gone wrong would reach Washington within hours. Within days, grappling for control of the war, President Nixon announced that there would be no more large-scale enemy engagements. His administration couldn't stomach the bad press.

13

"BRAVE MEN STILL DIE"

Throughout 1969 the news out of Vietnam, even in a military rag such as *Stars and Stripes*, often sounded like a weather report: "Fighting continued light and scattered throughout most of the nation. . . . " Nixon, barely four months into his presidency, was struggling to come up with a solution that would bring peace with dignity. May 1969 marked the one-year anniversary of the start of the Paris Peace Accords. Over the course of a year, as diplomats on both sides sat down to discuss matters at hand in talks infamously bogged down in bickering about the shape of the negotiating table, twelve thousand Americans had been killed. An *Associated Press* reporter would write on May 14, 1969, in a *Stars and Stripes* article, "In a sense, the Paris talks have resembled the Vietnam War itself. Optimism has alternated with bewilderment. Euphoria has given way to frustration. Henry A. Kissinger, President Nixon's national security advisor, has called this 'the classic Vietnam syndrome.' "

This newspaper article greeted Nixon, by then obsessed with the antiwar sentiment, on the very day he was to publicly address the nation on his Vietnam strategy. In this televised speech he hoped both to demonstrate to Hanoi that he sought a diplomatic deterrent and to convince the American public that he was winding things down. "Since I took office four months ago," he began,

> nothing has taken so much of my time and energy as the search for a way to bring lasting peace to Vietnam. I know that some believe that I should have ended the war immediately after the inauguration by simply ordering our forces home from Vietnam.
>
> This would have been the easy thing to do. It might have been a popular thing to do. But I would have betrayed my solemn responsibility as President of the United States if I had done so.
>
> I want to end this war. The American people want to end this war. The people of South Vietnam want to end this war. But we want to end it permanently so that the younger brothers of our soldiers in Vietnam will not have to fight in the future in another Vietnam someplace else in the world.
>
> The fact that there is no easy way to end the war does not mean that we have no choice but to let the war drag on with no end in sight.
>
> For four years American boys have been fighting and dying in Vietnam. For twelve months our negotiators have been talking with the other side in Paris. And yet the fighting goes on. The destruction continues. Brave men still die.

Nixon went on to offer his first comprehensive plan, proposing that all foreign troops—both American and North Vietnamese—leave South Vietnam within one year of a signed peace accord. He warned the enemy not to confuse flexibility with weakness: "Reports from Hanoi indicate that the enemy has given up hope for a military victory in South Vietnam, but is counting on a collapse of the will in the United States. There could be no greater error in judgment."

The world was watching.

There was no serious response from Hanoi, Nixon would write in his memoir. The situation was too complex to be resolved with any eight-point plan.

Anti-Communist Asia watched the war in Vietnam with great concern. Nixon's speech aroused some suspicion that America might abandon its obligations under the Southeast Asian Treaty Organization (SEATO), a coalition of seven nations formed to combat Communist infiltration and expansion. A product of the Eisenhower presidency, which heavily endorsed the coalition, SEATO was among the most misunderstood sideshows of the Cold War and Vietnam.

Despite the coalition's name, only two Southeast Asian countries—the Philippines and Thailand—signed on with SEATO when it was created in 1954. Both joined because of their close ties with the United States and a fear of Communist infiltration by factions within their own countries. Participation among the other member nations—the United States, France, Great Britain, Australia, and Pakistan—was uneven and at times disorganized. For the United States,

SEATO mostly served as a justification for the country's involvement in South Vietnam; it was said in 1964 that SEATO and the Tonkin Gulf Resolution together spelled *war*. But SEATO as a whole—which, unlike the North Atlantic Treaty Organization, did not have its own standing military forces— never supported military intervention in Vietnam, and by 1969 the war threatened the organization's legitimacy and future.

In the late 1960s, as Vietnam heated up, Pakistan and France had stopped participating in the coalition's annual show-of-force exercises—land-and-sea war games meant to prepare its member nations to work together in the face of a Communist threat—in protest against the war. Meanwhile Australia, where the war was just as unpopular as it was in the United States, teetered on whether to stay in SEATO at all.

Nonetheless, SEATO forged ahead with its exercises— or tried to. Nixon, meeting with Australian Prime Minister John Gorton in May 1969, assured him that the United States' impending pullout from Vietnam did not mean that Americans would be leaving the region—an assurance Australia was anxious to have, since according to Eisenhower's domino theory (which still carried some weight, though it had lost much of its credibility), communism unchecked might be nearly at its doorstep. But very quickly this claim was undermined, when it came out that just the year before, Nixon had called SEATO an "anachronism," an antiquated alliance not worth holding on to.

Nixon had plenty of company in not taking SEATO seriously, among both friends and enemies. Communist China was the first to call SEATO a "paper tiger," an alliance too weak to be any threat. The Soviet Union had spent the latter part of the 1950s threatening nations who joined the SEATO alliance, but a decade later it was so busy squabbling with China over border issues that the organization wasn't even on its radar at times. An Associated Press headline in May 1969—SEATO FORCE IS "A FICTION," THAI FOREIGN MINISTER SAYS—didn't help matters.

Two weeks after that resounding vote of no confidence, SEATO delegates met in Bangkok to discuss the organization's future. The talks focused on the future in Vietnam and on Nixon's proposal; glossed over was the fact that France and Pakistan had declined to participate in exercises and meetings, Pakistan claiming to be merely "observing" the SEATO meeting, as was an unnamed Russian individual. As expected, U.S. Secretary of State William P. Rogers promised that the United States would stay in, despite Nixon's past criticism.

With the future of SEATO at stake and the United States desperate to show that it would continue to fight communism even after it left Vietnam, the exercise shaping up in Manila some 1,000 miles away would help solidify the SEATO members' resolve to maintain the fight against communism in the region. Or so the organizers thought.

14

<u>RELIEF</u>

After its time on the gunline, the *Evans* did what virtually every Seventh Fleet warship did when in need of recuperation for both men and machine. She cruised to Subic Bay in the Philippine Islands.

Knowing their guys were going to want to blow off some steam, the officers urged them to stick together, or not leave base at all. U.S. Naval Base Subic Bay did what it could to keep the men on base, with clubs, bars, and other entertainment. But if you wanted girls—and girls is what everybody wanted—you made for the bridge over shit river, past the kids bathing in the water, past the dead animals floating by, and straight into Olongapo City.

The Olongapo was a cesspool of low, gray buildings, bars, dirt streets, blaring horns, red lights, drunken sailors, and, as with any port, prostitutes. The bars played American music, about four years behind the Billboard charts, lovey-dovey tunes that reminded the men of senior prom, a girl they once knew, and home. Drinks were cheap in the Olongapo—26 cents got you a beer—and the *Evans* crew had money to spend; gunline duties put them in the tax-free zone, bumping their pay slightly. A young enlisted sailor with fewer than two years in the U.S. Navy never made more than $150 a month. A lot of these guys sent money home, sure, but they'd set $10 aside for fun and stretch it as far as they could—and that was pretty far.

The Filipino women took their style cues from old American *Vogue* magazines, their hair in high bouffants or long and stringy, pale pink lipstick against cocoa skin, Audrey's exaggerated brows. They wore miniskirts and knee-high boots, tank tops if it got hot—and it always did. The going rate for a girl was $5, and if it happened in the Olongapo, it stayed in the Olongapo.

Years later navy men might look around to see if their wife or kid was nearby, then tell their stories about this wild port in particular: "Remember when . . ." The photos were always innocent; boy-men sitting in a semicircle around a table, cigarettes dangling from their mouths, arms around buxom island girls they'd joke were their "nieces," some guys already so drunk they could hardly keep their eyes open in the fog of smoke. Then came the music, and the dancing. Nothing like Jim Morrison loving her madly or Nancy's Sinatra's boots made for walkin' to shake off the sea legs. They'd spin girls around, then spin around themselves, careful not to drop their cigarettes, asking a buddy, "Here, hold my beer." You could hear the guys in the background, laughing. *I didn't know he had it in him.* Eventually, the room would go dark, and everything would just fade.

In the morning they'd wake up and not know what the hell happened, or how they got back to the ship. Someone might have a black eye—*Somebody said something about our ship, so I punched him first*—or a new tattoo. A piece of a uniform might be missing, or a wallet empty.

The old chiefs, who knew better themselves by now, would just shake their heads. *Must have been a good night, kid.*

The hangover would only last a few hours. If they could, they'd do it all over again. And many did. They deserved the break, for in a day or so they were off to Manila to get ready for *something big.*

D estroyers are one of the most versatile classes of warships, the chameleons of the fleet. They began making headlines in 1965 as Vietnam War workhorses, vital for operations both open and clandestine. The United States could not have fought the war in Vietnam without them. They offered naval gunfire support as well as coastal surveillance, patrolling the coast for North Vietnamese junks and other small-arms supply vessels toting weapons to the Vietcong. William Westmoreland, the U.S. Army general in command of Vietnam operations for most of the war, believed that 75 percent of the enemy supplies in Vietnam came by sea.

The *Evans* showed up at the South Vietnam coastline in early May as a member of Destroyer Squadron 23, left the gunline ten days later, and arrived in Subic Bay by May 17 as a member of Antisubmarine Group 1, a hunter-killer group led by the aircraft carrier *Kearsarge*. They call this changing of the hats, switching from one command to another, being "chopped."

II

DISASTER BY
MOONLIGHT

15

SEA SPIRIT

May 1969

The foreign flags and uniforms were the first signs that something spectacular was brewing in Manila Bay. Past the island of Corregidor, the bay widened, with the Bataan Peninsula to the north—the haunts of General McArthur, places the boys on the *Evans* might have read about in their high school history books, back when their lives were circumscribed by the lush green panorama of farms, or by square city blocks of cement and brick. But now they were seeing this world for themselves. The blue skies, the cerulean waters, the exotic landscape stretching out beyond the gray railing they leaned on, it all might have been straight from a navy recruiting poster.

Manila itself, just north of where the *Evans* would dock, was an elegant city, with its palm-covered hills and lush tropical greenery, its colonial mansions mingled with high-rises in an urban landscape punctuated with manicured parks.

The lively hues of a Crayola box of American car culture—Ford Bel Airs and Studebakers, Buicks and Pontiacs the size of boats, with fins like ocean fish—enlivened its streets. Some claim that only Warsaw suffered more damage than Manila in World War II, yet in 1969 one would never know that; it had all the chaos and vitality of a world-class city.

The Manila that the boys on the *Evans* regarded was a hub of tourism, business, and gastronomic delight. Every street corner enticed with the mouthwatering aroma of Spanish adobo spices, roasting chicken, or garlicky broiled fish. Bright Coca-Cola signs lined streets thronged with businessmen, pretty ladies, and schoolchildren. It was a bustling metropolis, well into its golden age, the era of President Ferdinand Marcos, then a popular hero in the first term of his reign. Few then foresaw the figure of repression and astounding corruption he would become over the next two decades, though the first wave of protest against his government was right around the corner, in 1970's harshly subdued First Quarter Storm. The world would remember his beloved, the Mrs. Imelda Marcus, for her excessive shoe collection.

The hustle from Vietnam to Subic and then south to Manila gave the *Evans* crew an opportunity to focus on antisubmarine maneuvers. The crew practiced these from time to time; they'd done a few exercises over the past year with the *Kearsarge* off the coast of both California and Hawaii. But it was never enough, as admirals had complained at a fleet planning meeting earlier in 1969, discussing their plans for the overworked Pacific Fleet. Essentially, as fleet commanders understood it, the United States was fighting a war and a half: the Cold War on one side, and the undeclared war in Vietnam. The latter represented a threat to military readiness for a possible engagement with the Soviet Union; ships stationed off the coast of Vietnam weren't available to thwart the USSR's fledgling submarine fleet, and their constant need of repairs and upkeep drained Navy resources. The U.S. Navy, busy as it was with the war in Vietnam, knew it still needed to improve antisubmarine warfare. When in transit, train, it told its commanders; whenever possible, train.

This time, though, it would be more than a few casual drills. Exercise Sea Spirit, the largest SEATO had conducted in over a decade, was an ambitious undertaking for almost everyone involved. Forty vessels—allied frigates, destroyers, aircraft carriers, and submarines—from six different nations, took part, as well as more than eighty aircraft. The U.S. ships included, as well as the *Evans*, the *Kearsarge,* also moored in Manila.

Many of the crew on the *Evans* had still been in high school the last time the ship participated in such an exhibition of might. In 1965 the ship joined in Exercise Sea Horse, a similar antisubmarine drill, if smaller, with only thirty-one ships. At the time, the U.S. Joint Chiefs of Staff had asked the commander of the Pacific forces whether such exercises made sense, given the conflict in Vietnam and the need for naval resources in the combat zone. When Vietnam heated up, there was talk of bringing ships in from the Atlantic Fleet to help with Vietnam War support activities. The need for ships never changed, and by March 1969, according to a Seventh Fleet memo, naval gunfire support "ships requirements have always exceeded availability." The reply to the Joint Chiefs of Staff in the mid-1960s was as true then as it was in 1969: the exercise would take place so close to Indochina that ships could be pulled off the exercise and put to work quickly in Vietnam if necessary.

Meanwhile, the *Evans*, having just left the naval armory in Subic Bay, had on board a full war allowance of weaponry, as well as roughly twenty-eight new men in its racks, mostly fresh boots out of recruit training. As they waited for their first ship in the hot, muggy Philippines, they wore their sea bags over their shoulders, weighed down with thick wool pea coats they hadn't known they wouldn't need, as well as paper for writing letters, pictures of girlfriends, and homesickness. Rumor had it that they got no leave, and that they'd gone straight from graduation to the asshole of the U.S. Navy, otherwise known as "the P.I." From the tall and skinny to the short and dumpy, they all had the same look, the same story. In an era of few choices, with the draft breathing down their necks, they just showed up one day and joined the Navy. One had just lost a brother in Vietnam. He wasn't taking any chances. They looked like babies standing there, the stench of shit river cooking in the hellish heat that made Subic Bay just about the worst place on earth, waiting for this mighty big ship that they'd learn, pretty quickly, wasn't near as big as it looked, once you were on it.

McLemore knew he'd be picking up some new guys. They'd be welcomed; the ship's shorthandedness had made its ten days on the gunline much more difficult. The crew made space for the new guys in First Division in the forecastle, with some sailors packing up their lockers and heading for another space on board, many moving from the front of the ship to the after section. Even the officers, some pinning a new rank, moved to slightly loftier sleeping quarters in the rear part of the ship. These small relocations, a matter of few feet on a ship like the *Evans*, would later mean the difference between life and death.

The Sea Spirit exercises, as it was outlined in February of that year, would take the *Evans* on a "devious" course, its participants would note while pouring over maps, across the South China Sea, snaking south along the coast of Vietnam and then northwest into the Gulf of Thailand and to Sattahip. Following the stop in Thailand, she would turn around and head back to support the war in Vietnam, as she'd done in 1965. McLemore told his men that the *Evans* would return to Vietnam at least four times; they could expect extra combat pay as early as mid-June. In letters home they wrote of Christmas gifts they'd be able to afford and cars they hoped to buy when they got back, girls they would marry, new babies they would shower with gifts. To a deployed all-American serviceman, homesickness always focused on Christmas. Lucky would be the ones whose schedules put them back in time to light the tree. Even if there was a delay—and delays were commonplace—the *Evans* would be home for the holidays. Sweltering in the tropical heat of the Philippine Islands, its men dreamed of winter wonderlands and of a glowing and tinseled Christmas tree.

They just had to get through these exercises first, and, as always, a few more stints on the gunline.

McLemore's team of young officers included one who'd failed his first test to serve as officer of the deck in the earlier part of the year. In the spring he tried again, and passed. True, one more name on the roster of qualified officers of the deck—bringing the number of men the captain could use in rotation to conn the ship to five—was good news. But Lieutenant Junior Grade Ronald Ramsey's promotion that very month while moored in the Philippines had been low-key, without a lot of fanfare. There hadn't really even been an official test. McLemore usually liked to hold qualification boards, meetings at which all the department heads could grill a potential candidate for officer of the deck to judge his fitness for the job. The busy time on the gunline and the preparations for Sea Spirit left little time for formalities, especially when the U.S. Navy never officially required anything ceremonious. When it came down to it, the men were ready when the captain said they were ready, and McLemore judged that Ramsey, an intelligent Purdue University graduate with leadership potential, had improved enough to make the grade.

Upon arriving in Manila, the *Evans* crew was put to work preparing for Sea Spirit. The early workup stage of the exercises were aimed at ironing out communications quirks and getting officers accustomed to working with foreign navies. They would include operations on a darkened ship, nighttime maneuvers, and zigzagging, a carefully choreographed method of evading submarines. Ships zigzagging in formation looked like a small swarm of bees, buzzing along while making abrupt turns that appeared random. In fact, planning was essential; confusion could be deadly. Australian Rear Admiral Gordon

John Crabb, a flag officer on board the HMAS *Melbourne*, worried that communication would be difficult, given the complexity of the ships involved and the differences—of language, customs, equipment—between the various navies. For three days crews hammered out radio use, visited other ships, raised flags, and flashed signals, putting all the communications protocols to work.

With six international navies working together, language barriers between the more than nine thousand participating servicemen were significant, but they weren't the only challenges. Early on, it was unclear whether some allied forces might have had access to classified tactical guidebooks, instructions deemed essential for the foreign navies to work together. To handle this uncertainty, pegged as minor at the time, planners created a separate operation order for Sea Spirit. These instructions, mimeographed and fastened together, outlined various turn-by-turn zigzag plans, and when they should be used and rules for following them. The new plans were passed around, yet any navy unfamiliar with the original, preset zigzags might have been at a disadvantage. Some of the navies might have had access to plans slightly different from those used in Sea Spirit. One subtle difference was the way sketched-out maneuvers were paused and the way they resumed when working directly with a carrier, for example. Though the difference seemed small, it would contribute to confusion later on—a confusion that proved fatal.

Such tiny holes in the plan, nearly invisible in the big picture, would be glaringly obvious under the harsh magnifying lens of hindsight.

Manila was a little less wild than Subic Bay's Olongapo City, yet it proved to be no less entertaining. Sometime between reveille and supper one day, a few *Evans* sailors decided they'd find some Australian sailors to trade uniforms with. The Royal Australian Navy's summer uniform consisted of white short pants and knee socks—different, and perhaps comical to the young American sailors. When the Americans couldn't find an Australian to entertain this idea, a drunken British sailor obliged. So in the middle of four lanes of traffic in downtown Manila several crazy sailors stripped to their skivvies and swapped clothing. When they stumbled back to their ships later that evening, their costumes made for some mistaken identities and droll stories, just the kind you'd remember decades later, bragging, "We never did get caught," or wondering "Whatever happened to that uniform?"

What the sailors didn't know—what they couldn't have known—was that this jewel of a city, this exotic playground that they explored in wild, rambunctious packs, would for some of them be their final stop. That the friends they made— the ones who'd slept just a few feet from them, crammed into the racks, whose jokes were so dirty they couldn't be repeated, just the memory of them igniting laughter well into old age— would be gone, in one unlucky roll of the dice.

For this generation, in so many ways, the future had never been in their own hands. From the day that, faced with the draft, they joined the Navy instead, the course of their lives had been dictated by chance and by circumstance. They'd lost a brother or a friend, or they'd seen someone on campus or on television say that this Vietnam thing wasn't worth dying for, and finally they signed on for the safer bet. Or their fathers had convinced them to avoid the dirt-and-foxhole life of a grunt. Then they decided they'd work in the engine room instead of deck division, and yet again the path branched. For most of the time, it was not by their own choice that their course was set, but by the Naval Bureau of Personnel, working by number, filling in the racks of some ship somewhere in the world. Ships that desperately needed men. Ships like the *Evans*.

Each chance, each choice, each throw of the dice, was spelling out a future beyond their control—but also beyond their imagination, for most of them. They were just kids on a wild ride, their lives spread out before them like the vast, glistening, rolling ocean.

16

HAUNTED HISTORY

Hidden in the pomp and hoopla of a major sea exercise that would launch in days, something very real was haunting the captain of the HMAS *Melbourne*. The sea in his blood, forty-seven-year-old Captain John Phillip Stevenson had joined the Royal Australian Navy in 1935, when he was just thirteen years old. The son of an Australian Navy admiral, he studied for four years at the Royal Australian Naval College and received a commission upon graduation. By age seventeen, he was on his first ship, the HMAS *Canberra*, a heavily armed cruiser that would eventually find its way to Ironbottom Sound after the infamous Battle of Savo Island in 1942. Stevenson, by then on to his next assignment, would miss the hell in the Pacific but catch it that same year in the Mediterranean, when an Italian bomber hit his ship, the HMAS *Nestor*, eventually sinking her. During and following the war he was sent to various training posts, back and forth between England and Australia, collecting specialties in radar, navigation, gunnery,

135

and watch keeping and gaining experience in all aspects of ship handling. By his thirtieth birthday he'd been named commander of a frigate, the first of many command posts in a career that spanned a variety of ships and schools. An able and experienced seaman, he ranked near the top of the Australian Navy at the time he was made commander of its prized flagship, the HMAS *Melbourne*, in October 1968.

Stevenson was a handsome man with light blue eyes, sharp features, and the salt-and-sun-weathered skin of a lifelong navy man. Short and slender, he had the demeanor of a gentleman. Nearly everything about him radiated a sense of cool, confident control. Even as a television news crew interviewed him on the flight deck of the *Melbourne* while the ship conducted trials at sea, he simultaneously kept an eye on the planes landing on the flight deck behind him, by glancing at a mirror. "The ship always came first," an officer present during the filming would recall. Stevenson was regarded as more democratic than the average officer, and his crew of thirteen hundred men worshipped him. As a colleague would boast, "Captain Stevenson has done just about everything an Australian naval officer can do."

Stevenson was married to a beautiful television news reporter and former actress, a woman whose delicate features might have masked her iron will and intelligence, and the couple had two children. Stevenson's fairly new sea command put him on the road to better things. In April of that year he became convinced that an admiral's star was in his future. Nevertheless, he felt troubled while moored in Manila Bay that spring. There were too many uncertainties and variables. The massive HMAS *Melbourne* stood strong and fierce in the gray swarm of smaller foreign ships around her. Her very strength represented a danger. Something could go wrong, as it had in the past—a past not so distant, and deadly.

The solution to his discomfort was a dinner.

On May 25, days before the multinational armada was to steam away in a show of anti-Communist might, Stevenson would entertain his compatriots in the elaborately wood-paneled wardroom of his ship. The *Melbourne* had come off the line in 1945 as the British HMS *Majestic*, the first of the Majestic class of aircraft carriers. She was barely finished by the time the war was over, the final touches on her completed just as the ink was drying on the Japanese surrender. The Royal Australian Navy, celebrating the Allied success in the Pacific and eager to boost its crippled fleet, seized the opportunity to raise the caliber of its forces. By 1947 the *Majestic*, along with another aircraft carrier, the HMS *Terrible*, was in Australian hands. With some new gear and some retrofittings, she was commissioned HMAS *Melbourne* in 1955. By 1969 she was Australia's only carrier.

Smaller than most of the American carriers of that era, the *Melbourne* weighed 22,000 tons. Roughly ten times the size of her escort ships, she packed a lot of punch into a frame a little longer than two American football fields set end to end, carrying thirteen hundred men and up to twenty-seven aircraft, including both antisubmarine and attack planes and antisubmarine helicopters. In early 1969 she underwent an $8.5 million overhaul that gave her, alongside a long list of tactical and cosmetic improvements, air-conditioning. The pride of the Australian Navy, she provided an admirable venue for entertaining guests.

It was here, in the grandest of maritime settings, that Stevenson would entertain the captains of all the ships slated to escort the *Melbourne* in the SEATO exercises. He was eager to meet them, if also careful not to overstep. But something had to be said, and say it he would, despite a festive atmosphere more conducive to raised glasses and the genial breaking of bread.

Joining Stevenson on board the *Melbourne* were McLemore, the captains of the U.S. destroyers the *James E. Kyes* and the *Everett F. Larson,* and the captain of the British frigate the HMS *Cleopatra.* The captain of the New Zealand antisubmarine frigate HMNZS *Blackpool,* which would also serve as one of the *Melbourne*'s assigned escorts, had met with Stevenson previously and could not make the gathering. It was a formal yet friendly affair, and little would be recalled of the details—whether the stewards served roast lamb or prawns, whether there were sweet Anzac biscuits to follow. Discussion was kept on the lighter side, with a little business in the mix. First up on the agenda: the transport phase of Sea Spirit, during which the five smaller ships would escort the carrier. Stevenson wanted to ensure he knew all the key leaders; he wanted to feel them out. He took a liking to Commander J. J. Doak, the captain of the USS *James E. Kyes,* commander of Destroyer Squadron 23 and essentially McLemore's boss.

Overall, the exercises would be not unlike the childhood game Battleship, in that they focused on spotting and targeting enemy submarines. It was the nitty-gritty that needed attention, and Doak, a World War II veteran, took to the task with a great sense of duty.

The HMAS *Melbourne* carried antisubmarine helicopters and tracker planes used for scouting and surveillance. As part of antisubmarine maneuvers, the destroyers would be called upon to serve plane guard, a task that required a rescue destroyer to maneuver to the rear of a carrier that was about to launch aircraft, the plan being to rescue a downed pilot if he happened to abort. A simple maneuver drawn on a sketch pad, it could spell disaster if the two ships, maneuvering closely at top speeds—the carrier to produce enough gust to launch aircraft and the ship to be in place at a moment's notice—were to collide. A historical fact Stevenson could not escape, that night nor any other in Manila Bay, was that just five years earlier the *Melbourne* had rammed the side of the HMAS *Voyager*, a plane guard destroyer. Upon impact the *Voyager* had split in two and sank in the chilly waters of Jervis Bay, Australia, killing eighty-two sailors. This was why Stevenson was now discussing maneuvers with the captains of the ships he would be steaming with: he wanted to avoid another catastrophe.

The inquiry into the *Voyager* disaster had ripped at the heart of the Australian Navy, raising questions on everything from policies to personalities. Stevenson relayed the story to his foreign escorts in the wardroom that night, adding, "Watch my signals very closely before going to your next position. I do not think either Australia's Navy or its government can stand another collision at sea." Neither could

Stevenson, who was looking to be pinned admiral; he had lost a friend in the disaster, and another close friend had been disgraced during the inquiry.

For the United States, such a collision at sea wasn't exactly a foreign concept. In the midst of plane guard maneuvers in the foggy Caribbean in 1952, the carrier USS *Wasp* had sliced the destroyer USS *Hobson* in two, killing 176 crewmen. Seventh Fleet destroyers practiced plane guard duty regularly while working with carriers in the Gulf of Tonkin during Vietnam bombing runs. It was routine for the Australians too, but the patterns were slightly different. As one prominent officer on the *Evans* would later suggest, plane guard for the two navies was like the principal dancers of two ballet companies switching places in the *Nutcracker*: it was the same Tchaikovsky overall, but with subtle differences that an untrained eye might not even catch.

McLemore would later recall that he took Stevenson's comments about the *Voyager* incident as more of an aside, just one yarn among many around a table of career navy men. Perhaps they took it more seriously when Stevenson passed around the official mimeographed HMAS *Melbourne* escort handout, intended to give smaller escort ships guidelines for working with the Australian flagship. Among the main points made was that smaller ships should always turn away from the *Melbourne*'s path, since the carrier, usually going at full speed when launching aircraft, could not turn or slow down abruptly. The escort handout made its way back to the *Evans*, but it was never officially presented to the officers; it would become just another in the pile of documents related to the exercise that would begin at daybreak. Some would recall seeing it, others not.

The sun weighed heavy over the Manila harbor on the morning of May 28. Sailors stood at attention on the swabbed decks of their ships, waiting to get on with the show of anti-Communist might. The future of SEATO hung in the balance; its delegates had spent the last few days in Bangkok, doubtful of the organization's will after the bloody affair in Vietnam. But Philippine President Ferdinand Marcos's words during the opening ceremony for Sea Spirit were full of promise: the exercises would "reaffirm the willingness of participating nations to act collectively against a common danger." Next on stage was the exercise director, U.S. Rear Admiral William T. Rapp, whose speech quickly turned to the war in Vietnam and where Sea Spirit fit in. Vietnam sat just across the South China Sea, the joint naval forces' channel for weapons and men destined for the war zone. Rapp's words echoed across Manila Bay to the ears of men at war:

> During the present conflict in Vietnam, the free world nations have been called to support over 500,000 servicemen at a rate which has required approximately one ton of supplies per man, per month. Statistics available to me indicate that 95 percent of all those supplies, ranging from ammunition and fuel, to food and medical supplies, travel to Vietnam by ship along a 10,000-mile supply lifeline. Perhaps even more revealing is the fact that two out of every three servicemen in Vietnam have been transported to that country by ship.

The topic was an obvious choice for Rapp, whose instructions for U.S. ships in the exercise included Sino-Soviet radio jamming whenever possible. The South China Sea was a major route for enemy suppliers, and escalating border conflicts between China and the USSR made the sea the most viable option for the key Soviet supply line.

17

GHASTLY

On the *Melbourne*, Captain Stevenson couldn't believe what he had just seen. It could have been disastrous; it was exactly the scenario that had haunted him day and night as the exercise got under way. When he'd stopped swearing, he retired to his cabin for some urgent letter writing. "I think you believe in little spirits and the hereafter and so on and I must tell you about a ghastly but interesting experience," he would write in a letter to his wife.

In the dark early-morning hours of May 31, Stevenson was in the pilothouse of the *Melbourne*, about to launch aircraft as part of the antisubmarine exercise. As planned, the task group consisted of the *Melbourne* in the center, surrounded by five escort ships, all six vessels zigzagging in formation.

Stevenson called the USS *Everett F. Larson*, then steaming ahead and to the right of the *Melbourne*, to move behind her for plane guard. He watched the American destroyer first turn right and then immediately, turn left—*left!*—across the carrier's path. "I was watching him as Robbie was," he would write to Jo, recalling previous *Melbourne* skipper John Robertson's experience in the *Voyager* incident; "in seconds we were heading for disaster."

Stevenson continued: "I hit the voice radio, sounded the siren and put the full wheel on. Fortunately so did he. There followed the worst 30 seconds of my life, until he whistled down my starboard side no more than 100 feet off. It was a story so identical to the *Voyager* one, even down to the destroyer turning away first."

The *Melbourne* captain was quite shaken up, especially considering the dinner he had hosted only days earlier and the warnings he had given then. Before writing to his wife he had written two terse letters to Commander A. W. Rilling of the *Larson,* the second coming after an "unsatisfactory" reply to the first. Stevenson's subsequent letter went into the specifics of what went wrong, including the conning officer's assumption that the *Larson* was on the port bow when it was actually on the starboard bow. Whoever was conning the *Larson* had not consulted the guide before turning, and had then been slow to react once the two ships were on a collision course. Stevenson's letter was wordy and specific. And necessary, the Australian captain thought.

Stevenson relayed the scenario to Rear Admiral Gordon John Crabb, who followed with his own note to Commander Doak of the *Kyes,* requesting that the *Melbourne*'s escort ships maintain a distance of three thousand yards instead of the standard two thousand. The request was accepted, and the exercise continued.

While reports were made on the *Melbourne*, the *Larson*'s daily deck logs would not mention the near miss, though another incident would make the *Larson*'s logbook two days later: on the afternoon of June 2, Americans on the *Larson* would be rushed to their emergency general quarters after learning that the 26,000-ton British oiler HMS *Tidereach* had collided with the 2,415-ton Thai frigate HTMS *Tachin*. Though this later incident, which resulted in no injuries and only minor damage, was absent from the deck logs of other American ships, it at least put some sailors on their toes.

Later in the day on June 2, Rear Admiral Jerome King on the *Kearsarge* sent a harsh secret letter to all the U.S. destroyers in the exercise, chiding them for maneuvering "sloppily" and noting that one had come close to colliding with a carrier. On the *Evans* the message prompted McLemore to contact his squadron leader Doak, on the *Kyes,* to check whether the admiral was talking about the *Evans*. The reply was no. Still, though none of the ships knew of the *Larson* affair, it was clear to *Evans* officers that all was not well.

Doak, meanwhile, took a helicopter over to the *Melbourne* at the request of Rear Admiral Crabb, who wanted to meet the leader of Destroyer Squadron 23 to further discuss the *Larson* incident in person. The two men weighed the option of keeping a destroyer stationed behind the *Melbourne* for air operations, but the suggestion was shot down after Crabb insisted that, for antisubmarine purposes, it was not prudent to station an escort ship behind the carrier, where the escort would have difficulty searching for enemies. As long as a wing destroyer stationed to the immediate right or left of the carrier was used for plane guard, Doak responded, other ships ought to be able to maneuver safely; this was what American ships sometimes did when operating with the *Kearsarge*. The two men, with some disagreement, went over various ideas for how ships ought to screen the *Melbourne*. Much to Crabb's surprise, when replenishing was complete that afternoon the escort ships proceeded to screen the *Melbourne* according to his suggestions. The *Evans* would be the plane guard destroyer for the evening.

Working in shifts around the clock, *Evans* officers kept their eyes on the *Melbourne*. They were unaccustomed to these maneuvers, which were more exacting than anything the ship had attempted before. The *Evans* had served as plane guard destroyer for the carrier *Kearsarge*, but it had usually been stationed behind the carrier so that it might maneuver into place more easily and quickly. The present SEATO exercise called for ships to remain in front, to the right and left of the carrier. Maneuvering into plane guard to the rear when a destroyer was stationed ahead of the carrier was a more difficult task, requiring wide turns and coordination with other ships in the screen.

As Lieutenant Junior Grade Ronald Ramsey, the *Evans*'s most recently qualified officer of the deck, would later reveal, "The ship had been maneuvering quite beyond its normal tactics with the *Kearsarge* during the entire SEATO exercise with Commonwealth ships. They sharpened us up, you might say. They like to do a lot of playing around . . . and we have seldom if ever gone through zigzag plans and things like this." Another officer would later recall that the *Evans* officers were "scared" of the carrier, and that the Australian style of communication was unfamiliar to them. Even the accents were difficult to decipher over radio, a third officer would later explain. Confidence was waning. As *Evans* sonarman John Spray would write home that very week, "The ship is now engaged in a large SEATO operation. . . . The whole thing is a farce. None of the ships can cooperate with each other."

His final words would resonate within days: "I only hope that our well-being never depends upon such a group as this."

McLemore was exhausted. It was rumored that on June 2 he hadn't slept in two days. He would later claim that the exercise was "very complex in its concept. . . . Designed that way, there were many things coming up all the time."

They were well into Sea Spirit's transport phase. Within four days the ships were slated to arrive in Sattahip, Thailand, and the exercise would come to a close—if only they could get there. The ship had refueled that day, and that alone was no easy task. The *Evans* had had to move in alongside a massive oiler while the deck force worked to receive the fuel line. With two vessels maneuvering that close to each other at sea, one mistake could be disastrous.

As McLemore dealt with King's seething message, another came in from the *Melbourne*, ordering the *Evans* to serve as plane guard destroyer throughout the night and into the morning of June 3. McLemore would not recall seeing it, but another officer would recall that he had. Still, there was no doubt among those on watch in the pilothouse later that day: the *Evans* would go on to serve as plane guard destroyer no fewer than three times before midnight. It would also, later in the night, stray out of its sector more than once.

18

DARKENED SHIP

The South China Sea was blue as far as the eye could see, calm and glistening; the sunset was a blanket of orange light in the distance. The *Evans* cruised southwesterly along an invisible line that would become important much, much later on. She was just one blip on the radar in a war effort the Seventh Fleet tracked daily, plotting the coordinates of carrier groups. The scuttlebutt on board was only that they were somewhere near Vietnam, but two men, at least, knew exactly where their tiny ship was in the world.

The executive officer, Lieutenant Commander George McMichael, McLemore's number two and the ship's navigator, monitored the ship's loran, a positioning unit that could place a ship's coordinates. The loran would malfunction sometime after dusk on June 2, requiring McMichael's immediate attention just after midnight. The *Evans* was just outside what he would later refer to as the "combat pay and tax exemption zone" of the Vietnam War, skimming along the waterway between Vietnam and west of the Vietnam-controlled Spratly Islands—far from the fighting, but not far enough.

And then there was Ensign John Norton, who loved the natural world and, as his mother would say, had the sea in his eyes. It was likely that the tall, handsome officer was taking it all in that night, as he often did, marveling at the magnificent sight of nothing but blue water and the thought of what lay beneath, layers of sedimentary clay, sand, and rock. This was a place he knew well, better than most on the *Evans*, for he had studied it as an undergraduate at Columbia University. In the fall of 1967, his naval science engineering assignment had been to pick a place in the world and study its sediment. Norton had chosen the South China Sea, which he studied in maps and reports while interning at Lamont Geological Observatory in New York. His detailed eleven-page report included a map he'd made with fine strokes of colored pencils and a series of dots for the precise points of geology he discussed. Those dots traced, as fate would have it, nearly the exact path of the *Evans* on that June evening, as it steamed over some of the deepest sea trenches in the world.

Norton was likely amazed at the mere thought of being in that place he knew so well, above what he had described in his Columbia report as "the ooze of protozoa and clay and chemically precipitated limestone." As the sun went down, the waning full moon cast a path of light over the calm sea. This realm too—the space above the sea's surface, rather than below—was another he'd been fascinated with since childhood. He'd followed the race to space throughout the 1950s and '60s, clipping out *New York Times* articles and pasting them into hefty scrapbooks, documenting the drama of this battle for supremacy in what would become, as history revealed it, simply another facet of the Cold War. The U.S. space program was fighting to get to the moon before the Communists could, to demonstrate that their technology ruled supreme—and that they could launch rockets to faraway places. And guys like Norton fought a real war.

As Norton stood on the main deck of his very first ship, far from home for the very first time, the scene brought him back to something familiar from his boyhood. This would be his last sunset, the last time he'd gaze at the moon, and within a few hours, his final resting place. But at the time he could never have known it.

Nobody could have.

Norton wasn't on duty that evening, and officers not on duty typically hung out in the wardroom or in their berthing, writing letters. To get to the stateroom he shared with three other men, Norton had two options. The first was to head out of the wardroom onto the main deck and take a ladder down to the mess deck, where other sailors might be playing cards or watching a movie. If it were long past the evening meal, a sailor or two would be polishing tables and swabbing the decks, closing up shop until the following morning. The second option was to head forward from the wardroom, past the senior officers' quarters, and down a rickety steel ladder to the junior officers' quarters. It's likely that a ruckus could be heard in the vicinity; more than thirty men slept in the compartment just below, and about thirty more in a compartment under the mess deck. The chiefs were just forward of that. Shipboard life was a cluttered, noisy ordeal; when there was nothing to do and you wanted to be alone, you had just a few feet of space to yourself. Officers had a little more, but not much. When Norton turned in for the night, and the lights went out, the ship's gentle swaying would rock him to sleep.

Those in the enlisted berthing compartment just below were also winding down for the night. First Division was by then home to more than two dozen new seamen just weeks out of boot camp. Rumor had it that the new kids hadn't even been given leave following boot-camp graduation, poor bastards. Just over two months into its deployment, a span that included time on the gunline off Vietnam, the *Evans* was at last nearly fully staffed; it had left the United States vastly undermanned. The more experienced sailors would help the new men acclimate to navy life, much of which was spent simply counting down the days. Sometimes the advice and instructions sank in, and sometimes the information, coming in waves, just floated over the buzz cuts and wide, wondering eyes. The new sailors seemed to listen as most do, their eyes uncertain; maybe this was just another joke, another drill, something to highlight the fact that they were new and green.

The new men knew almost nothing about life at sea: where things were, how things were done, what it meant when the boatswain's mate whistled that high-pitch alert that could be heard over the swooshing of water on the main deck and the gentle hum of the engines below. They didn't know that the food could be worse—being closer to a base meant heartier provisions. They didn't know that it wasn't a door anymore, it was a *hatch*, and it could bang up your legs if you didn't pay attention to where the fuck you were stepping. It wasn't a *corridor*, it was a goddamned *passageway*. They didn't know that the place John Wayne had made look so cool was instead hot, muggy, and smaller than they could ever have imagined. They didn't know they would have to get out of their rack any time someone had to get into his locker—even if it was in the middle of the night. And that snoring, a symphony of gurgles and breathing, would be something they'd just have to get used to.

Just getting started, they knew they'd have to learn somehow how to survive the steady, rocking monotony, day after relentless day. Sleep was their escape. Many welcomed lights out; God knows the older seamen did. Another day gone meant one day closer to something else, perhaps something better. Surely it couldn't get worse. In the dark of night some must have wondered, What in the hell have I gotten myself into?

That night the exercise called for darkened ship, meaning that all exterior lights on the *Evans* were to be turned off, to make the ship invisible to submarines. Even the pilothouse, the workspace of but a few men, was dim so that those in charge could see out without glare. That night the exercise was in full swing, and the men of the task force were hunting submarines. In the dead of night on a dark sea they'd be lucky to spot a shadow or a silhouette on the horizon; those in charge turned to electronic devices to command and control, or to squinting into the darkness through binoculars. Complicating matters was the zigzagging, an unsettling maneuver in the dark.

The watch was busy, with two task forces on the primary radio—those of the *Melbourne* and the USS *Kearsarge* just thirty miles away. The *Evans* officer of the deck, Lieutenant Junior Grade Tom Bowler, made note of the busy circuits. McLemore, making his rounds, came into the pilothouse at about 9:00 p.m., just as the *Evans* was moving into plane guard position behind the *Melbourne* for the second time that night. On the Australian carrier, Stevenson would notice the smooth maneuver, the way the *Evans* had hooked out and away from his ship and come around her stern. Perfect—or at least a far cry from the near disaster of just two evenings prior.

Bowler, a class of 1967 U.S. Naval Academy graduate, was a natural. Among a batch of junior officers that came aboard in the fall of 1967, he was one of the first among them to qualify as officer of the deck. Eager to serve his country and fight communism, among his biggest fears during his plebe year at the academy was that the slow-growing fire in Indochina would be stomped out before he'd get his chance to see the flames. He'd seen then-President John F. Kennedy speak to midshipmen in Bancroft Hall 1963—months before his assassination—and he felt the call: *"I can imagine no more rewarding a career. And any man who may be asked in this century what he did to make his life worthwhile, I think can respond with a good deal of pride and satisfaction: 'I served in the United States Navy.'"* Bowler was confident and liked McLemore a great deal; he thought the captain brought a level of training on board that wasn't common—at least not under the previous captain. Thor Hanson, captain of the *Evans* from 1966 to 1968, had been known for "hogging" the conn, allowing little responsibility to his young officers. Under McLemore, the younger men were given space to learn. True, too much room to make mistakes could be risky—disastrous, even—but it would be even more detrimental to the Navy as a whole if its emerging leaders weren't given opportunities to command. There was a balance.

Bowler's junior officer of the deck was ensign Gregory Ogawa, who had just come on board in Hawaii. It was a pairing common on the *Evans*. The watch bill coordinator and third-highest-ranking officer, Lieutenant Gerald Dunne, liked to match watch standers by ability—an experienced officer of the deck with an inexperienced junior officer of the deck, and vice versa. Dunne, the only full lieutenant on the *Evans*, was a Class of 1964 U.S. Naval Academy graduate, following two old brothers—classes of 1954 and '60—through the academy and onto a life on the sea. He had stood out when he made it to the fleet just as the war in Vietnam heated up and the officer ranks became diluted with draft-induced fellows—men who signed up for the Navy after college to avoid the Army draft. The lieutenant's job was to gauge the abilities of the men and match them accordingly, so that on a ship with a shortage of fully qualified and experienced officers, each watch was "balanced." It was a delicate distribution of responsibilities, aimed at keeping the ship's operations on course and steady.

When Dunne decided who would serve on the midnight-to-four-a.m. midwatch on June 3, he was following this principle, balancing a capable man with a greener one. It was a balance that could be thrown off by one new factor in a matter of a few minutes, as a gust of wind might topple a shaky tightrope walker. There was always a risk, but in these times, you had to work with what you had.

19

The Watch

By 11:45 p.m. the *Evans* was nearly one hour into a scheduled zigzag maneuver: the ships turning in concert, following a preordained plan mapped out in three-hour intervals. From afar they might look more like insects buzzing around randomly in the night, but inside the control rooms of each ship, each turn was coordinated, course and speed varied according to schedule every three minutes. The exercise was tricky enough in itself, but under darkened ship conditions it was—as an experienced navy man would explain later, when the events of June 3, 1969 were dissected—among the most challenging of tasks. It called for an experienced ship handler who possessed the "seaman's eye"—aided by binoculars, the heavy "glasses" some officers wouldn't wear around their neck because of the muscle strain—sharp instincts, common sense, and a steady hand. Still, in the end it was basic seamanship. It was this that made what would happen in the next four hours all the more unbelievable to the droves of navy men who would later study it.

Lieutenant Junior Grade Ronald Ramsey passed through the combat information center on his way to the pilothouse just before midnight, having just had coffee in the wardroom with fellow officers who would be on watch. The information center—lit like the inside of a spaceship and packed with radars, screens, and radios, a spaghetti of wires, and buzzing machinery—was to be his right hand while he manned the pilothouse. The radarmen working inside would receive the same radio messages and top-secret codes, decipher them, and make recommendations. It was a fully staffed function of a ship, with the main goal of ensuring that nothing went wrong. While some might see the combat information center's job as that of second-guessing—some officers were known to ignore the combat information center completely—the men there had a duty to ensure, clarify, and, if the situation warranted, contradict the directives of the pilothouse. Getting acquainted with the combat information center watch crew is what any smart officer did, and Ramsey, on his way to the pilothouse for the midwatch, was doing just that.

Ramsey's light brown hair and small, innocent eyes gave him a boyish look, even though he was tall and walked with the confidence of a grown man. He was one of the few married young officers on board, and his wife was expecting their second child. Ramsey had come on board in 1967 after graduating from the Reserve Officer Training Corps through Purdue University in Indiana. His father was a retired chief, a machinist mate who likely taught his son to appreciate and respect his enlisted sailors, so much so that many enlistees on the *Evans* liked Ronald Ramsey best among the officers. One seaman would recall enjoying a concoction of whiskey-soaked cherries and Coca-Cola on board with the officer, who "wasn't a pain in the ass like the others who seemed to want to push around every single one of us and work us to death."

This brought some controversy. Ramsey was smart and capable, but he was also perhaps slightly overconfident, and other officers either didn't like him or were indifferent to him. Lieutenant Dunne saw Ramsey's overconfidence as a double-edged sword: it made Ramsey sure of himself, yet it could prevent him from asking for help when he needed it. Ramsey was the ship's communications officer, a billet usually given to a full lieutenant, though that alone was not necessarily an indication of his abilities; since the ship was understaffed in more experienced officers, many junior officers were obliged to take on higher responsibilities.

Bowler, the officer of the deck who Ramsey would relieve that evening, later recalled the first time he met the officer, in the fall of 1967; "Ramsey introduced himself as a brigade commander at Purdue," he said—unsolicited information that Bowler and the others regarded as a little pompous, and promptly discounted. When the young officers hit the beach together on liberty, Ramsey often disappeared. On several rolls of photographs taken by one of Ramsey's roommates from his 1967–68 deployment on the *Evans*, Ramsey appears only once, his face expressionless as he faces the camera, his arms folded and his "USS *Frank E. Evans*" baseball cap loose on his head and cocked to the side.

Ramsey's roommate at the time was the ship's supply officer, Lieutenant Junior Grade Robert Suhr. Suhr would later recall that Ramsey was a private person, and leave it at that. But there was some dissent. The former communications officer throughout 1967 and much of '68, Lieutenant Junior Grade Edwin Churchill (coincidentally, another Purdue University man), detested Ramsey. Lieutenant Churchill referred questions about the young officer's character to the cruise book from that year. A cruise book is a bit like a high school yearbook for a vessel on deployment, documenting in photos who was on the ship, where he went, and what he did. The Library of Congress keeps hundreds of these historical artifacts in its stacks, as does the Naval History and Heritage Command. Ramsey, while helping to put together the 1967–68 cruise book, in lieu of the customary official Navy portrait included a photo of himself underwater in heavy scuba gear, his face unrecognizable. His choice was seen as lacking decorum, even insulting. "We knew he wasn't serious about the Navy," his former boss would later say. Ramsey was also rumored to fraternize with the enlisted sailors too much.

In the early hours of June 3, Ramsey was just a name on a watch bill. He was a bit on the inexperienced side, having only served as a watch leader for two months, and thus not quite qualified on paper—a gray area that would become a sticking point later on. Working with him was Lieutenant Junior Grade James Hopson, who was more experienced as a junior officer of the deck than Ramsey was as an officer of the deck; the pairing was a balance that Dunne would later say "sufficed."

Hopson, a trained medical corpsman, was a mustang, a prior enlistee who had a bachelor's degree in mechanical engineering courtesy of the U.S. Navy and continued to serve as an officer. The *Evans* was his first ship. When he came on board in 1967 at the age of twenty-seven he was the oldest ensign—a fact that Captain Thor Hansen took advantage of to play a trick on an old chum. As the story goes, a destroyer was on the gunline off Vietnam, waiting for its new skipper—the shortage of qualified officers went right up the ranks—and Hansen decided to send Hopson over as the new captain, wearing Hanson's own uniform. Hopson lasted about a day on the ship before the crew suspected that he wasn't really the new commanding officer. It was a memorable stunt; apparently Hopson caused quite a ruckus when he pointed out that the crew was doing everything wrong.

Well into his second year on board the *Evans*, McLemore didn't trust Hopson. Although he put him in the billet of assistant engineering officer, he would go on to say that he hadn't been quite sure where to place him; in fact, the junior officer wasn't very good at the job.

Two officers were on duty in the combat information center that night, within a few steps of the pilothouse. Ensign Alan Armstrong was one of the ship's top junior officers, one who had also been enlisted previously. Ensign Robert Brandon, second in command in the combat information center, was an officer "head and shoulders" above the rest, McLemore would later say. The captain liked these two officers, and planned eventually to move them into higher positions.

It was standard practice, when the watch was changed, for the outgoing officers to notify those coming in what had happened over the past four hours and what was to be expected, details that included the planned course, speed, weather forecasts, and any extraneous information that could affect the evening's maneuvers—in this case, that the *Evans* had already been called to plane guard three times that night. Ramsey would later acknowledge that he knew the ship would be asked to maneuver into plane guard position, a thousand yards astern of the carrier, sometime during his four-hour watch. Other than that, the evening was supposed to be uneventful.

Having stationed four officers on duty, two in the pilothouse and two in the combat information center, McLemore turned in for the night. Expecting a lull in the SEATO operation—they would still be zigzagging, but no tedious seek-and-destroy exercises—he looked forward to his first chance to rest in over thirty-six hours. He often slept in his sea cabin, a narrow retreat with two doors, one leading to the pilothouse and the other to the combat information center. Each watch came with night orders, a list of requirements and rules for standing watch. One standing order for every watch stander, no matter where or when he would be in charge of a ship during his four-hour stint, was that the captain had to be notified whenever there was a change in course, speed, or sector. It was a confusing order, since the *Evans* would be changing course and speed every few minutes, as it executed the zigzag pattern required this evening. Generally, night orders also included scribbled instructions—that night, the words "be prepared" featured prominently—for certain tasks the captain wanted his watch standers to undertake. It was customary for each watch stander to read the orders and sign them before taking over the ship's controls.

Ramsey, getting ready to take over, was told to expect to maneuver the *Evans* into plane guard position sometime after 3:00 a.m. Given that the ship would be constantly zigzagging, he reckoned that he wouldn't need to notify the captain when he did this. It was a standard maneuver, and the captain knew it was coming—or so the young officer thought.

Whether Ramsey was right or dead wrong would be dissected much later. But by then the night orders for the USS *Frank E. Evans* watch standers would rest in a deep-sea crater, crushed in a mangled steel ship body some eleven hundred fathoms below the surface.

While officers called in orders, it was up to the enlisted personnel to send and receive radio messages, to operate the engine order telegraph, and to man the wheel. Most of Ramsey's pilothouse team had been in the Navy less than a year, and some had only a few months under their belts—just enough time to go to boot camp and get orders to a ship in Southeast Asia. But there was at least one star among the enlisted on duty that night: Seaman Robert Petty. A slender, blond nineteen-year-old, on paper Petty was qualified to shine boots, and little else. Yet the reality was very different. Petty was an independent type, one whose family circumstances in small-town Spring, Texas, had forced him to grow up fast. He had spent part of his teenage years in the merchant marines, and then joined the U.S. Navy to gain additional experience, eventually planning to return to the merchant marines as a career man. Petty knew a lot about sea life, and enjoyed the peace and beauty of the blanket of never-ending blue, no land in sight.

Petty's role that night was boatswain's mate of the watch, a sort of supervisor to the enlisted men working in the pilothouse. His job called for quick fixes on turns and engine orders—essentially, keeping an eye on the new guys. When a turn was ordered, the officers watched the rudder indicator to make sure the move had been executed correctly; that night there were some minor errors, but these were typical when new men were on board. Petty, who the officers relied on to help manage the new sailors, admired McLemore a great deal and thought wise the commander's decision to use the quiet overnight watches as training for inexperienced seamen.

Meanwhile, in the combat information center, a much more experienced watch crew balanced out the inexperience on the bridge. Inside the compartment stood some of the more capable radarmen on board. As a group, these men worked well together, so they typically served on duty at the same time. Each man had a station, a role to play: one would be on a headset, monitoring radio traffic; some would stand before a panel of circular radar screens and scopes; another set worked at a surface plotting table; and another set had a unique skill: writing backward in grease pencil on a glass board, so that those on the other side could see the ship's direction and monitor the exercise as a whole. The rest took up various posts along the sidelines, helping with code, manning certain apparatuses, or standing watch in radio rooms and sonar rooms. One man would be stationed in the interior communications and plotting room. Together their job was to keep track of the *Evans* as she zigzagged, and monitor the zigzagging of other ships in the vicinity.

Belowdecks, deep in the belly of the ship, where not one porthole existed, teams of snipes kept the *Evans* steaming, working in compartments lit as if by daylight. The engine and firerooms were like factories, a maze of levels linked by iron ladders and platforms. In the engine room the machinist mates waited for orders from the bridge: how fast, and when. The fireroom guys kept the burners lit, cranking out the steam that powered the vessel. In this hot, bright space, redolent of sweat, grease, and coffee, it was business as usual.

Outside, above the pilothouse and combat information center, stood lookouts, one on each side—visual spotters whose only job was to watch the dark, calm sea and the other ships, looking for nuances that the bridge might not catch. Near the mast over the pilothouse stood a signal shack, home to two signalmen on watch. Darkened ship status was like a night off—no flags, no flashing signals to other ships—and sometime after midnight the pair of signalmen decided to split their shift. One would climb on top of the shack and rest his eyes while the other sat inside or paced the platform outside the shack, looking at the stars, the sea, and the other ships in the distance, ink-black outlines under a moonlight sky.

With nearly two-thirds of the ship's men asleep, the quiet night had begun.

On the *Melbourne*, Stevenson's own watch team included men of various qualifications, none of which would ever come into question. The navigational bridge on a carrier is larger and more spread out, taking up two floors on the control tower, but its mechanisms are similar to those on a destroyer. The officer of the deck was Lieutenant Russell Lamb, who had been qualified for several years; Stevenson considered him to be the finest officer of the deck on board.

For a plane to generate enough lift to leave a carrier, it needs wind or speed. As Stevenson surveyed the night, the South China Sea was glassy; there was not the slightest breeze. That meant that the *Melbourne* would have to be at top speed when planes took off just after 3:00 a.m.; it wouldn't be a restful night. He'd alternate between visiting the pilothouse and writing letters in his stateroom, just a few steps away. When did a captain ever sleep? he wondered. Not tonight, not during this exercise—and not with the near collision of two nights earlier still fresh in his mind.

USS *Frank E. Evans*, DD-754. *Courtesy of the USS Frank E. Evans Association.*

August 6, 1965 issue of *Life* magazine, published one year after the Gulf of Tonkin incident. "In Action with the Navy off Vietnam, Fleet Lashes Out."

Commander Albert Sydney McLemore. *Courtesy photo.*

Master Chief Lawrence Reilly, 1960s. *Courtesy photo.*

Lawrence Reilly, Jr. as a child in the 1950s. *Courtesy photo.*

The Reilly family at James Reilly's wedding in 1968. From left to right, Luanne Reilly, Lieutenant Junior Grade James Reilly, Chief Lawrence Reilly, Boiler Tender Third Class Lawrence Reilly, Gerald Reilly, seated is Marion Reilly with Suzanne Reilly to her left. *Courtesy photo.*

Master Chief Lawrence Reilly, left, in conference with his son, Boiler Tender Third Class Lawrence Reilly. *Courtesy of the USS Frank E. Evans Association.*

Gary Sage, top left, Greg Sage, right, and Kelly Jo Sage, bottom. Niobrara, early 1950s. *Courtesy of Linda Vaa.*

Mothers Day gift for Eunice Sage. Three sailors: Boatswains Mate Second Class Gary Sage, Radarmen Third Class Greg, and Seaman Apprentice Kelly Jo Sage. *Courtesy of Linda Vaa.*

Machinist Mate Third Class Duane "Butterball" Conely at his home in Warren, Minnesota. *Courtesy photo.*

Seaman Apprentice William Thibeault playing guitar in the First Division berthing compartment of the *Evans*. Thibeault would decades laters write a song about his fallen shipmates: *Where's the Glory? Courtesy photo.*

Young Signalman Steve Kraus poses for a picture to send to Donna Kraus, his bride. Late 1960s. *Courtesy photo.*

USS *Frank E. Evans* firing off the coast of Vietnam, Operation Daring Rebel, May 1969. *Courtesy of a survivor.*

USS *Frank E. Evans* sailors drinking at a bar in Subic Bay. From left to right, Seaman Michael Clawson, Seaman Francis Garcia, Seaman Apprentice John Sauvey, Seaman Frederic Messier, Seaman Tom Vargo *Courtesy of the Messier family.*

Sage brothers opening mail on the fantail of the USS *Frank E. Evans* on May 25, 1969. From Left to right, Greg, Gary, and Kelly Jo, reading his birthday card from his mother. Kelly Jo turned 19 on May 29. *Sent to the Sage family from the United States Navy in July 1969.*

Photograph of the USS *Frank E. Evans* taken from the flight deck of the HMAS *Melbourne* during Exercise Sea Spirit. Thought to be the last photograph ever taken of the *Evans*. *Courtesy of the National Archives of Australia.*

Captain John Stevenson, commander of the HMAS *Melbourne*. *Courtesy of the National Archives of Australia.*

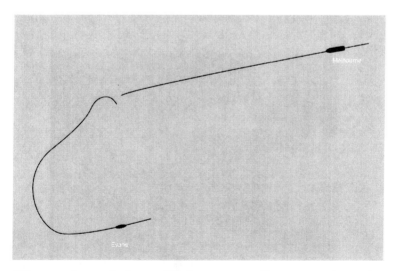

Illustration of the collision at sea between the USS *Frank E. Evans*, left, and HMAS *Melbourne*, right. *Courtesy of the National Archives of Australia.*

Frantic, Scared and injured, Americans sailors scrambling along the starboard passageway on the aft section of the USS *Frank E. Evans* of the immediately following the collision. *Courtesy of the National Archives of Australia.*

Muster on the aft section. Sailors were told to spread out, as this half of the ship was thought to be sinking. *Courtesy of the National Archives of Australia.*

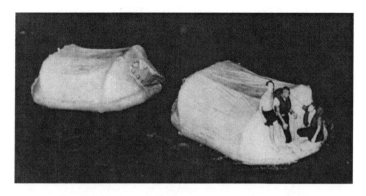

Evans sailors from the forward half, which sank in three minutes, climbed onto fenders while they waited for Australians in motorboats to rescue them. *Courtesy of the National Archives of Australia.*

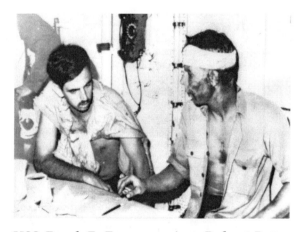

USS *Frank E. Evans* survivor Robert Petty, right, talks to another survivor while being treated on the HMAS *Melbourne* following the accident and rescue. Suffering injuries to his head and back, Petty was thrown into the sea from the pilothouse at collision. Instantly he swam back towards his ship and climbed aboard the sinking bow to open a hatch, rescuing sixteen sailors who were trapped inside. *Courtesy of the National Archives of Australia.*

The sun rose on June 3, 1969 to a bitter, gray morning as helicopters search for survivors. Behind the aft section of the Evans is likely the USS *James E. Kyes*. To the right is the USS *Everett F. Larson*. *Courtesy of the National Archives of Australia.*

What remained of the *Evans* tied alongside the *Larson* in the early morning hours as men assess the damage and gather personal items. The USS *Tawasa*, which will tow the *Evans*, arrived shortly thereafter. *Courtesy of the U.S. Navy History and Heritage Command.*

The collision caused a major gash in the bow of the HMAS *Melbourne*. The damage on the flight deck is likely where she rammed into the *Evans'* superstructure. *Courtesy of the National Archives of Australia.*

News outlets used information collected from the United States Navy, which put the collision "650 miles from Manila," to draw sketches of where the incident occurred. Vietnam, missing from the illustration, is roughly 200 miles west. *Associated Press map.*

Where the *Evans* was lost in reference to Vietnam. Despite being out of the combat zone, the *Evans* along with every American ship there on that day collected Vietnam Service Medals. *Map created by Charles Syrett at Map Graphics, Nelson, British Columbia, Canada.*

Eunice and Ernest Sage on June 5 listen to a reading of a condolence letter signed by President Richard Nixon. *Wire photo.*

Ernest reads a condolence letter and weeps as his youngest and only living son Doug Sage, 6, leans on his father. *Photograph courtesy of Linda Vaa. Used with the permission of the family of Lynn Pelham.*

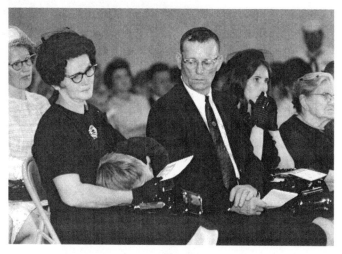

Ernest watched as Eunice Sage wept while comforting a wailing Doug Sage. Linda Vaa, to his left, holds a tissue to her mouth during the memorial service inside the gymnasium of Niobrara High School on June 11, 1969. *Photograph courtesy of Linda Vaa. Used with the permission of the family of Lynn Pelham.*

Eunice Sage at the L'Eau Qui Court Cemetery in Niobrara, Nebraska. Louise Esola took this final photograph of Eunice on September 12, 2010. The mother who lost three sons on the *Evans* passed away on September 24, twelve days later. *Author's collection.*

20

JULIET SEVEN

Gazing out on a clear, dark night from a ship, seeing only the moon and a glassy, calm sea, is quite soothing. It can also be disorienting, like riding on a slow-moving train, where it can look as if the platform moves away instead of the train itself.

It was just after 2:30 a.m.; the ships were still zigzagging, and Ramsey, who wanted to go over message traffic from the evening, decided to pass control of the ship over to his junior officer of the deck, Hopson. The *Evans*, code-named Juliet Seven, was steaming slightly ahead and to the left of the *Melbourne*, maintaining a healthy distance of 3,800 yards between the two ships. To the left of the *Evans* was the HMNZS *Blackpool*, zigzagging in its own sector.

Not until days later would it become evident that the *Evans* had already twice accidentally cruised into the *Blackpool*'s sector and then corrected itself, again accidentally, while attempting to follow a prescribed zigzag with which neither

Hopson nor Ramsey were familiar.

Switching duties in the middle of a quiet night kept the men from getting careless and bored; this was Ramsey's thinking, and the sign of a good watch stander, it would be said later. Ramsey knew the *Evans* would be called to plane guard duty sometime after 3:00 a.m., but he believed Hopson up to the task, as a capable officer, Ramsey would later go on to say, who would soon make officer of the deck. As he leaned over a chart table, reading the evening's messages, Ramsey was simply exercising good judgment as the leader of an ordinary night's watch.

Yet as events within the next hour would reveal, the situation was plagued with holes, some gaping, some tiny. A British psychologist by the name of James Reason would twenty years later analyze the role of human error in organizations. In what he called the Swiss cheese model, he envisioned layers of protection against possible catastrophes. Imagine several slices of Swiss cheese stacked upon one another, layers of defense, with the many holes representing both obvious and hidden weaknesses. When the holes line up—by chance, by an act of God, or through whatever agency in the universe one happens to believe in—disaster strikes. Calamitous human error can be a cruel game of chance, of holes lining up.

In the pilothouse on the morning of June 3, 1969, as the clock struck 3:00 a.m., the holes were hidden and small. On at least two occasions during the night the men on the bridge had disagreed with the combat information center's suggestions regarding the messages they'd decoded on speed and direction. They were minor disagreements, Hopson would later recall, but disagreements nonetheless. Twice the *Evans* had cruised out of its sector accidentally, and there would be speculation later that it was out of its sector once again in the three o'clock hour—though that alarmed no one at the time. Then there were the new recruits in the pilothouse, the ones who didn't quite get helm orders or engine order telegraphs right, those who needed correction. These were minor infractions, little things that Ramsey and others would quickly point out and correct—swiftly, but nonetheless often.

What would come to light later was that Ramsey had no formal qualification, no paper that announced, "Congratulations, you can officially man a ship." McLemore was a good captain. After Ramsey's first go-around on the tests for officer of the deck several months earlier, he hadn't thrown the young officer into the mix, but in fact had failed him, sending him back to study more. Nobody on board would ever call Ramsey inept; he was a smart and confident sailor. But his overconfidence, several officers would later claim, represented another hole, his ego a weakness that led to human error.

The war in Vietnam had caused other holes. Old ships like the *Evans* were overworked, undermanned, asked to do too many things. Had there been no Vietnam, the *Evans* would have been shit-canned for sure. After a hellish tour on the ship-shuddering gunline in 1967 and '68, the heavily used ship had been pulled into dry dock, its younger officers losing out on months of training as ship workers performed what seemed like miracles.

Antisubmarine warfare represented yet another hole. Essentially, antisubmarine warfare had been playing second fiddle to naval gunfire support and other roles deemed necessary for fighting the war in Vietnam. The admirals had acknowledged this overall weakness in a meeting in early 1969, calling for ships to bone up on antisubmarine skills whenever possible—which was not all that often, given that ships were in constant need of repair. The system of plane guarding introduced another hole. Destroyers did perform it often, both in exercises and in operations in the Gulf of Tonkin, supporting carriers that launched aircraft into North and South Vietnam. But the men of the *Evans* did it differently. Theirs had been more of a park-and-wait approach; they were not accustomed to being thrown into the middle of an antisubmarine exercise with a carrier under the command of an Australian who did things his own way.

In the pilothouse of the *Melbourne* at that very moment was yet another hole. That her skipper was already haunted by two incidents—a deadly one five years earlier, and a jolting one only two nights before—didn't help matters. And both incidents had happened on nights just like this.

At 3:12 a.m. Stevenson still had the *Larson* affair on his mind when, expecting planes to come in for a landing, he called the *Evans* to plane guard. Bucking normal procedure, Stevenson decided that in addition to ordering the *Evans* to station itself a thousand yards behind the carrier, he would provide the precise direction of the *Melbourne*, so there could be no confusion. If this were real-life antisubmarine warfare, he would have never given up his position and course over the radio. But remembering the *Larson* ordeal, he didn't want to take any chances. Following the radio transmission—a trail that began with a radio operator in another compartment on the carrier and then moved onto the primary tactical circuit, eventually making its way to the pilothouse on the *Evans* and to the four other ships in the formation—Stevenson also ordered his navigation lights up to full brilliance, even though the exercise had called for darkened ships. The knob for the navigation lights, if rotated past the setting for full illumination, turns the lights off again. The operator in charge of this function recalled first turning the dial, and then, moments later, noticing that he had accidentally turned it too far, past the brightest setting and back to dark, adjusting it back to full brilliance. The men on ships in the vicinity, however, mostly didn't notice this flash of light on the dark, calm water. Some even claimed it never happened.

Stevenson, on the open bridge, thought he couldn't take any chances. He couldn't forget the *Larson* incident. But surely, he thought, McLemore was in the pilothouse of the *Evans*. Why wouldn't he be? This was plane guard at night, a darkened ship amid foreign navies. Captains of American ships would in retrospect declare the situation to be among the most difficult for any officer, however experienced, to handle—and Hopson and Ramsey each had less than two years' time in the Navy.

But McLemore was asleep.

And there were still other holes.

The mimeographed plans aimed at keeping all ships zigzagging in sync were another weak spot. Some navies, it would later become evident, used an alternative protocol that called for zigzags to cease in the event of plane guard or other changes in station; some ships would stop, while others would continue with the zigzag plan. And then there was the profuse use of code—unfamiliar code, in some cases.

Hopson received the message in shackled code. Ramsey, still reading over the chart table, also saw it. No doubt a radarman in the combat information center also heard it over a headset. They had seconds to come up with a plan, yet they were slow to respond, an Australian communications officer would later recall. Due to a miscalculation as to where the ships were within the zigzag plan—and whether the zigzagging should halt after the order was given to plane guard—Hopson believed the carrier was heading south when in fact it was heading west. With no correction or objection, Hopson announced his strategy to Ramsey, who continued sifting through message traffic, unaware that he should be doing something else, something more immediate.

Another hole existed in McLemore's night orders for the officers in control, the paper-thin yet regulation-strong layer of protection put in place to protect the ship against mishaps while the captain was sleeping. These orders required the officer of the deck to wake the captain in the event of any change of course or speed. But the ship had been changing course and speed every three minutes, due to the zigzag plans. This made for a predicament; Ramsey felt that surely he was not obliged to wake McLemore every three minutes, and thus believed he should not wake him at all. The ship's executive officer, Lieutenant Commander George McMichael, would later dispute this, as would many of the other officers on board. If you are changing station—going from zigzag to something else like plane guard—they argued, you must wake the captain. But neither Ramsey nor Hopson thought they were doing anything other than what was required. The pair had good intentions—another trademark of human error.

With the HMNZS *Blackpool* in a sector to the left, Hopson ordered a right turn so that the *Evans* could cruise along the carrier's right side and come up just behind her. It would have been a perfect move, had only Hopson assessed the carrier's direction correctly. But as it was, Hopson's turn appeared, to Stevenson's horror, to bring the *Evans* onto a heading straight for the *Melbourne*.

Seconds later Hopson took his first visual sighting of the carrier—just a "shadow," was all he would profess to have seen—and suddenly became alarmed. Confusion took hold. Not panic—not yet; not until Ramsey and the others heard over the radio, "You are on a collision course." They heard this alert three times.

The lights on the carrier flashed on. She's about to launch aircraft, Hopson thought; turning to Ramsey, he said, "I don't get it." With the flattops, as carriers are known, it is difficult to decipher front from back. Were they behind her already? Navy men describe this terrifying moment of utter confusion as being "lost in the bubble." It was a situation in which neither Ramsey nor Hopson had adequate experience.

In these tragic minutes, neither *Evans* officer in the pilothouse would recall hearing anything from the combat information center, where inside the small compartment a screen showed two blips—those of the *Evans* and the *Melbourne*—moving alarmingly close to each other. And yet, it seemed, no one said anything. Silence from the combat information center at a moment like this seemed preposterous to those who would later hear of it. Petty, the enlisted seaman in charge—who stood between the helmsman at the wheel and the lee helmsman, sending orders to the engine room—noticed the rise in tension.

On the *Melbourne*, Stevenson was immediately alarmed by the *Evans*'s inaction after its first turn. In a maneuver that would look like a fishhook when drawn on a sketchpad, the *Evans* had turned into the carrier's path and not corrected itself. This was the one thing Stevenson had been adamant about. The escort handout had put it in writing; he had himself said it clearly over jovial dinner-table discussions only a week earlier. He was now in a fit, cursing; it was the *Larson* all over again. This time, though, he sent three collision-course warnings—and still there was no correction. Wake up, *Evans*! he thought. What the hell are you doing?

The *Evans* turned only slightly left—as it would become known later, by 10 degrees, a shift that wouldn't even get a driver into another lane on a freeway. And then nothing. She was still turning, that giant fishhook, right into the *Melbourne*'s path.

Ramsey, not yet outside on the open bridge where he could gain a visual sighting of the carrier, immediately ordered right full rudder, his tactic for getting the ship off the collision course that neither he nor Hopson had seen coming.

At about the same moment, Stevenson on the *Melbourne* ordered his rudder to port—left. The *Evans* was heading right. The turns were simultaneous, the radio messages nearly so, though the other ships in the vicinity, all on the same tactical radio, would recall hearing one message before the other. Some would say they'd heard the *Melbourne* first, others the *Evans*.

It was 3:14 a.m.

On the *Evans* there was raw panic. Petty saw the new men in the pilothouse hesitate at the rash of engine and rudder orders. There was a clash of new directions, and more hesitation. Petty took over, within seconds seeing a bright ray of light coming through the porthole. By then Ramsey was out on the open bridge. It was a deadly predicament, a game of chance. Seconds, centimeters. And the men in control of the *Evans* knew it: their tiny ship was crossing into the path of a ship ten times her size. Could they make it? Ramsey at first thought they could. And then he saw the carrier turning left. Why is she turning? he wondered. He knew the rule: the larger ship has right-of-way, and always maintains course and speed.

When the moment was examined later, both turns—Ramsey's hard right and Stevenson's hard left—became sticking points: Which had come first? When expert navigators later speculated over sloppy heaps of scrap paper, it was clear that of the nine possible combinations of maneuvers, this was one of only two that would lead to disaster. If the *Melbourne* had stayed on course, she would still have hit the *Evans*, it would be decided later on. Had both ships done nothing or both turned the opposite way, the disaster would not have happened. But, to disbelieving eyes, it had.

On the *Evans* both Hopson and Ramsey stood still; perhaps shock took hold. Neither pulled the collision alarm, which would wake the slumbering seamen below and warn them of the horror unfolding. In a last-ditch effort to seize the moment, to backpedal, Hopson ordered the engines all back full. This rare order, when received in the engine room three levels below, was like an alarm bell, the slamming of the brakes. *We never get an all back full*, thought a machinist mate who, under drowsy overhead lighting, had just brewed a pot of coffee. The all back full could do nothing to stop the deadly momentum of even a tiny ship moving at full speed.

Hopson yelled, "We're gonna get hit, we're gonna get hit!" Ramsey stood on the port side of the *Evans*, in shock at the sight of the bow of the *Melbourne* towering over them by at least the height of a five-story building, headed right for them. It looked like she was going to hit the combat information center. Right in the middle of the *Evans*, between the smokestacks.

A lookout on the *Evans* noticed the glowing snow-white froth, the surf unfurling, sliced by the gray sharp-nosed bow of a massive aircraft carrier that just five minutes earlier had been a faraway silhouette against the moonlit sky.

Stevenson sounded the *Melbourne*'s collision alarm; some on the *Evans* watch crew would later recall hearing the blare. There it was, the horror, coming closer and closer until it hit—right where Ramsey had calculated it would. Those on the *Melbourne*'s flight deck felt their mighty ship rise. And then the sound—oh, the sound!

A watch stander on the bridge of the HMNZS *Blackpool*, steaming 5,000 yards away, watched in awe as two shadows in the distance merged. On the *Kyes*, about 8,500 yards away, an American ensign watched two blips on a radar scope coming together and then—as if the naked eye would reveal something different—rushed to the starboard wing, squinting in the direction of the *Melbourne*. A combat information center officer stepped out to join him on the open bridge and quipped, "It looks like it's going to be a close one."

If only.

It was 3:15, just three minutes after what was supposed to be a quiet night was interrupted by a message from the carrier.

Three minutes during which everything went wrong.

Three minutes when the holes lined up.

21

DISASTER

At close to top speed the *Melbourne* rammed the *Evans* at frame 92—its precise middle, slicing it easily like "a knife through butter," one horrified Australian would remember, violently rocking the destroyer onto its side. Most of the men on the bridge were catapulted into the sea like rag dolls, some buried under the ship's towering mast, which now lay nearly flat against the water. They would clamber for the surface amid a sound one would later describe as fifty cars crashing and another as a high-speed train disaster: screeches of steel coming undone, rivets pulled, a terrible unbuckling, explosions, the hiss of steam like a giant can being opened. The smell of sulfur infused the salt sea air. Water rushed into every hatch that wasn't sealed shut, every tear in the *Evans*'s rusted steel hull. The *Melbourne* had cruised through her with 22,000 tons of momentum; Stevenson stopped the engines before impact, but it was too late.

When the tearing sound subsided, the front half of the *Evans* listed on its side, drifting along the port side of the *Melbourne*. The back half had also tilted, but would recover, as it scraped along the carrier's starboard side, taking with it various antennae, to an eerie, decapitated, upright position.

22

THREE MINUTES

From the flight deck of the *Melbourne* the scene was one of horror, one of panic. Stevenson ordered boats into the water, but he didn't have to; the *Melbourne* crew, a brave cadre of men not much different than those whose lives hung by a thread, was already on it. Those not working to lower rescue cutters helplessly watched the horrific scene unfolding on the port side. The front half of the *Evans* was sinking fast, its hull number, 754, glowing in the moonlight. In those seconds, in the darkness not yet relieved by searchlights, the men of the *Melbourne* could not spot one American sailor on the broken *Evans*, but saw small, frantic wakes that signaled men in the water.

At the rolling bow of the *Evans*, a blond figure, clad in blood- and water-soaked dungarees, was climbing back aboard the port side. For the Australians watching from the *Melbourne*, adrenaline kicked in. Within a few seconds, several had jumped forty-five feet down into a dark sea to save those they didn't know and couldn't quite see, but might see in nightmares later on.

Belowdecks in the sinking bow of the *Evans*, the impact had thrown sailors on top of one another and across their tomblike berthing compartments. Only minutes earlier they'd been slumbering in chain-strung coil-and-canvas racks, dozing to the gentle rocking of the sea, the white noise of engines at work, and the gentle *ping, ping, ping* of water against the hull. Their plummet onto the hard steel bulkheads and conduits came without warning; heads smashed, bones broken. Some never woke; trauma in deep sleep can often lead to a comatose response. Some lay unconscious amid the chaos and shouting, likely buried in a heap of old mattresses.

For the rest, the beating of their own hearts was all they could hear for a split second, maybe two. The compartments were black; the lights in the passageways flickered and then went out. The few battle lanterns that worked provided illumination, but some were already underwater. The water roared into the compartment, rising, and with it the panic and chaos, now in loud syllables echoing off hard steel. The shouting and crying gave way to a flickering hope; there had to be a way out. *Please God, help us.*

Yet amid the panic and helplessness, there were some heroes. In one berthing compartment, Gary Sage sought to gain control: "Stay calm, and we'll get out of here." It was confusing and dark, but one sailor would remember Gary searching for his younger brother Kelly Jo. In another enlisted berthing compartment next door, George LaLiberte hollered,

"Come on, let's go!" and directed the procession out. It was those heroes—the ones who told men the words they needed to hear, or grabbed and pushed the others forward and out—who would not survive.

Using the dead, light fixtures hanging loose overhead as ladders, sailors followed each other through the jungle of racks, through a hatch, and onto the mess decks against the dying light. The men of the division berthed just under the mess decks were the first to witness the obstacle course of a ship on its side. There they scrabbled with bare feet among the slippery table stanchions. They could hear shouting just forward and down, coming from another berthing compartment, where men started climbing out. In the hustle there was a mysterious and frantic banging, and more shouting. The ship was still rolling onto its side, and the water was rising fast. For some paralyzed by fear and uncertainty, shock took hold, mumbled prayers, especially when someone in front of them slipped, fell, and couldn't recover. And then somebody behind would jolt them, shove a little: "Come on, hurry, man."

They saw their shipmates get sucked back into compartments, whirlpools and waterfalls, violently tossing bodies, cracking skulls, tangling limbs. If you thought about it too long, you wouldn't make it. If you helped someone, you wouldn't make it. These split-second decisions would haunt the men ten minutes later, two days later, years later, decades later. There seemed to be two ways out; those who went one way made it, the others did not. There were two levels between their sleeping compartments and the main deck—they had but minutes, maybe only seconds.

"Here, this way!" one called out, a frantic shouting barely audible amid the sounds of an increasingly certain death. Behind the men climbing out of one quickly flooding compartment a steel ladder had come unhinged, blocking the door to the junior officers' quarters. The beating on the door and the cries for help caused a few to look back. The horror was everywhere as the ship continued to roll, now nearly upside down.

Only a few men escaped First Division before what was left of it flooded. The water followed the men, fast approaching the food-service steam line on the mess deck; there a portside hatch was the only way out. This narrow passageway was wide enough for at least two sailors to stand when the *Evans* was upright, but with the ship nearly upside down, it was like climbing under a bed. And it was a mess— steel metal food trays piled to one side, men slipping and falling. Those in front clambered toward the two-hundred-pound hatch, engaging all muscle and might to push it up and open as the water made its way through, engulfing the mess deck, a pool of floating debris and bodies.

This was the moment when life hung in the balance. The shouting continued and, more quietly, the pleading and the prayers. *This is it*, one sailor would say to himself. Another would think of his mother, a woman already in mourning after having lost another son, and wonder—irrational as it sounds— how he would ever tell her that he hadn't survived, that she had lost another.

And then they heard someone on the other side. Robert Petty, at the helm moments earlier, had been catapulted starboard into the open sea, metal debris ramming his upper back and shoulders, his head hitting a hunk of steel in the water. Amid a choking cloud of black smoke the young blond seaman, weak and disoriented, had heard someone, somewhere, tell him to go and open that hatch. *The hatch. There. Go.*

Later no one would recall having told the young, injured man to climb back aboard a fast-sinking ship, but he had. Petty swam frantically back, hit steel, and climbed and then crawled to open the hatch leading to the steam line into the mess deck. Behind it huddled a soaked and scared group of men, saying what they thought would be their last prayers. Petty pulled on the hatch, the men pushed, and it swung up. *Open.* The ship was flat on its side now.

Within a few seconds sixteen sailors, bloodied and in skivvies, climbed up and out, each pushing the one in front of him with desperate force as Petty held the hatch open. Some hesitated; some jumped into the water right away. One thought he needed to go back to get his wallet; another, next to him, said, "Like hell!"

As the ship inverted, exposing her underbelly and sonar dome, a number of chiefs who had congregated on the hull slid into the water. A few stayed put, among them a black man, out of breath, shaking and hollering. It was Chief Willie King; he couldn't swim. The escape from the chief compartment forward in the ship had been harrowing: the only way out of their pitch-black compartment had been a thin, rickety ladder, with torrents of water pouring in, and the sheer horror of not being able to see or grab the handle on the hatch. Chief Charles Cannington remembered he had a penlight in his locker, turned around and scrambled to locate it, then handed it to the first in line. Cannington, the ship's doctor, had spent a fair amount of time with the Marines on the ground, and was the kind who'd put the safety of others before his own. His penlight got six of his fellow chiefs out, yet he wouldn't make it himself, when water shot into the compartment as if from a fire hose.

When they got out, that's when it hit: they had no life jackets. Captain McLemore was there, telling everybody to jump. He made it out, his body lacerated and bruised, through a tear in the steel in his sea cabin. Nearby and inside still, two other chiefs and an officer would face pitch-black confusion as they were tossed into desks and bulkheads. The water, in an instant it seemed, had risen past their knees, making for an escape that involved swimming and feeling around for hatches, tables, and ladders with their bare feet and fingers. All three—Chief Reilly included—would make it out. They could see the moon, round and bright through an opened hatch.

They jumped into the water without hesitation. The bow continued to roll, to sink. The sea was flat, warm, and salty, with an oil slick like a bleeding wound. Some men vomited immediately. No one had a life jacket; those had been stowed somewhere else. And there was no time; those who could swim did so as fast as they could, turning around to watch the white-painted hull number 754 descend into the water amid smoke, explosions, and bubbles. They found pieces of debris and clung to them.

Bubbles at the surface, men kicking in the water and

pleading for help. One man heard a final human scream as he looked at his watch; it was 3:18, only three minutes after impact. Those who were the last to escape got sucked down into a massive whirlpool as the ship sank. They pulled for the surface and got sucked back in. They flailed, reached; some were lucky, some not.

And then the water calmed, the *Evans* gone. They shouted for help, grabbed onto one another, swam toward the debris that had bobbed up. Many thought the entire ship had sunk, and they were the only ones left.

As the men on the front section fought a watery death, those asleep in the rear section of the ship were tossed as it tipped and then righted itself almost immediately. Their compartments filled with water that then, just as quickly, receded. It would be easy to think of these men as the lucky ones; not so. The men inside scrambled for the main deck, rushing to their general quarters, but found only black sea and a slick of oil. The front half of the ship was gone; only mangled wires and torn metal remained, a ragged, ripped deck. The one smokestack that remained was tilted slightly. Most everyone there, thinking their minutes were numbered, scrambled to find life jackets.

And then came the screams.

Among those who would sustain the worst injuries were the men working in the forward engine room, one thin-metal wall from where the *Melbourne* had plowed through, one bulkhead from the ship's boilers. For these sailors who manned the factory of the ship, the power of the vessel, the collision was their meeting with God—or the devil. Hell-hot steam from burst pipes burned the flesh off bones, threw mechanics against panels of knobs, gauges, and dials. *Oh God, the sting.* There was screaming, praying, the darkness and the confusion of the search for a way out. And then the added sting of rushing salt water.

Within seconds the sea quickly filled the engine room, until the men there were only a head's height away from drowning; certainly these would be their last breaths. They huddled together. Bob Lockwood prayed, *God help us.* Joe Mulitsch, completely submerged, trapped under the steel grating of the engine room's lower level, thought of home, his mother, his sisters, his girlfriend, the sun, the trees and green grass—everything. *It's just like what they say, man, about when you think you're gonna die. Your life flashes.* And then a hatch above opened, and they were pulled to safety, badly burned—they'd never be the same—soaked and stone white, half dead. Few would ever forget their cries, the flesh melting off their bones. The shock as they stared into nothingness.

23

RESCUE

As they scrambled about the topside of the dead, floating half of their ship, the men were told to spread out. Small fires had broken out, and there was an ominous hissing of steam. They were terrified that this half too would sink. One climbed aboard the whaleboat, which dangled from one steel cable. He tried to cut through with a pocketknife. No good. It would later haunt him—perhaps he could have saved someone, had he been able to cut it loose. The others searched for life jackets—some in a panic, as they couldn't swim. One man looked overboard and was struck by the grim image of glowing white uniforms floating away over the calm, dark sea: the ship's laundry had been hit, split down the middle.

The *Melbourne* was attempting to pull up alongside what was left of the *Evans*. When she got close enough, the Australian crewmen tossed down a Jacob's ladder. The battered crew on the *Evans* lined up single file; helping one another, they climbed, broken and bruised, to safety. A few officers remained behind to salvage what they could. One of them found the boatswain's locker, grabbed some paint, and painted a line on the hull so they'd know if it was slowly sinking. They scanned the moonlit sea for the forward section, but it was nowhere to be seen.

After he hit the water, as his ship sank behind him, McLemore worked to gather survivors on a piece of floating debris. His first fleeting thought was that the war had begun, and his ship had been torpedoed. It wasn't unimaginable; just one year earlier the North Koreans had seized the USS *Pueblo,* capturing and torturing the crew, and the Communists had most recently shot down a U.S. spy plane in the Sea of Japan, killing thirty-one crew members. McLemore had, after all, seen sparks and smelled the smoke, heard the desperate screams. The carrier in the distance wasn't the *Melbourne,* he thought, it was the *Kearsarge. It wasn't an accident, it was war.* And then reality hit him as he saw part of the ship roll, her insides exposed, and billows of steam emerging from her mangled hull. And he recognized the *Melbourne.* And he saw that his ship had been cut in half.

The choppy sound of motorboats in the water was reassuring. The captain checked on the men, asked how they were, wondered exactly what had just happened and how. A fatherly type, he was concerned: for a ship that carried nearly three hundred men, there weren't many in the water. His mind raced back to his last trip through the pilothouse, giving instructions to Hopson and Ramsey, leaving the officers in charge, and then hitting the firm mattress in his sea cabin, exhausted.

Nearby, Hopson and Ramsey were hanging on to a floating piece of wooden deck grating. At impact they had been tossed and landed under the mast, sucked under several times, struggling to the surface again, fighting for their lives. A signalman swam over to Ramsey, who was confused and in shock, saying, "Why did he turn that way?" Hopson was chanting, "Oh my God . . . oh my God." Less than ten minutes earlier they had been in the pilothouse, fielding a call to plane guard. It had happened that fast.

Chief Reilly, among the last to leap from the sinking bow, was in the water, hanging onto another piece of deck grating, exhausted. His son had been on that ship, and the chief was among those who thought the entire ship had sunk. Something sharp grazed his leg. *Sharks!* he thought, but it was someone else's toenail. The water was dark and a searchlight wavered overhead. *Helicopters.* They would be rescued.

As a cutter from the *Melbourne* looked for survivors to pick up, some waved its pilot off, sending him to find those in more desperate need. In the water some of the men were wiped out, but had remembered how to float. They shouted to the others, those who couldn't swim and were panicking, flailing in the water, and looking for anything to grab hold of.

One man hollered instructions at those who were crying for help. "Float, you sons of bitches! Calm down and float!" One kid grabbed the leg of another man and pulled him down, back into the water. As the man came back to the surface, gasping, he kicked the kid off. It was the only way; otherwise, both of them would drown. "I have to live with that," the survivor would later say. Forty years later he would still have nightmares: people all around him drowning, desperate screams for help.

The rescue boat had made its rounds and was now nearly filled with survivors. It had found only one gray and lifeless body, that of Kenneth Glines, the starboard lookout from *Missouri*. A helicopter spotted one more man treading water several hundred yards away; he was the last to get picked up. The sea was glassy, a calm mirror. The boats continued the search in the dark, but hope was gone.

The sky was abuzz with helicopters, from the *Melbourne* and from the *Kearsarge*, the latter having arrived on the scene within the hour. On the flight deck of the *Melbourne* the survivors congregated, shivering with shock, grasping chilled Foster's beers, big as oil cans, provided by the Australians. And there was a calming sound, something soothing: a violin.

Stevenson had ordered the ship's band to the flight deck to play American music; his thought was that it would calm the men and help keep order. Most of the survivors from the front half were in skivvies, those from the aft in T-shirts and dungarees. Forty minutes after the collision, Captain McLemore climbed aboard the ship that had apparently sunk the *Evans*. He was naked.

McLemore, by then with a blanket wrapped around his waist, made his way to the pilothouse on the *Melbourne* as the rest of the crew assembled in the carrier's mess deck to meet with the Australian medical staff and fill out survivor forms. The *Melbourne* sailors were shaken; some had been there in 1964 when the carrier rammed the side of the HMAS *Voyager*, splitting it in two—the very incident that still haunted Stevenson.

Outside the pilothouse McLemore and Stevenson embraced; their eyes filled with grief, they apologized to one another. It wouldn't occur to Stevenson right then that McLemore had not been on the bridge during the ill-fated maneuver to plane guard. That knowledge, along with the shock and anger, would come later. Right now he just felt disbelief. And sorrow.

Chief Reilly climbed onto the flight deck from the cutter. He heard his name being called as a fellow chief made his way over to greet him. This man had gotten out, but others hadn't, he told Reilly. *So many others. Oh, God.* The chief who'd found Reilly amid the survivors was weeping, couldn't quite get the words out. Reilly was looking above the soaked young men and music, searching for the familiar face of his son. Still crying, the other chief mustered the words: "Larry's . . . not here."

The words hung there, words floating in the night sky.

It couldn't be.

Chief Reilly slumped, still looking around at all the boys. So many of them, standing there in skivvies, wrapping in blankets, in dead-eye shock. *Can you be sure? How can you be sure?* Larry Jr. was supposed to be sleeping—his rack was aft—but at 8:00 p.m. on June 2 the schedule had changed; they'd needed him in the forward fireroom. Still crying, this chief—the very one who had changed the schedule just hours earlier—explained, "He was on watch, Chief, he was on watch." Larry had been on watch in the forward fireroom, below the combat information center, exactly where the *Melbourne* hit.

Reilly, an old salt, knew there was no chance. His son was gone.

24

VIETNAM

Even in the middle of the night, there was no reprieve from the fighting at the Vietnam Office of Information; someone was always on duty. The country never went to sleep, it seemed. There'd just been a fatal automobile accident, in fact, and an American helicopter had crashed under hostile fire. And there was all the action in Long Khanh. The week, like all the weeks that year, especially in the previous month, had been bloody.

A cable came through, and someone on duty in the naval public affairs office, likely a young public affairs operator, began to type.

THE AUSTRALIAN AIRCRAFT CARRIER MELBOURNE
AND THE US DESTROYER FRANK E. EVANS COLLIDED
AT SEA AT THREE TWENTY AM LOCAL TIME IN THE
SOUTH CHINA SEA, 200 MILES OFF THE COAST OF
SOUTH VIETNAM . . . MELBOURNE RADIOED THE USS
KEARSARGE, THE US AIRCRAFT CARRIER THEN 30

MILES AWAY THAT "MANY CASUALTIES" WERE LIKELY, AND ASKED FOR ALL AVAILABLE HELICOPTERS AND DOCTORS, WHICH WERE ON THEIR WAY MINUTES . . .

It was only a draft.

Mistakes were evident right away. In 10-point typeface at the very top of the document it was dated "3 MAY 1969." Someone else, someone superior, crossed MAY out and scribbled in JUNE.

And perhaps that wasn't the only problem with the cable. That the accident had occurred "200 miles off the coast of South Vietnam" was a damaging admission that would never make it to a reporter's desk.

In the minutes following the collision, as Australian sailors watched the forward section of the *Evans* roll and sink, leaving behind men treading water, waving for help, and screaming, others heard a whimper, almost childlike. They searched for the source of the sound, and found it: a man curled up in a ball, crying, bloodied. It was an American sailor, Marcus Rodriguez, who'd been on duty, taking a rest atop the signal shack of the *Evans*, when she was hit. He had flown through the air and hit the flight deck of the *Melbourne*, shattering half the bones in his body. Rodriguez had plans to be a baseball player, and he'd once been scouted by the Philadelphia Phillies. But at 3:20 a.m. on June 3, 1969, that hope was as shattered as his bones. They took him to the sick bay, but it didn't look good. Word spread that he'd died.

The men in sick bay took one look at Rodriguez and

said they would have to at least try. The tall young man was eventually strapped to a gurney, loaded onto an aircraft, and flown to a hospital in Cam Ranh Bay, South Vietnam—the closest, the men said, and a map confirmed that. Another man would be sent there as well, with third-degree burns.

Meanwhile, the Saigon press office was buzzing. Public affairs officers in khaki were organizing press pools and putting reporters on standby. The plan was for the newsmen to board the *Kearsarge* in the South China Sea, where they could interview survivors and cover the search-and-rescue efforts— but this plan was soon scrapped, "by higher authority." Commander Herbert Hetu, head of public relations for the Seventh Fleet's Saigon office, was on a plane out of Saigon, headed for Clark Air Force Base in the Philippines. Within a day of that flight he'd brief McLemore and his second in command, McMichael, over two hours the U.S. Navy described as a "dirty question and answer session."

On June 6 at 8:00 a.m., Hetu boarded the *Kearsarge* to tell the American survivors, then getting ready to disembark, that the press could interview them. "I am not in any way suggesting that we do not want the press to get all the facts possible. . . . We want to help them get it," Hetu told the men, saying that it was their choice whether they wanted to be interviewed. He suggested some possible points the men might make, encouraging them to recount acts of heroism and praise the swift rescue operation. Yet the list of cautions and warnings he rattled off was so daunting and confusing that the shaken young sailors ended up hesitant to speak out at all.

As soon as the Office of the Assistant of the Secretary of Defense began directing the affair, it was clear that much was at stake, and that the collision was likely the Americans' fault. While the Australians ran to the press with their side, the Americans were ordered to keep quiet. Both the magnitude and the location of the accident made for a public-relations nightmare: seventy-four dead Americans, too close to Vietnam. By the time the press releases made their way into newsrooms everywhere, the accident was reported as having taken place "650 miles from Manila," or, more vaguely yet, the "South Pacific," as one prominent New York City paper would report. A map sent to the Associated Press didn't even include Vietnam; the sliver of a country had been chopped off the map's edge. The collision, according to this sketch, had occurred near Borneo, perhaps, or Manila, shown in the far upper-right-hand corner of the map.

Photographs of the low-lying aft section of the *Evans*, taken in the gray morning light over the South China Sea by photographers on the *Kearsarge*, arrived at the air base in Tan Son Nhut near Saigon for processing. The Seventh Fleet press office there sifted through hundreds of images taken by Navy photographers, but released only five to the press.

As the tragedy unfolded in those dark morning hours in the sea off Vietnam, folks in the United States were just wrapping up their day's work. It was Monday there, still June 2. By the time the sun had started to burn through the clouds over the South China Sea, Walter Cronkite was almost finished with his nightly newscast when he was handed a sheet of paper.

25

THE BOYS

With three of her boys away all at once, Eunice spent her evenings writing letters, pieces of home that went through some big post office in San Francisco and onto a plane, and then on a boat across the ocean. It made her feel close to them. Her kitchen table was a light shade of Formica, framed in aluminum, and her pencil was sharp. Her handwriting, almost scribbled, would fade. She wrote often of the farm, of the sports teams, of the weather, and of poor Doug, all alone, no big brothers around to spar with. The boys' rooms upstairs were dusty and lifeless. Doug would go up there and play from time to time. He'd try on Kelly Jo's ragged old work boots, which he decided to wear, big and floppy as they were on his six-year-old feet, until Kelly Jo came home. That Kelly Jo had his older brothers with him was a comfort for her at times, but then— her mind would wander into places, things, she couldn't bear to think about. If you thought it, it could happen.

An uneasiness kept Eunice awake at night, but it was

soothed by the letters her boys sent her; these were her connection across ten thousand miles. The boys made the front page of the *Niobrara Tribune* the week just before Memorial Day. It was that picture her daughter-in-law Linda had thought of. The perfect gift for Eunice: all three sailors smiling into a camera. She cherished it, true, but at the same time it haunted her. Three boys, all on the same warship. Gary, on the farm barely three months ago, was the only one who had mentioned this anxiety to another townsperson: the fact that if something happened, some tragedy, Eunice and Ernie could lose all three boys at one stroke.

The calendar in the kitchen read June 2, 1969. Ernest had just come in, taken off his boots, and washed his hands. Doug was having a sleepover with a friend, the two boys bouncing on Ernest and Eunice's bed—doing everything, it seemed, Eunice had told him not to do. It was not yet dark, and Ernest— interested in world affairs and the latest from the Vietnam War—had tuned in to the *CBS Evening News*. Only a week earlier his sons' ship had made the *Nebraska Tribune* for having participated in Operation Daring Rebel, firing from the coast of Vietnam. The town, struggling with poverty exacerbated by a seesaw of catastrophic droughts and floods, had its own to be proud of. In its front windows the Masonic temple downtown displayed the pictures of all the town's boys serving in the armed services, along with scribbled addresses and birth dates, in case anyone wanted to send a card or letter.

Ernest always watched the news for his boys. That night the gentlemen in suits discussed the peace talks in Paris: angry words, and some politician hollering into a microphone about waste. *When is it going to end?* And then, of course, came the death toll; more than two hundred American boys just in the last week. Dogs made the news that night, dogs who'd helped the troops on the ground; it was soft news sprinkled into the unbearable. At least, Ernest felt, his boys were safe. They weren't on the ground, in the middle of that hell, but on the calm periphery.

At the very end of the newscast, Cronkite's demeanor changed. There was the shock of breaking news, of *this just in . . .*

"The destroyer USS *Frank E. Evans* has been cut in half after a collision with the aircraft carrier *Melbourne*. The front half sank in two minutes. No word on casualties."

Hearing it from the kitchen, only steps away, Eunice rushed to the television set. Looking at Ernie, she put her hand to her mouth. *My God.* And then she fainted. On a gray screen the newscast credits were rolling. Doug rushed in. Startled by his mother on the floor, and what his father would repeat—the *Frank-Eeee-Evans*—he started screaming. There was another ship possibly over there, a USS *Frank Evans*, Gary had once told Ernest, warning him not to get the two confused. Ernest repeated the name Cronkite had just given. He was sure: it was his sons' ship.

There was no phone in the white frame farmhouse, and it was five miles to town. Ernie ran outside, jumped off the stairless old porch into the dirt and matted grass, and headed for his pickup truck.

As Eunice came to she called out, "Ernie? *Ernie?*"

But he was gone, a trail of dirt and gravel in his wake.

The village of Niobrara occupied just a few blocks. Its chief of police, Rollie "Buck" Noyer, had recently gotten his first radio—a big deal, making headlines in the *Niobrara Tribune*—so he could communicate with officers in nearby towns if he needed assistance. That was a rarity in Niobrara, though—a dot of a town, home to seven hundred residents, two hundred miles from anywhere important. Newscasters in the upcoming days would struggle even to pronounce the town's name: *Ni-ya-brare-ah*.

Ernest sped into town. Once he got down a hill, made a right, and crossed a bridge, it was a straight shot. A hard left onto Main Street was all that was left. He parked and dashed out when he saw Buck parked in his cruiser, the one with the new radio. "Buck, I just don't know what to do. I just heard the ship my boys were on was cut in half. What should I do?"

The sun had set. The waning full moon was starting to show over the straight, long road out of town, and night was falling like a thick, dark curtain.

Buck looked at Ernie. The new police radio could get clear to Yankton, maybe, a few miles north in South Dakota. The father was desperate, full of the helpless despair of not knowing, and no way to know. Not tonight, at least. The police officer, the town going quiet behind him, said all he knew to say to a face he would never forget.

"Just pray, Ernie. Just pray."

The telegrams marked SAGE arrived the next day. Navy Lieutenant Rex Crowder, along with a chaplain, would drive two hours to deliver them. Crowder, who worked at a

U.S. Navy recruiting headquarters in Sioux City, Iowa, had done this sort of thing before, but never on this scale. It was one thing to tell a family that a son had been killed—another altogether to bring the news of three dead, all at the same time. His visit to the Sage farm would haunt him forever.

The dark car made its way along the dirt roads, through tall grass and lush trees. By now, members of the extended Sage family were there; they'd all heard something and rushed to the farm to await any news. Eunice, in a housedress, her legs neatly bandaged against the pain of varicose veins, was already showing signs of strain, worry, and dread. It was record temperatures for the early part of June. The sun blazed through the window, and the propellers of a box fan spun a light breeze into the living room. There were soft sounds in the kitchen; somebody was making something. The waiting was hell.

It happened very quickly.

Somebody's here.

Eunice and Ernie rushed outside, the screen door slamming behind them. There was the sound of car doors shutting, the glare from the morning sun, the shining shoes on the dirt path—black shoes, official shoes—and a stiff white officer's cap in one hand; signs of respect. And three sheets of paper in the other hand.

What to say now?

Everybody there knew; everyone in God's country heard Eunice's cries for her three boys.

26

A SEA LIKE GLASS

Twenty-six years earlier a woman in Waterloo, Iowa, had received a letter from her son, who had been serving in the Pacific. "Isn't it too bad about the Sullivan boys?" the sailor wrote home in early 1943. Startled, this mother bundled up for Northern Iowa's icy cold and went straight to the house at 98 Adams Street in town to talk to Thomas and Alleta Sullivan, who had five blue stars in their front window.

Alleta was a heavyset woman, with thick, dark hair she wore parted. When she greeted the neighbor, she admitted she'd heard nothing. She couldn't believe it, she told the woman, who read parts of the letter from her own son: "I heard that their ship was sunk." A glance at the calendar ignited the worry: Alleta and Thomas hadn't heard from them—any of the five—in two months. Since November 8, 1942, to be exact; and it was now January 1943. The visitor began to cry. Alleta comforted her, and told her not to worry, it was likely a mistake. Still, when the woman left, Alleta couldn't shake the dread. When she went to bed that night she could hardly sleep. Terrible dreams, she would tell newsmen later on, of her boys in trouble, crying out for their mother.

The Sullivan boys had been a public relations gold mine in early 1942, personifications of the spirit of a country that worked together, bought war bonds, and enlisted together. They joined just after Pearl Harbor to avenge the Japanese attack, which had taken a boy from one town over. The caveat: they would serve together, make no mistake about it. "Together," the headlines would read, nobody could beat them. The Navy was reluctant to allow them to serve together, but it conceded. On the USS *Juneau*, standing around an opened hatch on the newly commissioned cruiser, all five smiled for the cameraman. They were a human fortress: George, Francis, Albert, Joseph, and Madison.

Increasingly confused and desperate, Alleta wrote a letter to the Bureau of Navy Personnel. "It is all over town now and I am so worried," she wrote, listing the names of her five boys—George, Francis, Joseph, Madison, and Albert—when she realized that her worst fears as a mother might have been realized. "It was hard to give five sons to all at once to the Navy." She added that, no matter what, she'd do her duty. Alleta had promised to christen the USS *Tawasa*, a small Navy tug scheduled to come off the assembly line in Portland, Oregon, in February of that year: "I am so happy the Navy has bestowed the honor on me to christen the *USS Tawasa*," she continued. Her letter's sole purpose was to calm what she hoped was a rumor.

The reality would devastate her. A reply from the secretary of the Navy arrived within days, delivered by Navy personnel and a chaplain.

"Which one?" Thomas Sullivan asked the uniformed gentlemen at the door.

"All of them," a man replied. All five brothers had been missing and presumed dead since November 1942, just after the second naval battle at Guadalcanal. The Navy hadn't been able to say anything; before Alleta's letter came, her sons' deaths were deemed classified information.

Alleta, despite her unimaginable grief, fulfilled her promise. On a cold, windy day in February 1943 she sent a champagne bottle crashing into the hull of the USS *Tawasa*, a small ship, minute in the scheme of things. "Build ships faster," she told reporters, her lips quivering as they had in earlier interviews. "I feel satisfied that if more ships had been out there the Juneau would be afloat today and my boys would be on board." Within months she would do the same for the USS *The Sullivans*, a destroyer. The loss of the five brothers loomed so large in naval history that another USS *The Sullivans* would be launched in 1997.

The tiny *Tawasa* would go on to serve in two more wars. By the time of the Vietnam War, the *Tawasa* was an old boat, but an able one. On June 3, 1969, she was the only Navy tug around, on duty off the coast of Vietnam, when she received a call to a shipwreck nearby.

At sunrise the sea was as smooth as glass, and the *Tawasa* was only one of many ships disturbing the calm surface on their way to the collision site. News of the *Evans* disaster had traveled to other ships in the vicinity and beyond, many of which had been called to the scene. The *Larson*, which had been cruising with the *Evans* just hours earlier, was tied alongside the warship's aft half, which was miraculously still afloat, and crew members salvaged paperwork and other valuables held there. The *Kearsarge*, anchored a hundred yards away, collected boatloads of survivors motored in from the *Melbourne*.

Arriving just after noon, the *Tawasa* was instructed to prepare what was left of the *Evans* for a tow to Vietnam, the closest land available, where an investigation, it was hoped, would help connect the dots.

But the order was changed at the last minute, by "higher authority," a U.S. Navy public affairs officer documenting the ordeal would later note. What remained of the *Evans* would go to U.S. Naval Base Subic Bay instead, a journey of over six hundred miles, rather than the two hundred to Vietnam. The *Tawasa*, its crew haunted by the notion that it was towing a corpse, almost lost her twice in the complicated journey east.

The SEATO exercise had already been canceled by then; the participating ships had regrouped and been sent elsewhere. Most of the American vessels not involved with the rescue and recovery received orders for Vietnam's coastal waters, either to provide naval gunfire support or to support carriers in the Gulf of Tonkin. The *Kearsarge*, after dropping survivors off in Subic Bay, headed for the Tonkin. The war would go on for most ships. Every U.S. ship there, on the night of the sinking and on the scene—even the *Tawasa*—would collect Vietnam Service Medals for their efforts, even in the days of the SEATO exercise prior to the collision. The USS *Frank E. Evans*, decapitated yet still a commissioned vessel, would also collect such a medal, its last. The date on the commendation: "2 Jun 1969—"

In the war effort, in her small place in the world—the reason she was there to begin with—the *Evans* faded. What she left behind were questions and a list of names.

III

IN THE WAKE

27

THE LOST 74

The number was fifty-seven, some headlines first read. But soon later the official number of seamen lost in the collision became seventy-four. Only one body, that of Kenneth Glines, was recovered; the rest of the American boys had vanished, either gone down with the ship or drowned and lost. It was a tragedy of multitudes, one whose file—neatly typed casualty reports that would one day go missing in the Navy's official archives—was thick with sheets of paper, identical reports of causes of death, likely "drowning." Only names, ranks, and service numbers distinguished one from the next. One name was misspelled; another was wrong entirely.

Like so many lost in that place and that time, the crew members of the *Evans* died young. Some had babies at home, or pregnant wives. Their sweethearts were planning winter weddings, and misting letters with perfume. One was to celebrate his birthday that day; another had celebrated his the night before. Some came from big cities like San Francisco,

Philadelphia, or New York; others were farm boys who grew up in places nobody had ever heard of. They were fortunate sons, some of them. One came from a house so pristine and handsome that it would later be used as a movie set. Others were dirt poor; to some, the U.S. Navy presented their first real bed and a shot at three square meals. It was hard to imagine, but hearty scoops of sloppy and steamy on an aluminum tray were the best meals they'd seen.

The young men ran toward the life of big ships on the high seas, dread of the Army draft weighing heavy on their minds. Canada was not an option; these boys would serve their country as their fathers had, for some of their families had strong U.S. Navy legacies. Some of their dads had fought in grime and glory in World War II and pushed their sons into this life of clean sheets and warm meals. Two fathers had survived the Japanese bombing of Pearl Harbor; one had helped build the warship that would take his proud son's life. Some had no mothers; others had mothers who're still crying to this day.

Some boys were hometown athletic stars: football players, record setters in track and field. There were high school dropouts as well. Many of them smoked cigarettes and drank; boys will be boys, after all. They played pranks and told jokes, most of them dirty—too dirty to repeat but oh so funny to hear. They sang along to "Wooly Bully" and gave each other nicknames. They loved their cars and their women. Some had baby faces; some had chiseled jawlines and scruff. Some cussed, some prayed. And they all likely wondered, How did I end up here?

Their VFWs and American Legions would remember them forever. Their photos would hang proudly. Some wore government-issued, dark-rimmed Coke-bottle glasses and posed stoic and proud; others had boyish smiles, goofy grins, and a gentle-eyed callowness that said *I have my life ahead of me.*

In three minutes, they were gone, like a bright light flickering out to black.

The ships in the vicinity held memorial services at sunset on June 3, 1969, closing a day that for many would live on forever. The haunting echo of "Taps," its first line "day is done," could be heard for miles in hearts and minds. It was the one sunset they'd never forget.

The U.S. Navy knew within hours who had made it and who hadn't. They knew then that the death toll would be shocking; one-third of the *Evans*'s crew had gone to the bottom of the South China Sea. They knew three brothers were on that list. Newscasts and headlines begged: How had they allowed that? What about the Sullivans? Scrambling, the Navy told the press it would review its policies.

The news was catastrophic for all the families. Many of their sons were firstborns—*the one who made me a mother.* Some couldn't believe what the man at the door was telling them; one mother broke a dish she had been washing when the doorbell rang and she saw, through a gap in the sheer curtains, the car as black as death. Another took off running down the street when she opened the door and saw the men in uniform. She had been watching the news. It was illogical to run—run where?—but logic never seems to come into such an equation. One threw herself onto the hood of a truck. These mothers cried out the names and nicknames they had given their baby boys. They looked up at the blue sky and begged, *No . . . please, no . . .* One father sat in a blue 1968 Chevelle SS, the muscle car his son had loved. A little brother listened to his big brother's records over and over. Mothers and fathers stared at the carpet, the exact spots where their sons had taken their first steps, as these men in uniform said, "We regret to inform you . . ."

For some, the first telegram that arrived would state MISSING. In a day—or only hours, in some cases—a second would arrive, stating that the boy in question was gone, with no remains. What some read into this was possibility. *What if they could find him? Later?*

As the men in uniform sat talking in some kitchen and families congregated, wondering what next with no body to bury, the children watched *Gilligan's Island* reruns. They wondered what it would be like to be stranded on an island somewhere, whether drinks tasted good served up in coconut shells. They wondered how their fathers and older brothers would get home, stranded on that island and all. One wide-eyed little sister would go—months later, after the family was provided a fallen serviceman's tombstone—to the cemetery late at night in her pajamas. Four blocks downtown, all by herself, because she thought he was there. Where else could he be?

The families of those who survived wouldn't get the news for days. Choppily worded telegrams were sent from the *Kearsarge*—"safe . . . okay . . . cuts and bruises"—but were slow to arrive. One survivor would answer the door of his rural Texas home to receive the very telegram he had sent a week prior from the South China Sea. The survivors would pose for photographers. When Mrs. Frank E. Evans, then living in Louisiana, discovered that one of them lived near her home in Lake Charles, she rushed to meet him, to embrace him, and to welcome him home. Alleen Fisk Evans was a passionate, sentimental woman; within a week's time she would write compassionate letters to the seventy-one families of the lost.

Their stories were unfathomable.

John Spray, the sonarman who had called the SEATO exercise a "farce" in a letter home, writing that he hoped that no one's life ever depended on such an operation, was gone. Norton, the young officer in love with the moon and the mountains: gone. The beloved Willie King, a black man who had climbed the ranks but never learned to swim: gone.

In the mess deck on the carrier *Kearsarge* a group of aviation mechanics sat around talking about the collision and what lay at the bottom of the South China Sea with the bow of the *Evans*. There were cameras, recorders, gifts purchased on liberty for sweethearts back home. Then one of them looked at Chief Reilly, to them just an older guy in a disheveled uniform, a poor bastard from the *Evans*.

"Hey, there, you lose anything?"

Reilly was quiet for a moment. Then he shot back, with pain in his eyes, "My son."

He spent hours watching the sea in the day that followed, waiting for the okay to go home early and be with his family. His son was out there somewhere.

In 1967 Carlos Sanchez and Natalia Melendrez of Whittier, California, had lost their son Robert Melendrez in a jeep accident in Binh Dinh Province, South Vietnam. Their middle son, nineteen-year-old Andrew Melendrez, was on watch in the pilothouse on the *Evans* at the time of the collision. They had pushed him toward the Navy; he was of draft age, it was safer. Andrew went to boot camp in February and boarded the *Evans,* along with more than two dozen other young men, on May 17, 1969. Barely three weeks into his first stint on the ship he was gone.

Only one of these twenty eight fresh boots, Danny Salisbury, made it out. A letter he'd written arrived at his childhood home in Caney, Kansas, one week after the *Evans* sank. "There isn't much to say," he wrote; "the boy from St. Joseph's, Missouri didn't make it." That was Steven Guyer, a friend from boot camp. Years later Salisbury would think of his friends and wonder if he had jinxed his ship when he joked with his mother and father that he would be home for his birthday in mid-June "no matter what." He'd wonder if he could live with that.

Duane Conely and many of those he worked with belowdecks made it out with a few cuts and bruises but with their spirits torn to smithereens as they saw how close they had come to death. In Minnesota, Conely's father sat and watched the news reports, watching like all other parents for his son in the footage of sailors walking off the *Kearsarge* and lining up for a plane ride home.

Butterball, who would retain his nickname for the rest of his life but never set foot on a cruising warship again, was a survivor, like his Third Army paratrooper dad. "I knew you made it," the father told his son. "I just knew you would."

28

FLAGS AND FATHERS

The Reilly's Costa Mesa home sat in a quaint community of two-story townhouses strung together around intimate gardens and landscaped courtyards, with trees offering shelter from the blazing California sun. The streets of the Monticello subdivision had been given names associated with the Revolutionary War: Lexington, Valley Forge, and Yorktown, to name a few. In her home on Minuteman Way, darkened by closed drapes, Marion Reilly spoke with a *Daily Pilot* reporter, offering the young man coffee and other provisions. It was a Navy home, the journalist would note, finding the strong coffee to be "full of a sense of resignation."

Marion, whose hair had lightened quite a bit with age and the sun, had known that her son was missing and presumed lost for a little less than a day. Her daughter-in-law Joyce Reilly was there, and Marion's one-year-old grandson Larry III was asleep upstairs. Jerry, the youngest brother and yet the protective type, sat nearby. People she hadn't spoken to in years had been calling and bringing things by. "Everybody brings doughnuts, and nobody eats them," she said, this lifetime Navy wife, courteous and cool, all the while watching the clock, waiting for her husband's return. Master Chief Lawrence Reilly had phoned from the Philippines the night before, promising he'd get home as fast as he could. "He said don't hold out any hope at all," Marion told the reporter. "I don't know how he'd get home, all his gear went down with the ship and he has no money or clothes."

The chief was waiting in Subic Bay for a flight home. At first the U.S. Navy brass had refused to let him go early, before the other crew, but given the circumstances, an admiral overrode the decision. He was flying standby, and had already lost his space on a connecting flight out of Guam to those more official; at least once he'd been bumped for something called a computer. He was wearing a faded, borrowed uniform and had a disheveled look. A naval officer at the airport had chided him on his appearance. When the chief replied that he was from the *Evans*, that his son had been killed, and that he had lost everything, the officer had joined Reilly, the two men—one pristine, the other unkempt—sitting together in silence.

In California, Marion was in no better shape. "I don't think I want my picture in the paper . . . not with my face all cried up," she told the young reporter, careful not to reveal the family's plans for getting their father home. The chief was to arrive, penniless and grief-stricken, at about midnight, if not later. His eldest son, Lieutenant Junior Grade James Reilly, a public affairs officer, would meet him at Travis Air Force Base in northern California, and the pair would fly together to Los Angeles, where younger son Jerry Reilly would meet them and rush his father past the news crews parked in front of their home.

The young officer Reilly, known in the family as Jimmy, had been married for seven months and was stationed at Naval Base Charleston along the South Carolina coast, having already completed a stint at Seventh Fleet headquarters in Saigon. He had been having lunch on a rooftop hotel during the Tet Offensive in 1968, watching all hell break loose in the distant sky. He was the one Marion worried about at the time; family lore has it that he once wrote his mother a letter while sitting underneath a desk in Saigon. At that same time, Larry Sr. and Larry Jr. sat on the *Evans*, firing away at the coastline from a safe distance.

Twenty-three-year-old Jimmy had found out about the collision as soon as it hit the Navy's public affairs channels. He knew where his father slept and where his brother worked on the *Evans*. In a panic, he phoned a friend at Navy headquarters in Washington to inquire about the list of the missing and presumed dead.

"Can you tell me?"

"I have the list in front of me, but I can't."

"Don't screw me around." The junior officer was outranked yet determined. "Tell me. Is there a Reilly on that list? Tell me."

"There is."

"Who?"

"Lawrence Reilly."

Jimmy's heart sunk. It could be either. He waited.

"BT, Third Class."

It was his twenty-year-old brother.

Jimmy decided to call his mother immediately.

In Costa Mesa, Marion was shopping for a dress for her daughter Luanne's eighth-grade graduation ceremony when the collision made the news. When she answered the phone later that afternoon, she knew it was Jimmy. He would have found out, she knew; Jimmy was a rock, dependable. And he was calling with news that would shatter her. There was no easy way, so he just said it. Luanne would never forget her cries; nor would Jimmy, who sat stone silent on the other end of the phone, an entire country between them. Marion had early on given a nickname to her second son, the little one who had her eyes, the one who never left her side. Now it was all she could cry: "Booper . . . oh, my Booper."

Jimmy hung up the phone and headed for the airport in Charleston.

When Chief Reilly stepped off the plane at Travis Air Force Base into the sun, Jimmy was standing there in his Navy whites, his eyes masked by glasses and his face further obscured by his stiff cover. He embraced his father; the older Reilly was tired and weathered, his khaki uniform stripped of insignia. Cameramen and reporters approached him with a barrage of questions, asking him if he could have gotten to his son in time. *What was it like? What happened?* Originally the press had thought the chief would be flying into a different airport—a last-minute change made in secret, one reporter would write. There was no avoiding this onslaught of the press; the collision was still a mystery stateside, and Reilly would be the first survivor to set foot onto continental U.S. soil. The chief spoke quickly during a press conference, arranged in hopes of keeping the media from bombarding the family home in Costa Mesa.

"There was no time," he told the cameras and reporters as Jimmy stood by his side, his arm around his father. "It sounded like a huge can opener, you could hear metal ripping . . . I was asleep."

All Chief Reilly wanted to do, from the time he stood motionless on the *Kearsarge*, looking at a calm, flat sea, to the hours he spent at various military airports—Clark to Guam, Guam to Travis—was get to Marion.

On the other side of the world, the *Evans* survivors walked off the *Kearsarge* at Subic Bay, a gangway that led to their first steps on dry land after an ordeal that was already giving way to nightmares and shot nerves. McLemore was in bad shape, it was said; at least one sailor recalled seeing the skipper crying on the *Kearsarge*. Within days he'd say good-bye to most of the crew, 134 of them boarding a plane to Long Beach, given thirty days of leave that, much to their disgust, would be taken out of their allotted vacation time. Even the Red Cross was charging them for phone calls, coffee and doughnuts. They had nothing, really. For many of them, everything they had went down with the ship. Some of them had bad feelings about the Navy—an angst that asked, Why this? Why them?—but for their captain, many never had an ill thought. As the stewardesses prepared for takeoff, McLemore climbed aboard the plane and told his men that they had done a great job and served their country well, that they ought to be proud, and that he had never worked with such a wonderful crew. Virtually all on board fought tears as they said good-bye to their beloved captain—a father figure, many would call him. As their plane vanished into the clouds, they could see the captain, a tiny figure walking away from the tarmac; they wondered what would happen to him, and then wonder moved to pity. Later on, as the men looked down at the ocean below, they felt a deep sorrow. Could they have done something more for their shipmates?

It was guilt of a most terrible kind.

The flags at Long Beach Naval Station rustled at half-staff that first week as preparations for a memorial service—to be attended mostly by families, as the surviving crew was still in the Philippines—got under way. It was Friday, June 6. Several dozen American flags, ordered for the occasion, sat neatly folded into triangles, waiting. Gull Park sat at the end of the long Navy Mole, where alongside the roadway was moored some of the Navy's reserve fleet. Grassy with trees, it was a beautiful spot at the entrance to the harbor, overlooking the vast ocean—the final resting place for seventy-three of the men who'd gone down with the *Evans*. (The body of Kenneth Glines was going to Missouri for burial.)

By 11:00 a.m. mothers clinging to husbands and wives to surviving children had made for the park, a solemn procession of thirty-four families who lived close enough to attend the service. Of those killed, twenty-seven were Californians. Three U.S. Navy chaplains attended, their words—*mindful of our frailties and mortality and we must learn to be ready when it comes time for us to follow these brave men*—echoing in the quiet air, save for an ocean breeze rustling the trees nearby. One woman in a light-colored two-piece suit held a folded flag to her heart, tilted face up to the sun, her eyes closed, a beautiful face submitting to a grief for which there were no words. She was the mother of Jon Stever, standing between his twin Ron and his father Kenneth. They'd driven in silence from their home in Altadena, California. The older gentleman stood stoic, the younger one leaned in toward his mother, his head turned toward a lectern. Nearby, Chief Reilly sat next to his daughter-in-law Joyce, with Marion on the other side of this young widow, weeping behind a black veil.

There were the usual hymns and prayers, the embraces, the sobs, the silence, the looking around at the strangers who shared in this sudden grief. And there was, abruptly, a tiny voice that echoed throughout the park, one of innocence, one of longing. Sitting on his uncle Jimmy's lap, a milk bottle clenched in his chubby hands, the one-year-old Larry Reilly III gazed at the many sailors in uniform, calling out to them excitedly, with one word that tore at the heart of everyone there, a tender summons they would forever remember: "Daddy!"

The memorial came to a close with a three-volley salute, fired by U.S. Marines in concert, piercing the air. Then came the playing of "Taps," echoing over the sea that seemed to surround the mourners. As families embraced and said their farewells, a curious boy of seven crawled over the concrete where the Marines had fired. Small and fragile, he scraped his pants as he gathered all the shell casings—still warm from the firing—he could hold in his small pockets.

Later on, when Mike Lehman became a man, he'd go on to become a radarman just like his father, Eugene Lehman, and he'd wear one of these casings strung around his neck on a silver chain. Eventually he'd find himself on a ship passing through the same deep waters of the South China Sea where rested the remains of seventy-three American sailors, among them his father. Standing in the ocean breeze, tall, blond, and handsome, with feathered hair and moist baby blue eyes, he'd throw a pack of Marlboro Reds overboard. It was then that he'd swear, for a brief moment, when he glanced toward an outside passageway, that he saw a figure standing there. His dad, he thought. He felt it. It sounded strange, he'd later say.

That little boy in Long Beach would later pass along the other shell casings to his siblings and uncles and then, eventually, to the other kids he'd come across later in his life, the ones who'd also lost fathers that June day. Too young to understand the newspaper articles, the little boy picking up shell casings that day in Long Beach would eventually sign up for that navy life, making it all the way up the ladder to chief. He did it because, truth be told, he wanted to know what had really happened to his father's ship.

29

THE INQUIRY

The road to George Dewey High School on U.S. Naval Base Subic Bay passed through bright green fields, a calm, verdant landscape now cut in two by a line of dark official vehicles. Inside, the school was chilly, the air-conditioning on overdrive to compete with the Philippine Islands' notorious heat and humidity, and the opening and closing of doors as an army of press and uniformed officials filed in. Going from outside to inside the flat, one-story building was refreshing and chilling at once, especially for those who would face a panel of investigators.

It had been six days since the collision between the USS *Frank E. Evans* and the HMAS *Melbourne*. The collision had occurred so quickly, so unexpectedly, that virtually every man told he might be called on to testify was nervous—even a lowly officer who had been asleep in his quarters on the *Evans* at the time of collision. Could he have missed a message sent when he was on watch, twelve hours before? A young seaman with barely one year in the Navy, who'd been sitting alone in the aft steering compartment, wondered the same thing: Did I miss something? The board would have no punitive powers—it was a fact-finding mission only—but it still did not sit well with all the parties called to testify.

The investigation into a mysterious and potentially damning incident that involved the navies of two separate but friendly nations would be tricky. A dual-nation investigation hadn't happened in nearly half a decade. But this wasn't the only Australian-American incident in recent years. In the dark morning hours of June 17, 1968, American Air Force jets had mistakenly fired on the Australian destroyer HMAS *Hobart*, and two Australian sailors were killed in the attack. There had been reports of hovering enemy aircraft, and Air Force radars couldn't distinguish helicopters from surface ships. Two other American ships were also targeted, leading the U.S. Navy to conduct an inquiry of its own with the assistance of three Australian advisers. That incident received little press compared to the tidal wave of reporters now interested in the collision between the flagship of the Royal Australian Navy and an American destroyer. And this time the Australians believed they would be more involved in the investigation and the outcome.

The inquiry would be held in the high school library, it was decided, with special classrooms set up for reporters—sixteen typewriter stations, along with a bank of telephones. No one knew how long an investigation into five terrible minutes in the middle of the night on the dark, deep ocean could take; it could be hours, days, or weeks. Men sat, some in barracks and in game rooms, others in the corridors and classrooms, waiting to say what they knew and didn't know, what they thought had happened and what could have happened.

The Joint United States Navy–Royal Australian Navy Board of Inquiry got under way on the morning of June 9, 1969. A group of older navy men in starched white uniforms and stiff gold shoulder boards entered the room, followed by several dozen reporters and photographers. One after another they placed their gold-and-white dress covers side by side on the tall bookshelves and took seats before tables covered in dark green linen cloth. Recorders had been set up, as well as a witness box to the left of the table. A drawing pad sat on a wooden easel nearby. Separate desks had been set up for a court reporter and counsel; it had already been arranged that the Americans, per the U.S. Navy's judge advocate general's rules, would be given the right to an attorney.

The journalists and members of the public, sitting in the rows of wooden chairs set up roughly fifteen feet away from the board, couldn't tell the Australian board members from the American. As they smiled for the cameras, posing alongside one another, they appeared to be a friendly bunch of weathered navy men. Some were graying, some balding; all had tanned forearms and leathery, wrinkled skin. This was the group whose job it would be to pinpoint the precise cause of the catastrophe: a destroyer cut in half and seventy-four dead Americans in a glassy sea on an otherwise quiet night.

The Australians had selected Rear Admiral Hugh D. Stevenson, the Royal Australian Navy deputy chief of naval staff (and no relation to *Melbourne* Captain John

Stevenson). Stevenson had much navigation experience and four commands at sea under his belt, and political onlookers deemed him an ideal candidate to help investigate the incident. Next was Captain E. W. Shands, another experienced navigator; ironically, he'd been the skipper of the HMAS *Hobart* when American missiles smashed into her hull.

The third Australian pick was odd. Captain John Davidson had been in the Royal Australian Navy since 1956, but he was a supply officer, with little to no navigation experience. His duties included ensuring that ships had enough tea, biscuits, and ordnance, but he had nothing to do with complicated navigational matters.

The U.S. Navy appointed Captains Stephen L. Rusk and Clyde B. Anderson, both experienced ship and squadron commanders with plenty of navigation experience. As commanding officer of Naval Base Subic Bay, Anderson had been flown to the *Kearsarge* to witness—if not participate in—the early interrogations of both Ramsey and Hopson prior to their disembarking.

The U.S. Navy's third pick, forty-nine-year-old Rear Admiral Jerome King, was deemed one of the best, most capable surface operations officers in the navy. Admiral Thomas H. Moorer, the chief of naval operations, was said to have noticed this rising star sometime in the 1950s. A longtime mentee of the head of the Navy in Washington, King had been appointed head of the board of inquiry. He would preside over the questioning of witnesses, and enforce the rules as he saw fit. Authoritative and confident, with decades of navigational experience, he seemed perfectly suited to the role. But this was not the only reason he stood out. King was also the current head of Antisubmarine Warfare Group One and a flag officer, flying his own command flag on the *Kearsarge* during Exercise Sea Spirit and operating with U.S. ships in other training exercises since taking on that role. In essence, the USS *Frank E. Evans* had been under his command on the morning she cruised into the path of an aircraft carrier. For that reason, King was a controversial choice for the U.S. Navy, and many Australians saw him as such. In the words of one experienced Australian Navy man, Commander A. I. Chapman, "Certainly it should not have been a flag officer involved in the exercise." As Captain John Stevenson would say, much later on, "He should have been sitting in front of the board, answering questions with the rest of us." The *Evans*, in the chain of command, was considered one of *his* ships.

King had grown up working class—"poor," in Depression-era terms—and religious in Youngstown, Ohio. He was smart and hardworking; he had his first job, selling magazines, when he was just five years old. He attended Yale University on an academic scholarship, hitchhiking to and from the school because, he liked to joke, he didn't have any money, and if he did, he'd rather use it to entertain girls. When he first arrived on campus in New Haven, Connecticut, he was pulling hayseeds out of his hair. As the joke went, he signed up for the Naval Reserve Officer Training Corps by mistake, thinking he was in line for the post office; he only meant to send a postcard to his parents, telling them that he'd gotten there okay. He'd only seen the ocean a couple times, and never been to sea, but he had little in common with the fast-talking New Yorkers at

Yale, and he'd fall in love with the Navy.

King earned his commission in 1941, months before the Japanese attack on Pearl Harbor. He began his twenty-eight-year career on the cruiser USS *Trenton*, and then went on to destroyers—*Sumner*-class vessels just like the *Evans*. After attending various postgraduate schools, including the prestigious Massachusetts Institute of Technology, he moved on to training programs and eventually, naval leadership roles in Washington, D.C..

A navigator at heart, King loved posts that took him to the pilothouses of ships; he wasn't fond of going belowdecks to the engineering spaces. As he saw it, you were either one or the other, a navigator or an engineer. A likeable character, he was one month shy of his fiftieth birthday. Within a few years he'd be pinned vice admiral, becoming the first Naval Reserve Officer Training Corps graduate to join ranks usually reserved for graduates of the U.S. Naval Academy.

King was as frustrated with the Vietnam War as anyone who had been a part of both that and World War II. Years later, he'd say, "It's a totally different scene, totally different. . . . In '41 through '45, the people were dedicated to the war, you didn't fight it. Vietnam—that horrible scene—was filled with people who were fighting against the war every step of the way and leadership which was trying to cut and fit an impossible pattern." The board of inquiry was a delicate assignment, and he was determined that everything be done correctly—all the more so, given the palpable tension in the air as the inquiry got under way.

By the time the board convened, reporters had already had

several days to dissect the incident. While the U.S. Navy had remained mum, per the instructions of their superiors, many among the Australian force had already pleaded their case to the press, laying blame—covertly in some instances, blatantly in others—on the Americans. Charles Kelly, minister for the Royal Australian Navy, had publicly hinted that the accident was the Americans' fault, which infuriated King.

The Associated Press had just run a story quoting unnamed U.S. naval officers in Washington, D.C.. It's usually the destroyer's job to avoid collisions at sea, they said; smaller, more agile ships should avoid crossing in front of a carrier. The article closed with a comment from a congressman who called for the secretary of defense to shake up the force, citing the "four most recent bungles of the Navy": the North Korean seizure of the spy ship USS *Pueblo* in 1968; the North Korean downing of a reconnaissance plane in April 1969; the sinking of a new submarine in Vallejo, California, only one month earlier; and now the *Evans* catastrophe.

Just as the board members were taking their seats, the U.S. Navy would receive another blow. That it was meant to be humorous—journalistic satire at its best—didn't help. Already on newsstands, the July 1969 issue of the popular men's magazine *Esquire* featured a three-page spread headlined in stenciled army font, Esquire's Official Court of Inquiry into the Present State of the United States Navy, with a subheading taken from a hymn—"Oh, hear us as we cry to Thee, For those who peril on the sea"—and a cartoon of a life ring at the bottom of the sea, surrounded by jellyfish and seaweed. The feature listed, in annihilating bullet form, every accident and mishap on an American vessel since 1965—minus, of course, one collision at sea on June 3, 1969.

The Australian press, meanwhile, would declare the *Melbourne* a jinxed vessel, citing the *Voyager* collision as well as a second inquiry that had ended in 1968, finding the skipper of the destroyer primarily at fault—which was usually the case, as the inquiry noted. The Australian presses would also uncover a startling admission by the Royal Australian Navy that the carrier had also rammed into a Japanese cargo ship near Sydney earlier in 1969.

At the beginning a total of forty-one press passes were issued. Virtually every news outlet—ABC, NBC, CBS, the Associated Press, Reuters, *Newsweek*, the *New York Times*, the *London Daily Telegraph*, and the *Sydney Sun and Herald*, to name just a few—had sent a reporter, and they'd all been kept busy. Many were from the Saigon press corps, avid for more information about a collision deemed mysterious from day one. In the early hours of June 3 many of these South Vietnam–based journalists had assembled for a courtesy flight to the *Kearsarge,* orchestrated by the Seventh Fleet public information bureau at Tan Son Nhut Air Base near Saigon, to interview survivors and cover the search-and-rescue mission.

But a "higher authority"— so stated the newly established board of inquiry Command Information Bureau—would cancel this press junket at the last minute, leaving reporters scrambling for more information. At the board of inquiry, they would likely get the scoop.

30

THE TOLL

The phone rang in a tall townhouse on a tree-lined street in Bay Ridge, Brooklyn. Lena Norton—still hopeful despite the yellow telegram she clutched, now crumpled in her hand—answered, grabbing the receiver with white knuckles that also clasped a wet handkerchief.

"Hello? . . . Hello?"

Her voice was kind and soft despite the dread, despite the fact that she had been crying all morning, and in a quiet state of shock for days. And the phone calls—some of them were awful.

The silence gripped her. *Not again.* Then a cruel voice spouted cruel words, and Lena slammed the phone down. *Whoever would say such things?*

Likely it was that newspaper article.

It was days since that handsome blond reporter with the odd questions and the pushy manner had sat across from her husband in the living room, asking questions about the war and about her firstborn son. It was the onslaught of whys that made her shudder, that she couldn't bear to answer. The words in the article were harsh, uncompromising:

Was the sacrifice worthwhile?

"I can't help thinking. It's such a terrible—" Mrs. Norton could not finish her sentence. "No, I shouldn't say that," she added, looking at the photo on her piano. "But he had such a future, and he brought us so much hope."

She pressed her hand against her eyes, as if to hold in the tears.

The reporter had gotten to Lena. But no matter how much the young man with the notebook probed and prodded, John Norton Sr., alive nearly twenty-five years to the day after he set foot in France in one of the most lauded and successful invasions of all time, wouldn't budge. The old man's words were "measured," the reporter would later write: "I am very proud of my son and what he did . . . and needless to say, I shall miss him very much. But I think his death was in the finest American tradition of dying for a cause which is intended to help other nations." It wasn't a popular sentiment at the time, especially in a beatnik place like New York City.

The *New York Post* reporter went on to include Johnny's part in the Vietnam War, recounted in one of his last letters home: his warship's role, firing away along a pristine coastline, tracers lighting up the thick jungle beyond the beach.

And now everyone knew their name and that they lived in Bay Ridge—everything down to the house number. Everybody knew their son had died, and that he had been a part of that mess, the bloodshed.

It was bringing out the crazies, like the violent protests in the streets, kids screaming about God knows what. *Don't answer the phone*, Lena told herself. But she did; she answered every ring, every knock, that day and the next, even decades later, when the kids were grown and the tall house on Narrows Avenue seemed too big. She was reluctant to sell and move away. "He wouldn't find us. He wouldn't know how to find us," she would tell her husband. "I know, I'm going crazy." That there was no body to bury, no closing of the casket, gave Lena an irrational hope that would haunt her for the rest of her life.

It was like that for many of them.

The *New York Post* was then a staunchly liberal—and thus antiwar—paper, but it was as sensational and insensitive as it remains today. Such details did not occur to the elder Norton, a bright, clean-cut attorney who had risen due to his own merit, a veteran who didn't like what he saw out there on the campuses. That it was the *Post* that came knocking, a paper whose reporters other families would swat away like killer bees, likely didn't occur to him as he invited this ambitious young reporter into his living room to talk about the shock of it all and how the family felt. Lena stayed quiet for the most part; she let John talk while Bobby, nineteen and home from college, looked on, annoyed with the insensitive baiting in the name of journalistic inquiry: *Who was your son, John Norton Jr.? How are you feeling about the war?* Bobby had seen these guys around campus. The article the next day didn't surprise him; the inevitable rhetorical question, just after a few paragraphs about how wonderful Johnny was: "Was the sacrifice worthwhile?"

Lena wouldn't save the article, not even for one of those scrapbooks the mothers would eventually put together. It was page 14 news. The headline story on the front page that same day taunted the masses: NIXON DEFENDS THE MILITARY. It would infuriate some, and some it would send over the edge— to the telephone, perhaps, to vent their wrath to a grieving mother. The anger was everywhere. The world was upside down. "Those times," she'd say decades later, "were simply awful."

Lena was of another era entirely, an era of USO dances and ticker tape parades. To get away from that phone, and so six-year-old Beth wouldn't see her crying, Lena would climb a narrow, creaky staircase to a gabled attic bedroom, where the light from a tiny window overlooking the street slanted across a twin bed and a set of carved wooden ships on a small desk— all that was left of her Johnny. At six foot four, he must have felt like a giant in here.

Could they find him? The head knows the answer, but the heart never catches up. Lena would say that clear into old age, still not over it, still stuck in that moment, the ringing of the buzzer, the men standing there on the doorstep, the fancy car pulled up out front. The heart never catches up. After the telegram, every day was a tug-of-war: to accept the fact of it, to try to keep the memory alive, to wonder, at morning light every day, whether it really could have happened. Was it just a bad dream? How could it be that someone so big, someone whose life had almost defined her very existence, was gone, just like that?

In a Campbell's soup or Rinso soap advertisement from the 1950s you might spot a Lena Norton. She was the mother who made soup on snow days, the wife who starched her husband's shirts just before he set out to catch a train into Manhattan, the housewife who did endless mounds of laundry with a smile. From the time she held a nine-and-a-half-pound baby in a crowded Brooklyn hospital in 1947, it had been love. The nurses had played "Dear Little Boy of Mine"—*Oft when I'm lonely my memory swings back to your baby days...*—as they passed Lena a little bundle, eyebrows perfectly etched, a perfect hairline, "like he'd just been to a barber."

She could tell right away he'd look like his father, a former male model who used his handsome earnings to put himself through law school. Baby Johnny was so robust and healthy that people stopped Lena in the street. "Everybody wanted to see him," she'd say. Three Norton boys would be born before the world welcomed another decade, that "beautiful time, baby carriages, pregnant women everywhere." She spent the better part of the 1950s hiking up flights of stairs, first with fat babies and later with squirming toddlers. She changed diapers, fed the boys, took them to school. She remembers seeing Johnny off. It was the first day of kindergarten in a cold, hard public school building. She watched his little body walk away and wave to her, to little Bobby by her side and Kenny in the stroller. "Your heart will break two hundred times just like that," she said, "when you are a mother and they grow up."

And then the 1960s arrived, and her boys had grown tall and independent. People of the future couldn't imagine it, but

Johnny and Bobby, both not quite in high school, rode the subways alone through New York City to visit museums. "Well, dear," her husband asked Lena, "what do you want to do now? School? Work?" It was neither, and that was a funny thing; it was just about that time that another woman would jump-start a movement with these words: "The problem lay buried, unspoken, for many years in the minds of American women. It was a strange stirring, a sense of dissatisfaction, a yearning that women suffered in the middle of the twentieth century in the United States. Each suburban wife struggled with it alone. As she made the beds, shopped for groceries . . . she was afraid to ask even of herself the silent question—'Is this all?' "

In 1962, as the printer's ink dried on Betty Friedan's culture-transforming *Feminine Mystique*, Lena, educated at prestigious Barnard College, would ask her husband for one more baby. She loved raising children. Everything about it was wonderful. In her later recollections, the good times would come back to Lena, and she would speak hurriedly, as though they were being taken away from her all over again.

"We were so poor in the beginning that we had to move the bed to get to the dresser." Then the seasons changed, and they moved on—to bigger and better. She remembered their first television set, on which that the kids watched *Howdy Doody* and *Adventures of Superman*.

Johnny was the tallest; by middle school his feet dangled off the southern edge of the bed. He liked to lie there, read books about his father's war, and listen to the *Victory at Sea* musical score. He loved the water; he was a certified scuba diver, and loved to take a skimmer around Peach Lake, near the family's summer home. Intellectually gifted, he graduated from Stuyvesant High School—the only of two kids in the neighborhood accepted one year—and went on to Columbia University. Athletic and well proportioned, he was on the crew team. Lena liked to think he joined crew for the food—team members were well nourished on campus. A picture-perfect young man, he could have done anything, been anybody.

"Everybody knows he's a great swimmer," said his young sister Beth when she heard that Johnny was missing at sea. "Don't worry, Mom, he'll swim home. Johnny can swim."

Narrows Avenue in Bay Ridge led straight to a bay, and the bay to the sea, and then to another sea. The ocean was so big. *Can you imagine?* "I can't explain what it felt like, losing your child," she'd later say. Something so big in a life, like an ocean on a map. "You never get over it. You just look for that child forever."

Now, with the summer of 1969 approaching, it was all in his room, still smelling of sharpened pencil, musk, and leather. Boy smells. Lena spent hours sifting through Johnny's notebooks and albums from Columbia. His senior year there, in 1967–68, had been marked by wild student protest, the collegiate antiwar movement, defiance, and the shedding of light on all that was wrong with the world: poverty, racial inequality, women's inequality, and more. In the midst of it all Johnny was apolitical, with short hair and a tucked-in shirt. In the Naval Reserve Officers Training Corps at a time when his classmates wanted to blow up that building, he wore his uniform to class once a week, fighting off those who would knock his cover to the floor and call him a baby killer. His was among the last NROTC classes to graduate at Columbia; the school would vote the program out in 1969, and it would stay out for more than forty years.

Lena found a scrapbook full of *New York Times* articles in the room, witness to Johnny's childhood fascination with man's race to space. One of them speculated that man might soon walk on the moon. And man would, one month later. In that front bedroom, hiding from it all, she read his letters over and over again. Here she found papers that at first said, with glowing certainty, that Johnny's service commitment could wait so the young scientist could study and teach geology at one of the four institutions that had asked him to do so—his professors even had written the Navy about the talented young man. But the letters that followed said, no, the Navy needed him, straight after commissioning—which, due to all the protests, would take place off campus.

There was the war, and it was Johnny's turn. Lena knew well how war could put things on hold. In 1944, young, beautiful, and newly wed to a tall, handsome lawyer she'd met through a friend at Barnard, Lena would put her own plans on hold because of the invasion of Europe. America "needed its cannon fodder for the invasion," she recalled, laughing at how she imagined John Norton Sr. would perhaps get a desk job in Washington, given his law background and FBI work. Yet he went to war. That war killed a lot of kids from New York, but he came back, and they started a family. And Johnny was her firstborn. And now he was gone.

Looking for her son in the things he'd owned, she tried to think of those better times and the memories—the smell of a baby, the love you didn't quite know, a tiny hand to hold. That he had grown to be such a fine man was her one comfort when the day came to say good-bye. At an airport just outside the city, in January, she watched him head off to a war the world was calling a lost cause. At the time, she'd wished he didn't have to go. And now this. *This! Was it worth the sacrifice?* Then she would catch herself and think about the last time she saw her son, his eyes the color of the ocean—"a sailor's eyes," she would say.

As the plane took off, she'd turned to her husband, and in a laid-back accent that was all things Brooklyn asked, "He's gonna be all right, right?" John Sr., who had fought the Nazis close enough to be able to bring back souvenirs, fought in the cold and muddy trenches in battles there would one day be books and movies about, assured her, "Well, dear, it's not really"—he paused—"a navy war." To a generation that had witnessed Guadalcanal, Midway, the Battle off Samar, the hellacious battles against the Japanese in the Pacific, it really wasn't. "I did everything in my power to encourage him to stay out of the infantry," John Sr. told that *Post* reporter.

And now this, one year after his commissioning and graduation; "such a future," the *Post* article would say. He was gone. Forever, she knew it, just like that. No body, no burial.

The mornings were the worst. There was death, and there was one step up from that escape: sleep. When you really try, when you're really worn, you'll fall asleep. That's what happens when you lose a child. And then you wake up. You think, back and forth, my baby, the man he became, the life he was going to live, the girl he was going to marry. The children he would have had—would they have had eyes the color of the sea? And then reality jolts you. And some cold heart out there in this big city phones to remind you it's true, that it really happened, and that perhaps, the way the caller saw it, *it was deserved.*

The small window in Johnny's room faced north, toward a brick building, and then a park, then the East River and into Manhattan. And there, lost in a jungle of brick and the bustle of the city, is another mother just like Lena.

The woman was in her Sunday best on a Tuesday, standing on a street corner in Harlem on a hot mid-June morning, waiting for the traffic light to change. Across the street a towering man in a suit, his hair parted in a shellacked, right-leaning pompadour, saw her immediately. He would remember her forever, this immensely dignified black woman, dressed in black, eyes glistening behind her glasses, standing alone and holding—as if on a tray—a fresh American flag, folded in a proper triangle.

A day later, the image of the black woman still fresh in his mind, *Life* magazine's executive editor Hedley Donovan entered the green-glass Time & Life Building in Manhattan, ready to review the layout for the June 27 issue. The 48-story building sat across from the glitzy Radio City Music Hall and featured furnishings and décor that designers would forever laud as midcentury: boxed and curved side chairs, tables that combined carved wood and chrome, and artwork of curious angles. Lobby pieces designed by Eames himself. Space age, some would say. *Life* magazine's proposed front-page feature for an upcoming week was now a series of films spread over a lighted platform on the 34th floor of the building. For Donovan this was part of the process, as mundane as ordering an editorial assistant to brew coffee. He hit a button in the elevator, not knowing what he'd be looking at this time; he never knew. Two weeks earlier the magazine had covered the moon expedition; one week ago, life in the womb, the connection between mother and child.

Inside the newsroom, the editorial team sat nervously. Ralph Graves had just been promoted to managing editor, and this was to be his first issue. He wanted to shine. "Readers will care about this magazine only if we talk to them about the right things," were his first words to the editorial staff on June 16. The last two years had changed the world, and "books" like the *Saturday Evening Post*, with its wholesome Norman Rockwell covers, couldn't keep up with the sultry rock music, stringy-haired hippies, and wild politics. It was a low point in magazine journalism. The *Post* had shut down four months earlier, and to some it felt as if the grim reaper was working his way down magazine row. Graves knew something had to be done. They needed to tell the truth about these times. American readers wanted to see *faces*.

Graves glanced around the newsroom, waiting for Donovan, a man of few words who might crush it all with one shake of his head. Still, he thought, it would be unforgettable; no one had done it before. The magazine had raised eyebrows when it published photographs of two dead Marines on a beach in New Guinea twenty-five years ago, but this was different; readers would see their eyes, their young faces, their smiles— like a high school yearbook, only much more grim, because they were all gone. An average week in Vietnam at that time meant two to three hundred dead. He looked at the font, bold and brazen, and hovered over the pages: 217 American boys, all laid out on lighted panels.

Donovan will never let this fly, Graves thought. Even bringing it up might result in quite a showdown. Donovan was, after all, the man who'd written in 1967, as casualties mounted, that America needed patience. He'd described the Vietcong as merely a "very bad police problem," a force that fought barefoot and from fishing boats. The North Vietnamese Army was no match for American might, Donovan argued; he envisioned a big Victory in Vietnam Day with a ticker tape parade in only a few years' time. But then came the Tet Offensive. Walter Cronkite called the game a loss and a waste of precious life, campuses everywhere were on fire, and a slew of protest songs filled the airwaves. By 1969 most of those on the *Life* editorial floor had taken a strong stance against the war in Vietnam, but not Donovan.

Graves knew the cards were stacked against him, but the consensus in the newsroom was that they at least had to try. *Life*'s team of journalists had been getting close to the story, knocking on doors, sitting with grieving parents, rushing to gather photos; their hearts were in it now.

The feature was actually longtime journalist Loudon Wainwright's idea. A sensitive man, he had tired of the press releases from Washington: just names and ranks, three hundred each week, like stats on a scorecard. These were America's kids. Wainwright had written the only copy that would appear in the thirteen-page spread, which included part of a letter written home by one of these boys: "I am writing in a hurry. I can see death coming up the hill."

The glass door swung open, and in walked Donovan. All eyes followed as he walked to his desk, glanced at messages, chatted with an assistant, took a phone call. And then he called to Graves, "Ready now?" Graves nodded, and they all headed into the room with the lit-up table and the magazine feature that they hoped would forever change the face of an American institution. And it did: nearly every memoir, article, book, or doctoral dissertation on *Life* magazine would include details surrounding the June 27, 1969 issue.

Donovan, towering over the table, stared at it a while, up and down, side to side. Moments felt like hours. And then two words: "Run it."

There was no cheering, not yet; they waited until Donovan had left the office and was well out of earshot. "We were high with it, very high," Wainwright would later recall, likening the group to schoolboys who'd turned the principal around.

For Donovan, the woman in the black dress had evoked something. He couldn't forget that folded triangle and the red eyes behind the glasses. He thought that if people wanted to support the war—he hadn't changed his hawkish stance— they needed to see the toll: the images, names, ages, ranks, and hometowns. He'd been a naval officer in World War II; he understood war's cruel implications, and these included death. America needed to know.

As the editorial team finalized the galleys for "The Faces of the American Dead in Vietnam: One Week's Toll," the photography chief on the same floor was examining photojournalist Lynn Pelham's latest work. Over the years, Pelham had photographed the glory and the grimaces of John F. Kennedy and Nikita Khrushchev; he'd documented the moon race, socialism in small towns, dictators with polished brass buttons, and American beauty Elizabeth Taylor. These new images were good, there was no doubt about it. And they represented what *Life* did best: telling the story of everyday folks, of major world events hitting the home front.

That sweltering June, on a farm in a beat-up Nebraska town with nameless dirt thoroughfares, Pelham had captured it once again. The assignment was to find a particular family, grieving from unfathomable loss, and see how its members were holding up. His eyes, his lens, found the story: the stares and the silences. There were the baby pictures, captured from the frames in the run-down living room of the creaky-floored farmhouse. There was the house itself, and its weathered, whitewashed exterior; the beaten-dirt paths crisscrossing the property, the old trucks and rusted tools. And there was the land itself, its hills and tangled trees; the poverty of the town and its people; freckles and curly hair, the mother and father, and the little boy lost in it all, barefoot on a tractor, smiling for all the newsmen and cameras. This was the most attention anyone had ever paid to the town of Niobrara. There were hundreds of proofs, more than enough to craft a compelling piece about this loss, the editors reckoned.

But the June 27 issue was already awash in death. Graves once estimated that nine out of ten stories didn't make the final cut. Donovan would never allow this one too—not right now. They couldn't push it, the editors agreed. These poignant black-

and-white images, the story of the Sage family, torn apart by war, three sons lost in one blow, never made it.

It was not unusual for stories to get the ax. A typist put it more gently in a letter to the family dated June 23, 1969: "I hope that you will not be too disappointed that the editors of *Life* Magazine decided not to run the story. This is what happens each week—several stories are dropped, usually because of the lack of space." This from a famous building in the middle of the nation's biggest city, in the center of the universe, thousands of miles from this place no one had ever heard of before June 3, 1969.

31

"WE SHARE IN THEIR GRIEF"

One week after the disaster, the wide downtown streets of Niobrara were empty. The dozen or so American flags that lined the streets flew at half-staff. The businesses on Main Street were closed this Wednesday afternoon. Neon signs were dark, doors were locked, and the streets were silent save for the cool, rattling breezes off the Missouri River. Nearly every one of the town's seven hundred or so residents was headed to the gymnasium at nearby Niobrara High School, the only venue large enough for the memorial service.

The town had watched the Sage brothers grow up from fair-haired farm boys at their mother's side to young men: tall and full of life, ready to take on the world. Everyone knew Gary, Greg, and Kelly Jo in one way or another. Perhaps they'd seen Greg and Kelly Jo on the football field, and knew that Greg still held the record for high jump in track and field. Or they'd heard Kelly Jo's motorcycle tearing through town. Or maybe they knew Gary as a kind, quiet boy who smiled a lot and liked to sing, or that he had recently sent a girl in town a pretty necklace.

The people of Niobrara huddled together, hugged one another, and wept. Intermingled in this mass of puffy red faces and swollen eyes, of kind people wondering what to say, were the reporters. They were everywhere.

In Cunningham's Drug Store, eighteen-year-old Mary Cunningham told a newspaperman that she knew Kelly Jo well, and that he was "the kind you like to have around. He always seemed to be having fun." A schoolmate, twenty-year-old Cheryl Hargens, recalled for reporters a conversation she'd had with Gary when the boys had been home that March, in hindsight foreboding: "He told me then that he didn't like the idea of all three brothers being on the same ship. He said that if anything happened, that the family could lose all three." That they were not coming home weighed heavy on everyone there. "This has hit all of us," police chief Buck Noyer told a reporter. "My boy, Billy, played football with Greg and Kelly and he feels like we lost someone from our own family."

In a town this small, the Sage boys were everyone's sons and brothers, young men who had sailed off and would never come home, not in life or death. This memorial would be their final farewell.

Eunice Sage wore a short-sleeved black suit and matching gloves; a gold rose pinned to the center of her blouse glistened in the sun. A plaid coat rested on her shoulders, though it wasn't cold, and a black pillbox hat perched on her thick, dark hair. Her face looked paler than usual against her mourning attire. Dark-framed cat's-eye glasses hid her eyes, which were red from crying, and her mouth was frozen in a grimace of anguish behind her handkerchief. She nestled herself into her husband's shoulder. Ernest, standing tall in a dark suit, gazed over the crowd, holding Eunice steady, though it seemed to Eunice that she had to hold him up.

A week had passed in which to process it all. The afternoon Eunice and Ernest had received the telegrams, both sat together on a plain, weathered wooden bench on their front porch before a cluster of newspaper and television cameras, a deal Ernest's brother had made with members of the press: they would let them be after these few brief moments in the public eye. Ernest wore rolled-up jeans and a plaid shirt, looking down at the splintered wood porch and holding Eunice's hands, his squared, rough fingers rubbing her fingers gently. Eunice, in a loose and fading striped housedress, leaned her cheek again Ernest's shoulder, her eyes filled with worry, her mind racing, trying to make sense of it, what it meant when they said they would never find them, her three boys, lost at sea somewhere far, far from home. What did those words mean, *lost at sea*?

There they were, on the porch of the largest house they had ever lived in, where just three months before the peeling wallpaper had witnessed the laughter of three young men, the aroma of bacon and eggs filling the kitchen as all three of them crowded around the small table. What had been a full life was now empty.

There were no words.

As the Sage family left the Niobrara Lutheran Church and made their way to the large memorial service amid a hundred or so family members and close friends, news crews caught up with them again. The church had hosted an earlier, more intimate service and luncheon in memory of the three boys, but now the Sages faced the world once again, a world that was, in these dark times, kind to them.

The family had received hundreds of cards and letters, condolences from France, Australia, England, Canada, and all over the United States, with pastel glitter, doves, angels, and images of God's perfect hand reaching out. Many more would arrive in canvas postal bags in the weeks to come. Months later, Christmas would bring on another wave of greetings. Responding to this expression of concern and love from a world of strangers, from a world mired in hellish war and protest, the couple made a statement that day to the cameramen present. "We don't blame anybody," Eunice said. She shook and wept before the crowd, hiding her face between syllables. Her words were mumbled yet audible, though Ernie repeated them just to be sure. And both said, one after another, like vows, "This is the way the boys wanted it. . . . We thank everybody . . . the whole world."

Nearby, six-year-old Doug, with his spiky blond hair, trotted about the grass, squinting in the sun. Moments before he had been standing there alongside his parents, eyes wandering over the faces of those around him. Of the youngest, surviving brother one journalist would write, "How much, you wondered, did he understand?"

Inside the high school gymnasium, rows of folding chairs used for holiday pageants, class plays, and graduation ceremonies had been lined up for this more solemn occasion—the only such affair to ever be held there.

The Navy sent the Bluejackets Choir from the Great Lakes Naval Training Station, along with the base commandant, Rear Admiral Henry Renken, a man who would later become known among family and colleagues as "Mr. Navy Image," his own 1986 obituary would note, because of his tall, lean stature, white hair, and serious dark eyes. The Sages took their seats in the front; Doug sat between Eunice and Ernest, and Greg's widow Linda Sage, a youthful twenty one year old in a black hat and veil, sat on Ernest's other side, numbly wiping tears from her cheeks.

The ethereal and haunting tune of the official navy hymn, "Eternal Father, Strong to Save," accompanied a slow, ghostlike procession of four young sailors in white carrying four folded flags for the ceremony—one for Linda and three for Eunice and Ernest. As the music swelled, the words—*And give, for wild confusion, peace / Oh, hear us when we cry to Thee / For those in peril on the sea*—hailed truer than any of the sermons and prayers that would follow. Two pastors and a Navy chaplain spoke to the crowd of over twelve hundred. These attempts at theological enlightenments for how such things come to be were revealed before a congregation whose silence was broken only by sobs.

Reverend Charles Lindgren had come to know the Sages well after only being in Niobrara for two years. He offered these words:

War and its counterparts come because we live in an evil world, of evil men, with evil devices and ambitions. So comes our present tragedy, our racism, our economic and social injustices. For this reason we have our Vietnams . . . and communism, and even the troubles of our cities and campuses. What shall we say to these things? We can say today God lives—all need not be as it appears today. Today the faithful believer echoes the words of Job when he said, "I know that my Redeemer lives" in contrast to the theology, God is dead. This tragedy of the sea can and will be God's opportunity. Our God is not a God of destruction, but of life and salvation.

The governor of Nebraska, Norbert Tiemann, attending with a delegation of other state officials, said, "We share their grief," then went on, "The brothers were serving their country when they were needed. There is no more noble act than serving one's country and no greater sacrifice than to give one's life for one's country."

The ceremony was kept brief; it was hot inside the gymnasium, with so many townspeople crammed into one spot. After the sermons and eulogies, the admiral presented Ernest and Eunice with the flags and medals earned during their sons' brief time in the Navy. Ernest held two folded flags on his lap; Eunice held the third, sobbing.

Doug fidgeted throughout the service, watching the procession of sailors with folded flags in their hands, waiting perhaps for something else. He listened to three brief eulogies that painted the picture of American farm boys, all three baptized into their Lutheran faith on the same day, hardworking young men who had held jobs before joining the Navy. At one point Doug collapsed into his father's lap and wept.

Ernest comforted his last remaining son, all the while keeping his own composure, quieting a whisper inside himself, one that would haunt him for the rest of his life. As he told one reporter the week of the memorial, he himself had urged his older sons to join the Navy. "I was an Army man during World War II and I told them I thought maybe they'd have life a little better in the Navy. It seemed like good advice then but now I feel bad about it. I hear reports now that there's no chance for survivors. But you still cling to a little hope. A Navy man told me that both Gary and Kelly were on the deck crew, and if they were asleep . . . they just didn't have a chance. "

He'd never let that go. There just was no chance.

The truth was, Ernest blamed no one but himself.

And that's what he told the world, when the world was listening.

32

THE HILL

Catching wind that *Life* magazine was up to something in early June, the Pentagon pleaded that the publication not go through with their cover, not put on display the names and faces of more than two hundred dead Americans. It would harm the war effort, they argued to unwavering editors. The name Hamburger Hill, in particular, was rolling off the tongues of nearly every antiwar activist and lawmaker. A rallying point for activists, a crisis at the wrong time, Hamburger Hill was a fiasco for an embattled President Nixon, then facing an onslaught of criticism that began on May 1 when Senator George Aiken (R-Vermont), a senior member of the Senate Foreign Relations Committee, gave a speech on the Senate floor. In a barrage of words, Aiken criticized Nixon's handling of the war in the first few months of his presidency, and demanded that Nixon begin "immediate and orderly withdrawal" of Americans in Vietnam: "It should be started without delay."

Aiken's speech was seen as opening the floodgates, marking the end of a self-imposed moratorium on criticism of Nixon since he took office. The tsunami of fault finding it released was not quelled by the eight-point strategy for ending the war the president outlined in his landmark speech. Nixon's words reassured few in his own country and were practically ignored by Hanoi, perhaps because of Nixon's admission that his administration had "ruled out either a one-sided withdrawal from Vietnam, or the acceptance in Paris of terms that would amount to a disguised American defeat."

The headlines got progressively worse. There were the officially denied rumors of an escalating war in Vietnam, a new offensive likened to the public relations mess that was the Tet Offensive of 1968. There was news of doubled increases in U.S. casualties, from 184 to 430 in one bloody week alone. That Hamburger Hill would be abandoned, that enemy fighters would reposition themselves there once again, sparked a firestorm of controversy, just as seventy-two dead Americans made their way home in flag-draped caskets. In defending Hamburger Hill and the fact that more than a thousand North Vietnamese soldiers were moving back in line, one Army general said that he was "prepared to commit everything it takes . . . to do the job"; one antiwar lawmaker responded, calling for the generals in command to "personally lead the assault."

In a move to sway public relations, in late May Nixon introduced a new Army draft plan for young men in the United States to make life easier for those whose lives had been derailed by the war and the draft. A headline later that month would read GUESSING GAME—WHO'S GOING HOME FIRST? By the end of May 1969 Nixon was obsessed with headlines. As leaks to the press made clear, the war was a quicksand in which he was deeply mired.

In the first week of June, the president's days were filled with speeches and planning for peace talks with President Nguyen Van Thieu of South Vietnam, along with tweaking the final wording on a first official announcement that troops would start coming home. Defending the military, Nixon would tell the 1969 graduates of the Air Force Academy in Colorado Springs on June 4 that it was "open season on the armed forces." After the Hamburger Hill controversy, he had ordered no more large-scale enemy engagements in Vietnam. More bad news from Vietnam was the last thing the administration needed. It was the sheer number of dead soldiers—so many names and faces of American boys—that haunted Nixon.

Nixon, the man, had been raised a Quaker, and the doctrine of peace was a part of his upbringing; he wanted the war behind him. Nixon, the politician, however, wanted to get out with his pride intact. He was a sensitive man, no doubt; he had spent years in the Pacific during World War II. In his memoirs he would recall "the futility of war and the terrible reality of loss that lies behind it," words that came to him on Wake Island in July 1944, where his plane had stopped to refuel as it headed home. Wake Island had been a hot spot in World War II, as Japanese planes plummeted into Pearl Harbor. It was there, in the middle of the night on a dark island surrounded by ocean, that Nixon caught sight of a war cemetery close to the runway: "white crosses, row after row after row of them, stretching out into the darkness on that tiny island so far away from home." Doubts—what was worth all this fighting and dying?—crowded into his mind; yet he caught them, pushed them aside. The war of his youth was truly a necessary one. It had to be fought; there was no question. So there on Wake Island, in the summer of 1944, he faced the question all politicians and men of war must ask themselves—*Is it all worth it?*—and laid it to rest.

Nearly twenty-five years later to the date, in June 1969, he'd find himself asking the same question again, wrestling the same beast. It lay in a folder in a safe in the Oval Office in Washington; it hung over every newscast. *Was it all worth it?*

And now a new blow: seventy-four dead Americans, on a destroyer engaged in a multinational exercise two hundred miles off the coast of South Vietnam. Likely Nixon's longtime secretary Rose Mary Woods typed the letters, signed by the president, that offered condolences to the grieving families, telling them that their sons and husbands and brothers had died admirably, and that their nation would forever remember them. "Of all the burdens of the Presidency, the cruelest to bear are the losses of men such as your husband in the service of our country," read a letter to a twenty-year-old wife and mother.

"I was deeply shocked to learn that your sons Gary, Greg, and Kelly Jo, are missing in action as a result of the accident which took place in the South China Sea," Nixon's letter to the Sages in Niobrara, Nebraska, would say. "You are constantly in the prayers of Mrs. Nixon and me in this dark hour." But sorrow aside, the Sages represented another thorn in the side of the U.S. Navy and the Nixon administration. How had three sons from one family been allowed to serve on the same ship in a time of war? reporters inquired. The Sullivan family made news once again in 1969. Headlines also revealed that other brothers—threesomes, even—were also serving together on ships in the Gulf of Tonkin. The Navy would later rule—again—that this was allowed, as long as it fit personnel needs and the family approved.

Meanwhile there was an acute, unreported embarrassment on the part of the Nixon administration, revealed later on in the form of new requirements that it be informed of the details of all multinational exercises. It's likely that when Nixon received word about the loss of the Sage brothers and seventy-one other men on the USS *Frank E. Evans*, he hadn't been informed that the exercise was taking place; he had ordered no more large engagements that could produce such large casualties. But, in the words that would roll off the tongues of Navy officials and the sets of brothers still serving on ships together, "it was a freak accident."

Nixon spent June 3 in a snit over press leaks about a possible base closure on the Japanese island of Okinawa. The leaks invited speculation: what implications would this base closure in the Far East have for the war against communism? He was also fretting about the U.S. obligation to SEATO, that ever-present worry over alliances in the region and what would happen to them when American troops filed out of Southeast Asia. But over and under it all ran a troubling, insistent drumbeat: the death toll in Vietnam. The increasingly unpopular war loomed over the president, clouding his every speech and action.

For the besieged president, the collision of the *Melbourne* and the *Evans* could hardly have come at a worse time.

33

A COLLISION OF TRUTHS

Inside the makeshift courtroom in the dank high school library at U.S. Naval Base Subic Bay, the Joint United States Navy–Royal Australian Navy Board of Inquiry continued with open witness testimonies and lengthy closed sessions. Rain outside the building had turned the ground to a watery, muddy mush. Inside, as it seemed, the insistent questions, maddeningly slippery answers, stern voices, and inflammatory sidelong glances did the same for the court of inquiry.

The very first witness, Australian Rear Admiral Gordon John Crabb, in testimony that lasted nearly the entire opening day, spoke of the USS *Larson* coming within fifty feet of the HMAS *Melbourne* on May 31, 1969, a startling incident uncomfortably similar to the *Evans*'s turn into the carrier's path. "I have told my captains of my ships that if [one] ever turned his destroyer into a carrier I would sack him on the spot. I'm not just saying that now. I made that statement last year." Crabb was an imposing man, with big bones and a swift walk, yet he was known around the Australian fleet as a friendly, down-to-earth admiral, beloved by many, the enlisted in particular. He flew his flag on the *Melbourne* during the fated exercise, and the line of questioning was oddly focused on whether he had tactical control of the ship during the early-morning maneuvers on June 3. He did not. "There was no reason to," he testified, as spectators wondered why the question had even been asked; it was clear that Captain John Phillip Stevenson had been in charge that night and there was little to no controversy on who was in control. Crabb was merely awakened just before the collision, in time to witness the *Evans* make its hard right turn under the carrier's bow. By 3:23 a.m. he had canceled Exercise Sea Spirit and was helping to direct rescue efforts. The *Evans*, he noted, sank particularly fast; that was the one thing that concerned him acutely.

Meanwhile the media had garnered its first headline from the inquiry: after a near miss just days before, ships had been ordered to keep a distance of three thousand yards from the carrier, rather than the standard two thousand. This was a revelation to the public, though likely not for the senior board member, Rear Admiral Jerome King, the Antisubmarine Warfare One commander who, on the eve of the collision, had excoriated the American ships for their sloppy maneuvering during the exercise.

On the second day, the board members took a field trip to examine up close both the sawed-off stern of the *Evans*, moored in Subic Bay, and then, with a quick flight to Singapore, the jagged tear in the bow of the *Melbourne*, already in dry dock for repairs, part of which would include removal of an embedded metal shard from the *Evans*. This piece of mangled steel included, ironically, the painted-on insignia of King's Antisubmarine Warfare Group One. The jagged gash in the carrier's bow, in the shape of a sharp-toothed grin, made her look like a steel monster.

Meanwhile, the *Melbourne*'s captain sat alone in a small, musty hotel room at Subic Bay, drawing diagrams and drafting points for his testimony as he waited to testify. Anxious to return to his ship and his men, Stevenson was agitated that witnesses were not told when they would be called. It was at the board's discretion and, as some Australians saw it, the whims of Admiral King—an unpopular senior board member at the onset of the inquiry, when many reckoned he would not be fair, given that the *Evans* fell under his command.

The board reconvened at Dewey High School on the third day, eventually, after closed sessions, calling its second witness: Commander Albert Sydney McLemore. The *Evans* skipper made his way to the witness box, his shoulders down, his tall body slumped slightly, as was his normal stance. Facing the board, he appeared calm and stoic at first, speaking in confident tones. Within minutes, however, as the questions went from his career path to what he'd been doing on the night of June 2, he began to show the strain, cracking like ice under a heat lamp. He would testify for two days straight under an intense interrogation that pried into every facet of his command, his men, and how he'd left things when he turned in for his last night on the ship.

McLemore had been in the pilothouse on the evening of June 2 as the ship was maneuvering behind the carrier—for the third time that day—yet he testified that he did not know that the *Evans* had been designated as "plane guard destroyer" on the night of June 2–3. The documents he had seen since the collision, he said—manifests from both the *Kearsarge* and the *Larson*—indicated that the New Zealand frigate *Blackpool* would be on plane guard duty. That was originally the case, but exercise planners had decided to assign plane guard to the *Evans* early on June 2. At least two *Evans* officers would later testify to having seen the memorandum to that effect. It's likely that McLemore had been looking at the older document, but the fact that he witnessed the *Evans* going to plane guard at least once on the night of June 2 contradicted his testimony. In the event, the paper trail that might have refuted McLemore's testimony went down with the ship. Although he went to bed that evening aware that the *Melbourne* would be conducting flight operations sometime around 3:30 a.m., he would tell the board that he thought the call for rescue destroyer "could have gone to any ship," not necessarily the *Evans*, which would serve as plane guard destroyer at least three times throughout the night. It was controversial testimony, made even more gasp-worthy when the headlines that day blared, as though in neon lights: SKIPPER NOT TOLD OF SWITCH.

Another startling disclosure from McLemore was that U.S. Navy ships conducted plane guard maneuvers quite differently from what was practiced during Exercise Sea Spirit. When the *Evans* and other screening ships operated with the *Kearsarge*, the smaller ships remained behind the carrier and "the requirement then for moving into rescue destroyer station was simply one of closing in slightly and then when flights were over, opening slightly," he testified. The first wide turn the *Evans* made toward the carrier that night, a fishhook like the one Stevenson had sketched on a sheet of paper a day earlier, was apparently unfamiliar to McLemore's crew. This became another headline.

Then came the questions as to whether McLemore had left qualified officers in charge. Ramsey, it was revealed, had only been formally qualified to serve as fleet officer of the deck for ten days, yet had been overseeing watches on the bridge since the *Evans* left Long Beach. McLemore used the word *formal* but, as was the U.S. Navy way, there was nothing formal about it—it had been the sole decision of the commanding officer. "Commander," King asked, "in relation to qualification for . . . [fleet officer of the deck] are any written examinations, or formal courses of study required or any particular length of time or experience required for qualification in addition to the final judgment of the commanding officer?"

"No, sir," McLemore replied.

In fact no paper existed in the entire world, not stockpiled in an office or eleven hundred fathoms deep in the South China Sea, that could prove to the board that Ramsey was indeed qualified.

A day later the board called Stevenson to testify; it would be another two-day testimony. The Australian skipper was exasperated; it was Friday, and he had been waiting to testify all week. Putting on a confident face, he went into detail about the *Melbourne*'s mimeographed escort handout that he distributed to all the commanders of the escort ships during the May 25 dinner he had arranged. He explained that he essentially instructed them to first turn *away* from the *Melbourne* while in maneuvers with her—which neither the *Larson*, first, nor the *Evans* had done. The *Evans*, it was revealed in Stevenson's diagrams, had crossed the carrier's bow *twice*, with the second turn leading to the collision.

There was also "no doubt," he testified, that the *Evans* was designated plane guard destroyer. She had acted as plane guard destroyer several nights prior, in fact, yet maintained a course behind the carrier and merely moved in closer to plane-guard position when she was needed—the very maneuver McLemore and his crew were more familiar with.

Stevenson closed the second day of his testimony with a wordy list of all the steps he took to avoid a collision, starting with his May 25 dinner party, to practicing plane guard during the early stages of Sea Spirit, to "adherence to the set and practice procedure for moving to plane guard station," to use of navigation lights at "full brilliance," to signaling the *Melbourne*'s course prior to calling to execute the plane-guard order to eliminate confusion, and back again to "discussion with the commanding officer prior to the exercise at which time the imperative need for care in order to keep clear of the *Melbourne* was emphasized." His final words to the board: "If attention had been paid to even one of these cautions this collision could never have occurred."

Stevenson then requested to return to his ship, a request that was denied and stricken from the official record. Nobody could leave Subic Bay until the board understood what had gone wrong in the early-morning hours of June 3.

Later that day the board would turn its attention to those

who'd been on duty on the bridge of the *Evans*—namely, lieutenants junior grade Ronald Ramsey and James Hopson. Both were told that they were suspected of hazarding a vessel, among other crimes, and that although the fact-finding board would not issue punishment, legal proceedings could follow. Given the seriousness of the charge, both young officers sought council. Ramsey's attorney, bright twenty-seven-year-old U.S. Navy Lieutenant Frederic Tilton, had just been assigned the case. His eyes magnified by thick-rimmed glasses, the attorney asked for more time to meet with Ramsey, "to familiarize ourselves more fully with everything that is going on here in the entire situation." Tilton was bewildered by the hearing, which did not seem to follow the procedures of other inquiries. The young lawyer, a reservist who was a member of the South Dakota Bar Association before he was called to active duty, had spent much of his time in the U.S. Navy Judge Advocate General's Corps dealing with minor mishaps and—true to the times—drug infractions. This would be his most serious trial—and a trial is what it became to him, when he saw that his client had been named as a suspect. Ramsey appeared confused by the inquiry, and was clearly upset at having lost friends. Understanding from the onset what he was facing—at worst, seventy-four counts of negligent homicide—Tilton pitied the young officer.

What began as a friendly joint fact-finding inquiry into the collision of the USS *Frank E. Evans* and the HMAS *Melbourne* turned into a kangaroo court in the first week, a mash-up of rules and regulations setting the stage for harsh criticism. The rules appeared fluid—each navy followed its own protocols and bill of rights, and somehow they both met in the middle—but nevertheless they incited controversy. An Australian naval lawyer, sent to ensure that the board was acting fairly, was not allowed to sit in on the proceedings, a decision that angered some Australians. Counsel wasn't allowed to cross-examine witnesses or review testimony, a nuance that puzzled Tilton and others. And whenever matters of national security—such as an analysis of the exercise's zigzag plans—arose, the sessions would be closed for hours on end.

Tilton was incensed that Jo Stevenson, the Australian skipper's wife, sat in the third row throughout the inquiry. Strikingly attractive, petite and blond, she sat near the front of the press corps, keeping an eagle eye on the proceedings and taking copious notes in longhand. For her it was a matter of vindication of her husband, a matter of love.

The U.S. Navy's team of public affairs officers had been immediately suspicious when they recognized Jo Stevenson's name on the press form—vaguely identified as an "Australian magazine journalist"—and had tried to keep Mrs. Stevenson out of the press box, to no avail. A frustrated Tilton collected an affidavit from at least one school cafeteria worker who'd seen this pretty, brave woman sitting with her husband at a long table there, going over a stack of scribbled notes.

The American-born Jo, who left her two school-age children in the care of friends in Sydney, was worried that her husband would not be treated fairly in the inquiry. She'd seen this played out five years earlier, after the *Melbourne*'s collision with the *Voyager*, when the first inquiry placed blame on carrier captain John Robertson, a friend of the Stevensons, though a subsequent one vindicated him—a little too late, since his career was already irreparably tarnished. She had received her husband's letters detailing the near miss with the *Larson*. Whether anyone liked it or not (and most liked her, at least), Jo Stevenson was not going anywhere.

The day Ramsey appeared was one Jo had been greatly anticipating. "Slim, very self-possessed, neat, small brown eyes, nice looking," she jotted down in her notepad when Ramsey first walked into the room. But as annoyed as Tilton was at her presence, she was just as frustrated that Ramsey had been provided with an attorney. "How unfair then the Australian lawyer had not been permitted in the court even as an observer," she would later write. That he was given extensions to testify—first one day's, and then another, and yet another—riled her even more.

Hopson, the junior officer of the deck on duty the night of the collision, elicited pity from everyone there—including Jo Stevenson. The testimony from Ramsey and Hopson would put the board and everyone listening before them in the pilothouse of the *Evans* that night. It was a story she and others couldn't wait to hear.

Hopson looked young to Jo. In his testimony he described the ships' courses, their intended path relative to true north. He went into what their directions were, what he thought that meant, and where he had eventually noticed the *Melbourne* actually was in reference to the *Evans*—a visual sighting he failed to take when he ordered the first dangerous turn into the carrier's path, an order that followed the first radio signal and a hurried estimation of what to do next. The truth of the matter could be summed up in three words he would use during his lengthy, fumbling testimony: "I was confused."

What the board expected next was Ramsey. What they got, however, would complicate matters even further.

34

KEY WITNESSES

Lieutenant Frederic Tilton stood beside Ramsey at the end of the eighth day of the inquiry. Ramsey's extensions were up; the board wanted to hear from the young *Evans* officer who had ordered that final right turn into the path of the *Melbourne*. They had patiently awaited the long-delayed testimony of a man who might fill in some, if not all, of the blanks. Instead, in the young lawyer's eloquent, measured words, they got this:

> Gentlemen of the board, Mr. Ramsey and I recognize and appreciate the grave responsibility and extremely difficult task for which you have been called here to perform. We also fully recognize and understand the limitations of this board and certainly we appreciate the courtesy and understanding you have extended to Mr. Ramsey… Furthermore, it is Mr. Ramsey's very sincere desire to bring forth all the true facts concerning this tragic naval disaster in which so many of his personal friends and fellow shipmates lost their lives, in the hope that such an event might never happen again.

The board looked at the pair, still waiting to see where this was going. There was no doubt that Ramsey could be found at fault—it was he who had ordered right full rudder even though he did not have the conn and had not taken a visual of the carrier. But it was Hopson who had ordered the first turn into the carrier's path, and then become confused. Certain that Ramsey had done what he thought to be right at the time, and feeling the pressure of the entire U.S. Navy against him, Tilton was convinced that, as counsel, he needed to protect his client. Eyeing the board nervously, the lawyer continued:

> Both Mr. Ramsey and I are certain this board recognizes that the truth will prevail and that the true facts will be known and will be made available to the navies of all free nations of the world. Our own history tells us, however, that the truth can be best reached in an environment in which all the constitutional rights and guarantees of the individual are fully and completely safeguarded. This board . . . after carefully considering our request and reviewing its own authority, concluded that it was without authority to make testimony of prior witnesses available to me as Mr. Ramsey's counsel and that it was without authority to grant the right to recall prior witnesses, and that it was without authority to grant the right to confront and cross-examine all witnesses. Earlier, this board prohibited the presence of counsel during testimony presented by other witnesses though in fact the public, quite properly, were permitted to attend such sessions.

Tilton had met with the Subic Bay naval legal officer to

ensure that what was to come was a proper move for the young naval officer facing a profusion of charges. Admiral King was an imposing character, to say the least, and Tilton knew what the young lawyer was about to announce would rattle him. It would rattle everyone; inevitably, some would wonder what Ramsey was thinking, or perhaps hiding. Tilton was aware of the repercussions, but he was wholly convinced, after soliciting the opinions of like-minded lawyers, that he was protecting Ramsey. Everyone said the inquiry could be a raw, messy deal for Ramsey: seventy-four counts of manslaughter. It was too much. Somewhere in his file, Tilton had an article noting that even Senator Ted Kennedy, from his office in Washington, had criticized these lopsided proceedings at Subic Bay. This was the only thing Tilton could do to protect his young client. He adjusted his thick-framed glasses and went on:

> You have also advised Mr. Ramsey that he has been suspected of a military offense of negligently hazarding a vessel. In view of the complex nature of this offense and the total inability of counsel to effectively advise Mr. Ramsey without a complete and thorough knowledge of all the facts, I have accordingly advised Mr. Ramsey that he should not under these present circumstances waive his constitutional rights by making any statement to this board.

Jo Stevenson all but dropped her notebook at the idea that Ramsey would not testify before a board that, she felt, had badgered and humiliated her husband and the other Australian men he served with. *Constitutional rights?* Adding to her disgust, the very next morning, the board excused Ramsey from the proceedings, continuing as if nothing had happened.

Few understood the complexity behind Ramsey's decision, at the urging of his attorney, not to testify. In the days that followed King would call Ramsey and Tilton into the hotel room that served as his quarters on at least three separate occasions, asking the pair to reconsider, explaining how much was at stake. Tilton later recalled that while these weren't threatening encounters, they certainly did not sit well with him. King was using his rank to influence those below him, which was not proper behavior when it came to Judge Advocate General affairs. Tilton told Ramsey to keep his composure; it would be over soon.

King was by now frustrated by the testimonies, and it showed. He asked Australians to speak more slowly because he couldn't understand their accents—an ironic twist, since this was an investigation into an incident involving two foreign navies, in which communications played a major role. The press disgusted Admiral King, and he was particularly bothered by the bad timing displayed by *Esquire* magazine; the July 1969 issue, with its satirical enumeration of naval mishaps and blunders, made his Navy look like a league of buffoons. He also knew, deep down, that McLemore was unfit. He liked the captain as a person, but as a commander he'd been careless in how he led the officers on the *Evans*—"sloppy practices," the admiral would reveal in a later interview, that had dealt a death blow to the seventy-four young men under his command. Still, the admiral kept in line his pride in the U.S. Navy, making headlines when he responded with rapid-fire comments to an Australian commander's testimony.

Navy Lieutenant Commander R. A. Arundel, the fleet communications officer on board the *Melbourne*, testified that the *Evans* was "a little slow in reacting" to directives from the carrier. In general, he continued, much to the chagrin of a boiling Admiral King, "American ships are a little slower to react than Commonwealth ships."

"Commander Arundel," King interrupted, looking straight at the witness, "are you intimately familiar with the training of tactical operators in the Commonwealth navies?"

"Yes sir," snapped Arundel, looking straight back at the agitated American admiral.

"Are you intimately familiar with the training of officers of the deck in the U.S. Navy?"

The Australian hesitated. Lowering his eyes, he answered, "No sir."

Yet the American admiral knew that something on the *Evans* had been amiss. For one thing, in those final, confusing minutes Hopson had only heard one thing from the combat information center: the word "Hey," heard over the radio from a compartment in which were ten men whose main job was to double-check the radio signals and decisions made just a few feet away in the pilothouse. "Hey" and nothing else went against protocol. There was supposed to be someone on the earphones, receiving the messages, another at a chart table, another watching blips on the screen, another deciphering codes, not to mention backup personnel and, overseeing the operations, two extremely capable officers whose sole function was to ensure that mistakes weren't made. The crew in the combat information center that night was one of the finest on board; radarmen were usually kept in line, and they stayed there willingly. Sometimes the man in charge in the pilothouse didn't listen to their advice; it could be frustrating depending on which officer of the deck the radarmen were dealing with. It was a mystery: what had gone wrong with the system, and why hadn't more been said? It was impossible to know; nobody in the combat information center lived to tell the story.

Perhaps a *Navy Times* article on June 18 was the first to adequately summarize the ordeal that would continue for weeks without answers: "The full story of the events which led to the cutting in two of the USS FRANK E. EVANS by the bow of the [antisubmarine warfare] carrier HMAS MELBOURNE may never be known." It never was.

It's easy to see that an expert navigator such as Admiral King might find the series of events almost incredible. He told reporters he wanted to see that something came out of the inquiry, that it was done right. He became fixated, it was said, on the issue of lights. Stevenson had testified that he'd switched on the *Melbourne*'s navigation lights prior to calling the plane-guard maneuver. How could the men on the *Evans* have failed to see the carrier? Adding to the confusion—and King's frustration—was that the testimony of those stationed on both American and foreign ships in the vicinity on whether they had seen the carrier's lights was inconsistent. Some said they saw lights, others only shadows.

King couldn't let go of these discrepancies. Of the six hundred pages of transcript from the inquiry, an estimated one hundred dealt with lights. Jo Stevenson, who detested Admiral

King, would scribble in her notebook, "Admiral King, obsessed with lights."

King was also upset that by the time they actually testified before the board, some witnesses had changed the accounts they'd given in preliminary interviews and statements. One Australian radio operator did just that when talking about the last two signals transmitted between the *Evans* and the *Melbourne*. These final communications were considered a vital detail in the inquiry—and the board couldn't nail down which ship radioed first. It was clear that the *Evans*'s sharp right turn and the *Melbourne*'s hard left—attempts to avoid collision that in fact led to disaster—were the ships' last decisions. But witnesses disagreed on who had signaled first, as well as who actually turned first.

The Australian procedure, it would be later revealed, was to turn first and then tell the tactical operator, working at a desk fourteen feet away from where Stevenson stood, to signal the turn being made. The American procedure was to signal first and *then* turn, and operators and officers worked closer together in both proximity and timing. The difference in timing was only a matter of seconds, but those seconds were vital in figuring out what had happened. And the board would never know.

The inquiry was not without emotional moments. One *Evans* seaman would tell of the heroism he had witnessed in the mess decks in the three minutes it took for the bow of the *Evans* to sink completely. A few *Evans* officers—recounting a rumor that several sailors climbing out to safety had seen a ladder blocking the doorway to a compartment, condemning four officers to death—commented that the ship's design might be flawed. There were the accounts of men on the aft section, frightened yet not panicked, helping their fellow sailors to safety.

And there were, of course, the details regarding the gusto and bravery with which the Australian men carried out the rescue, jumping forty-five feet into a dark sea to save drowning Americans, risking their lives to save others. "I saw a chap in the water, I jumped in and put him on a raft," testified a burly Australian diving officer, Lieutenant Robert J. Burns, noting that when he heard another cry for help in the water, he swam over and put that man in the raft, too. He estimated he swam as much as two hundred yards before reaching the first *Evans* survivor, and again as far to reach the second. Fueled by adrenaline, he and other Australians continued to help with little regard for their own safety.

King—for the only time in the entire inquiry—rose from his seat and went to the witness box to shake the Australian hero's hand and thank him for his efforts. Such efforts would forever haunt Burns and the other brave men, who could never believe they'd truly done enough. At about this time many of the *Melbourne* sailors had put together a lump sum of money— over $30,000 when the press got wind of the story—to give to the children of the fallen American sailors in the form of scholarships. They did what they could yet many Australians remained haunted. Late at night, they would wake in horror and guilt, many times over, overwhelmed by visions of young American men struggling to stay afloat. Decades later they could still hear their cries.

Within days almost all of the reporters had cleared out. Back home, news of the proceedings in Subic Bay was buried in newspapers' back pages, and missing altogether from the nightly TV news. The inquiry, it seemed, was going nowhere. Likely the jargon was just too much for many reporters, with the profuse use of acronyms, and jumble of directions on a compass, given in three-digit numbers that meant little to the untrained navigators in the room. Was it "moonlighting" or "navigational lights," and what did "relative bearing" mean? The U.S. Navy's public affairs team kept a log of which reporters were there each day and the headlines that followed. These officers, all from the Seventh Fleet's public relations detachment in Saigon, spent hours explaining ship handling to journalists on deadline. This was made more complicated when regular journalists were replaced with "stringers," warm bodies hired by newspapers and wire services when something deemed more important—Nixon finally ordering troops to pull of out Vietnam, for instance—broke. Often these reporters, uninformed or uninterested, would for the most part tune out the testimony, sometimes excusing themselves altogether and just waiting for the verdict.

An air of outright slapstick crept into the proceedings when, just days into the long procession of questions and indecipherable navigational lingo, the British HMS *Rorqual*, attempting to tie up alongside the USS *Endurance* in Subic Bay, crashed into its hull instead.

By the final week, with the Fourth of July holiday approaching, answers remained elusive. Called back to testify before the board several times, a strained McLemore commented on several factors that might have contributed to the demise of the seventy-four Americans under his command. One of these was confused radio communications, he testified: "There was just too much traffic and too many people on one radio telephone circuit, in my opinion." He also suggested why the *Evans* had sunk so rapidly: "I had about a full war allowance on board. My forward guns were fully up to allowance." The *Evans* had also been refueled early in the day June 2, her forward tanks topped off for the journey to Thailand and then the coast of Vietnam. The other ships in Destroyer Squadron 23, as well as the *Kearsarge,* had also refueled and just after Sea Spirit was canceled and the rescue concluded, headed back to the Vietnam coastline. It was why they were there. Even as McLemore gave his testimony, the American ships that steamed out of Long Beach that spring were in or just south of the Tonkin Gulf.

McLemore seemed to damn the exercise as whole when he commented, "One of the little irritating things more than anything else about Sea Spirit was the fact that we had to regress in many areas to the use of [zigzag] publications which we hadn't used for some time." In summary, he said, it was "a very complex exercise." Perhaps, the implication was, too complex.

35

DERELICTION OF DUTY

After three weeks of prodding seventy-nine witnesses, Admiral King announced that the board would not hear any more testimony; it was ready to deliberate. A final report would be prepared in the upcoming weeks, he told a half-empty room—to be exact, "four newsmen and no public," as a public affairs officer would type in his own report. After only a week and a half of closed deliberations, the board reconvened, admitting into evidence three unsworn statements by Lieutenant Junior Grade Ronald Ramsey, one of which consisted of a scribbled note found the morning of June 3 in the sick bay on the *Melbourne*. Read aloud to the board by an American Navy official, one after another, the statements revealed that Ramsey thought he could have avoided collision by ordering that final right turn; that the final left turn from the *Melbourne* surprised him; that there was no panic in the pilothouse, contrary to what Hopson had testified; and that Ramsey did not wake the captain because the young officer in charge did not think it was necessary, nor required of him. It was never made clear why Ramsey failed to alert the captain when tragedy was imminent.

By July 18, the board had its final report. The transcript, featuring testimony from forty-eight American, twenty-eight Australian, one British, and two New Zealand witnesses was tallied at 550,350 words over 611 printed pages. Open sessions had lasted 60 hours and 33 minutes, closed sessions came in at 32 hours and 25 minutes, and classified sessions sat at 8 hours and 23 minutes. For every minute in open session the board spent 30 seconds in closed session—much had gone on behind closed doors. The report included photographs, mimeographed pages from sloppy logbooks, drafts of night orders on the *Evans,* and a study of the condition of the beheaded American destroyer. (She could be repaired only at a cost of $20.7 million, a separate report would conclude; a brand-new destroyer would cost about $23 million.) More than one hundred hours had been spent studying the collision between the *Evans* and the *Melbourne*—from the seemingly absurd minutiae required of such proceedings to the down-and-dirty testimonies on what went terribly wrong in the minutes following the order that had put the *Evans* on plane guard.

What the board of inquiry found was this: both navies shared in the blame—unequally so, a bullet-point list of transgressions would reveal, but both were culpable. The board had no authority to punish; its duty was only to probe.

Included in the findings was a chart that looked for all the world like a game of tic-tac-toe. Its nine boxes represented nine possible scenarios: nine possible courses of action the two ships might have taken when collision, according to the *Melbourne* skipper, was imminent. Had only the *Melbourne* turned—either right or left—disaster would have been avoided, though had the carrier turned right against the *Evans'* right turn, it would have been a close call, 100 yards or less. If the *Melbourne* had not turned, the ships would have still struck each other given the *Evans'* right turn. In fact, it appeared from the chart, it was Ramsey's hard right turn that had proved most disastrous.

The board's assessment, summed up near the end of its thirty-four pages of findings, was that the *Evans* "had the duty to remain clear of the *Melbourne* in taking station in column astern of her, and she did not do so, [and thus] primary responsibility for the collision rests upon the *Evans*." The mistakes made by Ramsey as the conning officer took up an entire page of fine type, with the word *failure* used fifteen times: failure to wake the captain when the call to plane-guard was ordered; failure to take a visual sighting of the *Melbourne* or ascertain her precise course before turning; and failure to ask the combat information center for more information before turning, among the litany of transgressions. Hopson's initial wrong turn rested on Ramsey's shoulders; since Ramsey was officer of the deck, Hopson fell under his command that night. McLemore was also to blame, the inquiry would find:

> As [commanding officer of the] *Evans*, Cmdr. McLemore had the responsibility to ensure that adequate provision was made for the safe navigation of his ship under all foreseeable conditions. This included responsibility to ensure that a qualified and

trained watch was posted. That adequate instructions, including standing and current night orders, were provided as to calling him during the night to advise, among other things, of signals for *Evans* to change station within the formation. That adequate measures were taken to insure that his orders and instructions in these respects were carried out. [Commanding officer of the] *Evans* adequately discharged these responsibilities. Although the board finds no acts or omissions of [commanding officer of the] *Evans* which contributed to the collision, it recognizes the inherent accountability of the commanding officer for his ship, and his absolute responsibility for the actions of his ship.

The findings did not, in essence, clear McLemore, who was asleep at the time, but neither did they clear Stevenson:

Capt. Stevenson must bear a share of the responsibility for the collision since as task unit commander, he was responsible for the safe operation of all ships in the task unit. He failed to exercise due care in that he did not positively direct the movements of the *Evans* at a time not later then when *Evans* was determined by him to have come into a collision course.

That Stevenson had not slowed down was also listed among his alleged mistakes; speed would not have stopped the collision but would have "lessened the effects thereof." The Australian skipper, whom the press had referred to as a "cool hand at sea," was shocked. His wife was unsurprised; she would later reveal that she had been told that both navies would share the blame for the sake of politics between the allied anticommunist nations. Her husband's charges would later be restated before his very own court-martial, held in Canberra, Australia, the following month. That the *Melbourne* skipper had failed to better direct the *Evans* was the allegation, one that an Australian military judge dismissed in minutes, stating that there was "no case to answer." Stevenson walked out of a courthouse in Canberra a vindicated, smiling man.

Nevertheless, Stevenson had been tried, and as his wife would later say, his career had been blemished. Disheartened to learn that he would never pin admiral and instead was offered a junior desk job, he left the Australian Navy within a year.

By August 1969 Ramsey, Hopson, and McLemore were in the hot seat again at an Article 32 investigation, a preliminary hearing to see if courts-martial were necessary. After the joint board of inquiry, the list of charges against Ramsey and Hopson was lengthy: dereliction of duty; negligence; hazarding a vessel and, more specifically, failing to sound a collision alarm when the hazard of collision existed; failing to establish the correct position of the *Evans* in reference to the carrier *Melbourne*; and failing to ascertain a safe course of action for the plane-guard maneuver. McLemore's charges included dereliction of duty in that he permitted an "inexperienced and immature" officer of the deck to stand watch unsupervised, and "failed to require an alert and competent watch."

Held in a muggy Quonset hut on the Subic Bay base over the course of eight days, the proceedings would include further testimony from some of the same officers and enlisted men who had answered questions at the controversial hearing in June. Ramsey was once again represented by Tilton, the young attorney this time working with the U.S. Navy Judge Advocate General Corps manual as his guide. This fair trial would permit Tilton, and the attorneys representing Hopson and McLemore, to cross-examine witnesses and review testimony, privileges not permitted in the lopsided joint board of inquiry earlier that summer.

The investigation ran much more smoothly. Several Australians, though not required to be there, came of their own accord to testify. Captain Stevenson, then dealing with his own court-martial, gave testimony similar to what he'd given to the board of inquiry. One new revelation, however, was that the skipper had not been entirely sure that the *Evans* was on a collision course when it first turned into the carrier's path. Stevenson saw the maneuver— a risky one he had specifically asked screening ships not to undertake—and panicked, ordering his radio operator to tell the *Evans* it was on a collision course because he "wanted to shock them into action before the situation got more acute." It's not known what would have happened had the Australian skipper not sent that initial warning.

Another revelation concerned the position of other ships in the screen at the time of the *Evans*'s first turn into the *Melbourne*'s path. The HMNZS *Blackpool* had been patrolling a sector to the left of the *Evans*, forcing the American destroyer to make a wide right turn in front of the carrier, but at a distance so great that it could be adjusted.

Captain Clyde B. Anderson, who had sat on the joint

board of inquiry, testified as an expert witness during these proceedings, stating as an experienced destroyer commander that he, like Hopson, would have "come right in order to cross the carrier's bow without closing the range. Once clear across her bow we would continue to turn further right and go down her starboard side and turn into station." Yet the heading of the carrier had been miscalculated, adding to the confusion.

Anderson, perhaps damning McLemore's decision to go to sleep that night, leaving Ramsey in charge, called the zigzag maneuvering of ships under darkened conditions one of the "most difficult to be encountered" by any ship handler; "The officer who stands the deck watch under these circumstances should be extremely well qualified."

Yet in the middle of questioning another revelation emerged, in some ways vindicating McLemore. Had the collision not occurred, the *Evans* would have earned the distinction of being named the best ship in Destroyer Squadron 23. Even Stevenson had called her "a good ship" during these proceedings.

Within a month of the Article 32 investigation, McLemore and Ramsey were court-martialed. Ramsey pleaded guilty and received the mild punishment of loss of seniority in the officer ranks, a sentence he called fair in his first press conference following the proceedings. Days later McLemore pleaded not guilty to charges of negligence, but was found guilty under old navy rules dictating that what happens on a captain's ship is his responsibility, and given a reprimand. Hopson was never court-martialed, but he was reprimanded under a separate code.

All three American officers were given shore duty that fall. The Navy sent McLemore to an undersea warfare group in Long Beach. Both Hopson and Ramsey were sent to Mare Island Naval Shipyard, near McLemore's hometown of Vallejo, California, also home to McLemore's alma mater, California Maritime Academy. The hometown newspapers there had covered the collision from the beginning, but the headlines got smaller as time went on and other events took precedence as news. It was a busy summer, one for the history books.

While the board of inquiry deliberated and a nation celebrated its independence, nineteen-year-old Michael Magee and twenty-two-year-old Darlene Elizabeth Ferrin were shot in a parking lot of Blue Rock Springs Park in Vallejo, booting McLemore from the front cover of his hometown newspaper. This July 4, 1969, attack would become the first committed by a mysterious individual who would send cryptic letters to the San Francisco area newspapers, prompting reporters to eventually dub him the Zodiac Killer. This was the final summer of a decade that had changed the world. In a matter of days the first troop withdrawals from Vietnam would begin; later in the month astronauts Neil Armstrong and Buzz Aldrin would walk on the moon; and a few weeks after that, hippies were twirling in the mud at Woodstock. The summer was unforgettable.

In a living room near Seattle, Washington, newly-wed Patricia Armstrong would watch the black-and-white screen and hear, over the fuzzy transmission, a man with her own last name—though no relative—say, "That's one small step for man, one giant leap for mankind." Mourning the loss of her brother Alan, whose last letters home had put him on the *Evans* off the coast of Vietnam, she wondered at that very moment: How can we put a man way up on the moon, but not operate ships in the sea without running them into each other?

36

GOODNIGHT SAIGON

The families never got the answers they needed. There were seventy-one mothers and wives writing letters after the collision. One would write another that her letters to the secretary of the Navy had gone unanswered. "How easy it has been for the Navy Department to forget," wrote the mother of brown-haired, brown-eyed Linden Orpurt, of Chicago, Illinois, to the mother of Andrew James Botto, a dark-haired, bespectacled young man who in letters liked to tease his sister Frances back home in Stockton, California. Both men were in their early twenties and had been on the *Evans* for nearly two years, serving in two deployments to Vietnam before they were declared lost at sea in terse telegrams that included little explanation for how in the world it happened.

Master Chief Lawrence Reilly would spend his last few years in the Navy on shore duty near Long Beach. Consequently, he'd be asked to assist with military death notifications in the areas in and around Orange and Los

Angeles Counties. As a grieving father himself, he identified with the families of those killed in Vietnam. By 1969 just over half the official death toll from the entire war would be reached—many more would follow the seventy-four killed on the *Evans*. This devastating year was only the midpoint.

Many of the other *Evans* survivors went about their lives, transferred to other ships and bases, and tried to move on. A few of them went on to fight in Vietnam with the brown-water naval forces—that is, on smaller boats that operated in the country's rivers. Many left the Navy altogether. Some, when they could muster the courage, sought out the families of other lost seamen to deliver their sympathy in person, to pay their last respects, and to explain that as shipmates they had been best friends.

The aft section of the *Evans*, dragged 650 miles from the collision site to Subic Bay in June, was investigated and decommissioned within a month. She was later stripped of any old parts that might be reused—in some ways, she went back to Vietnam—and was left practically dismantled, surrounded by construction scaffolding, her insides exposed, ripped and left bare. The sight of the rusted, crippled hull stunned many on their way to some other ship at U.S. Naval Base Subic Bay. It was like seeing a dead body—few who saw it could forget it. Yet parts of the *Evans* would live on, for a few more years at least, on other vessels sent to fight the continuing war in Vietnam.

On October 10 the floating hunk of debris was dragged out to sea again, to serve her country once more. The men on the destroyer USS *John R. Craig* were mournful about the duty that lay ahead: half of a dead fighter floating in the turquoise water as target practice. That those who had died on her could have been them never escaped their minds as their own ship maneuvered into position. Vietnam, the war, the era really was a game of chance—they were the lucky ones. But there was no celebrating it. Young sailor Jan Thomas Igras described the scene:

> The day was fair and sunny; the seas calm. Our gun crews first used what I was told were "sand shells" to fire on *Frank E. Evans*. They were non-explosive rounds that made a dust plume to register a strike. *Frank E. Evans* was fired upon all day long. Only the gun crews were at their battle stations. For the rest of the crew it was normal ship's work routine. I, like most of my shipmates, went topside many times throughout the day to witness the morbid work in progress.
>
> The announcement came over . . . that *Frank E. Evans* was about to sink. We could watch the death throes of a once vital man o' war from our deck amidships. Perhaps 20 or 30 of *Craig*'s curious crew gathered there to watch her final minutes. She was less than a mile off our port side. Our ship began a high-speed run and both of our five-inch gun mounts, two guns per turret, opened fire. Several salvos found their mark. The explosions aboard *Frank E. Evans* could not be heard, but the large plumes of white smoke indicated that explosive shells had done their work. The last furious blows dealt by a friendly ship were too

much for the now twisted and sinking *Frank E. Evans*. Her end was not spectacular.

She neither rose at the truncated bow nor the stern. There were no explosions.

Frank E. Evans merely slipped beneath the gentle blue sea. It was as if the ship itself had given up in her struggle to remain afloat and had resigned herself to accept the watery grave that awaited.

Back in the United States, the *Evans* had been forgotten by most, upstaged by the news of the world. But she had left her legacy: the U.S. Navy would use her as a cautionary tale, one told through an official training video produced in 1975 titled *I Relieve You, Sir*. She would help solidify the U.S. Navy's need to instill pride in its surface officers with the creation of the Surface Warfare Officers designation in 1970. It was perhaps suiting that the first deputy chief of naval operations for surface warfare was Rear Admiral Jerome King, a Navy man who knew firsthand the dangers of poor training and lack of pride in the fleet. Years later the Navy would create the Surface Warfare Officers School to train incoming ensigns, for surface warfare was the only route for officers that did not include some form of post-commission schooling. Before then, newly pinned ensigns fresh out of college and officer candidate school had been sent to fill responsible billets at sea with no additional training—a lackluster education that made for a struggling fleet and deadly mishaps.

Outside the Navy few would remember the *Evans*. She was a blip lost in the larger picture of the bloody Vietnam War that continued several hundreds of miles away.

Five days after the *Evans*'s aft section sunk to the bottom of the sea, a nationwide demonstration in the United States called for a moratorium on the Vietnam War. Politicians from both sides of the aisle criticized Richard Nixon's handling of the war. The president, in turn, continued to grapple with it, hoping it would not venture beyond "Johnson's war" to one that would bear his own name. By November he would ask the silent majority of his countrymen to support him as he worked to end the fighting:

> I know it may not be fashionable to speak of patriotism or national destiny these days. . . . Let historians not record that when America was the most powerful nation in the world we passed on the other side of the road and allowed for the last hopes of peace and freedom of millions of people to be suffocated by the forces of totalitarianism. . . . I can order an immediate, precipitate withdrawal of all Americans from Vietnam without regard to the effects of that action . . . or we can persist in our search for a just peace, through a negotiated settlement, if possible, or through continued implementation of our plan for Vietnamization if necessary. . . . I have chosen this second course. It is not the easy way. It is the right way.

Vietnamization was the administration's label for handing over the fight to comrades in South Vietnam, with little interference on the part of American troops. This would be Nixon's peace. But the fighting would continue until 1973, when an accord would finally be reached and prisoners of war could come home; even the draft would end that year.

At about the same time, the battered World War II destroyers would be retired for good, and the USS *Larson*, which had last been seen in press images alongside the aft section of the *Evans*, would be hailed in headlines as among the last of the "six-gunned" destroyers to come back from Vietnam. In 1975 Americans would leave the embassy in Saigon via helicopters that hovered above its rooftop, the American perimeters already breached by the fighting and victorious North Vietnamese. By 1976, with American might crippled over the country's handling of the war in Vietnam, the Southeast Asian Treaty Organization would disband. The closing of the casket on Vietnam would take over half a decade looking forward from the crescendo that was 1969.

Meanwhile, the demonstrations continued throughout 1969 with more bad news from the war zone—breaking news about a terrible massacre in a place called My Lai and a blatant refusal to fight in the bloodied Song Chang Valley. In the first case, men had followed orders to a fault; in the second, they did not follow orders at all. Nixon balanced the news with an announcement in December that fifty thousand more troops—another drop in the bucket—would be coming home within months.

This year 1969 also closed with minutiae for the president to attend to. In a perhaps symbolic gesture, Nixon announced a long-awaited plan for the demolition of the old and debilitated Main Navy and Munitions Buildings. Eventual destruction of the flat concrete complex along Constitution Avenue in Washington, D.C. left an open space on the National Mall, a fifty-acre site that would become the Constitutional Gardens by 1976, when Gallup Polls found concerns over Vietnam near the bottom of the list for Americans. Most wanted to move on.

But some couldn't.

By the early 1980s, that lush greenery along Constitution Avenue would become the backdrop to an incision carved in the earth, home to glossy black panels of granite rising, powerfully, as if from the ashes of war. There, engraved on stone in breathtaking magnitude, are the names of the more than 58,000 Americans killed in the Vietnam War.

They were mostly boys.

They died in firefights and in ambushes. In the velvet night, in the rain, and under a blistering, unforgiving sun. They died at the hands of the enemy, in the hellish jungle, in a compound. They died in friendly fire and in accidents. They died in their helicopters and jeeps. They died in ditches, in fires, and explosions. They died silently. They died screaming. They died in the air and on land.

And at sea.

IV

THE SECOND WATCH

37

<u>LEST WE FORGET</u>

It was two days before Christmas in Pomona, California. The year was 1965. The morning sun warmed the cool, crisp air only slightly as a dark-haired young man retrieved the mail from a small box along the curb in front of a ranch-style house with blue trim. The neighborhood was hardly a decade old; its streets were wide, barely shaded by the baby palm trees that lined the sidewalks. Steve Kraus was nineteen; he had just finished high school, later than usual, having first spent two years in a seminary high school, intent on becoming a priest. The Kraus family had been living in Fair Oaks near Sacramento when the father Jeff, an engineer for outer-space test rockets, passed away suddenly at age fifty-two, only a few months after a lung cancer diagnosis. The youngest Kraus children were between three and seven years of age; the older three had all grown up. Steve, the middle child of the seven, was the one his mother Edythe Kraus could lean on. He knew that she had roots and family in Southern California, and given his widowed mother still had little ones, he had convinced her to sell the home in Fair Oaks and move to the Los Angeles area. They had landed in Pomona, on the eastern outskirts of the city.

Steve ran errands for his mother because she didn't drive, and made sure the bills were paid and all was well before he headed for his job as a box boy and clerk at Jenkins Market along Garey Avenue. Before that, he had worked as a "pearl diver"—a dishwasher—in a small café. The responsible type, he was the head of the household, but even so he rarely received mail.

That very morning Steve was getting ready to wrap up a semester as a full-time student at Mount San Antonio Community College. And that's when it caught up with him: one letter in the pile of mail. One standard envelope, addressed to Stephen A. Kraus, 1932 Miramar Way. It was official, typeset. Steve tore into the envelope to find one sheet of paper, tri-folded and terse, that sent his heart racing: a draft notice from the United States Army, telling him to report for his physical.

The letter came down like a hammer. The Battle of Ia Drang Valley had just been in the news in November, the first major engagement between Vietnamese regulars and U.S. forces; more than three hundred Americans were killed. The story was that Lyndon Johnson had upped his draft calls, eliminating some deferments.

Nowhere did the form letter say they would give him a gun and send him off to some jungle; it simply gave a string of report-to dates and other requirements. But Steve, whose older brother had served in the Army, knew what the piece of paper meant. Without much thought of what he had planned to do that day, he got into his shiny black 1959 Chevy and drove two miles away to the U.S. Naval Recruiting Office.

It's likely he had passed the building several times on his way to downtown Pomona to run errands for his mother or to watch a movie in the old "movie palace" cinema. The YMCA building at 350 Garey Avenue was distinguished, Mission style with red brick and dark-framed arched windows, a Mediterranean roof, and ornamental concrete. It had been built following World War I, and during World War II it had operated as a sleep-and-shower facility for servicemen passing through the area. In the 1960s it leased office space.

Towering palm trees lined the sidewalk like toy soldiers. The street was a busy one. As Steve headed toward quaint downtown Pomona, with its candy and dress shops, the building was on the left. A small sign in the window on the first floor marked the location of the recruiting office. Steve hooked a U-turn and parked; he made for the concrete stairs to the main door, and there he ran into a recruiter who had had just locked up and was heading out of town for Christmas. Steve must have borne a look of desperation, a familiar tri-folded sheet of paper in his hand. "Okay, kid," said the clean-cut chief in a khaki uniform. "Come back January 4." The chief took Steve into the office and brandished a card, one he could send to the draft board indicating that he had already enlisted in the Navy—although, in actuality, he hadn't.

When the morning of January 4, 1966 arrived, Steve said good-bye to his mother and made for the large building on

Garey Avenue, thinking he'd be marching off that very day. Edythe was worried for her son, but knew it was one way or the other, and this way was safer. Steve had already quit his job at Jenkins. But when he got to the office, a recruiter told him he could go on a delayed entry program. It would be 120 extra days of civilian life. He took it, and found another job scooping ice cream at a Baskin Robbins shop. That was a good thing, because in the time that followed—on the very day before he went to boot camp, actually—he was set up on a blind date with a petite young lady from one town over. Pretty Donna Marrs had thick black hair and tanned skin; Steve thought she looked Mexican. And Donna thought his eyes lit up. *Handsome.*

They went to a drive-in movie; *One Million Years B.C.*, *Alfie*, and *Batman* were playing around that time, but neither could later recall which film played in vibrant Technicolor on the big screen before them. Steve watched Donna; Donna watched Steve's hands. The next day he left for boot camp in San Diego. And then he was off to his first ship and, eventually, stationed off the coast of Vietnam. The romance blossomed through letters and quick visits home to Pomona. Within two years they were married.

Quite early on, Steve had set his sights on the rate of signalman, the neat-and-tidy job on ship that calls for visual communications using nautical flags strung up near the mast and a signal lamp the size of a hubcap. While the ship was moored in its home port of Long Beach, the signalmen went home first every day; the dingy, grease-covered engine-room guys stayed the latest. The radarmen were always sent away to various schools—*too far away*. The deck crew spent most of their time chipping paint and repainting. *Slave labor.* It wasn't for him. Intelligent and swift, he was a shoe-in for a signalman's post.

The USS *Henry W. Tucker* was an ugly, old ship. A destroyer in the *Gearing* class, the one that followed that of the *Sumner*, the *Tucker* was built at the tail end of World War II and kept on the line, like all others, for Vietnam. Versatile, she was a "Market Time" ship—a ship that provided surveillance along the enemy coastline, and was among the first to engage in shore bombardment in 1965. By 1967 she was also a plane-guard destroyer, aiding in the launching of aircraft off carriers parked in the Gulf of Tonkin.

July 29, 1967, was a brutal day in naval history. Under cloudless blue skies the USS *Forrestal* was preparing to launch an attack on North Vietnam when one of its jets, through an electronic mishap, accidentally fired a rocket into one of its planes, exploding at least two bombs and igniting a roaring fire and further explosions. It was a macabre sight indeed for those on nearby ships, who watched as the deadly fire engulfed the deck of the 75,000-ton flattop and thick black smoke billowed skyward. And worse for those on board; on a ship, in the middle of an ocean, there is no place to go.

Steve was on a platform on the *Tucker*, watching through a signalman's gigantic binoculars, when he saw that first ball of fire, and then another explosion, and then the ominous smoke. This fire would take the lives of 134 American sailors, the largest single loss of life for the U.S. Navy's fighting Seventh Fleet during the Vietnam War. The tragedy was particularly poignant for Steve at the time, still watching through the "big eyes," as they called them. This was his generation and its war, the war they were there to fight, as was made clear early in boot camp when the instructors introduced a black-and-white film titled—with no question mark—*Why Vietnam*. And it was deadly. It could have been him over there in that fire.

Fewer than two years after the USS *Forrestal* fire, Steve was in that same place, on a ship very much like the *Tucker* and in an identical maneuver with an aircraft carrier nearby, when he would become an integral part of the second largest single loss of life for the U.S. Navy in Vietnam. This time, however, the scene was one of pure darkness.

S teve and two fresh boots named Isaac Lyons Jr. and James Kerr took a plane, an oiler, an amphibious ship, and then a small motorboat to the USS *Frank E. Evans* in May 1969. Steve had just been stationed on the USS *Reeves*, a newer, larger, and more comfortable warship, when his new orders brought a wave of dread. The *Evans* would be another World War II tin can: rickety, smelly, and uncomfortable. The *Evans* was firing its guns that day; Steve came aboard on May 14 just as the crew was exhausting their ammunition and their stores. They were readying for a brief interlude at Subic Bay, then Manila, and then some kind of exercise.

D arkened ship meant the *Evans* wouldn't be flashing its amber signals that evening. With more than three years of experience as a signalman, Steve had been put on the watch rotation immediately. That night, just before the clock on board hit 0000 on June 3, he met signalman Marcus Rodriguez on the platform outside the signal shack. The pair decided that since it would be a quiet night, they would split the shift. Marcus could relax while Steve stayed up, and then they'd switch. The signal shack was the size of a broom closet and sat higher than the navigation bridge. There was a platform outside it, and just after 3:00 a.m., that's where Steve was. On quiet nights like this he usually wrote letters to Donna, who was then three months pregnant with their first child. The couple was renting a small one-bedroom apartment in a midcentury avocado green building, a quaint place on a tree-lined street in Pomona. That it was close to family was reassuring as Steve left for another stint off the coast of Vietnam.

Tonight there would be no letter writing; Steve's eyes burned red and tired. To maintain some form of duty and to stay awake, he walked about the platform and searched for the carrier HMAS *Melbourne*, the one they had been steaming with for days. He couldn't spot her—not even in the distance. He noticed his ship turning, a wide turn, going fast—about 22 knots. They'd been zigzagging all night at what appeared random times and speeds, sure, but this maneuver was different. It was wide, almost a semicircle. Where was the *Melbourne*? When Steve last checked, he'd seen the massive flattop's silhouette to the right, seemingly minuscule as it stood about ten football fields away. Steve walked to one side of the *Evans* as it turned. Still nothing, no *Melbourne*. And the *Evans* was still turning.

Again he walked to the other side of the signal platform. Suddenly there was a sharp turn to starboard, so sharp that the entire ship leaned to the right, and Steve held on to the railing. And then he saw the *Melbourne*, less than a hundred yards away and steaming fast, the frothy white wake under the moonlight clear as snow, her bow headed straight for the *Evans*. The larger warship's lights were on. A horn pierced the night air. Steve rushed back into the signal shack, banged on the roof—Marcus was up there, asleep—and grabbed the radio. "We're gonna get—"

Midsentence. At midships. The *Evans* was hit violently, bulldozed, and rocked to her side under the massive weight of the carrier, whose rectangular flight deck plowed into the *Evans* close to the signal shack. Steve was thrown to the door of the shack, his thumb stuck in the door, the shack now flat against the water. His thumb, then a hand and then an arm, and then—one final push—he was out. The water was there, flat, black, full of oil and determination, pouring into the front half of the ship just below him. There was no leap, no plunge; Steve just swam away, frantically, as explosions went off and steam billowed behind him.

The nightmares weren't that bad, Steve would say later. There was one terrible one once, the kind where you are falling. Donna remembered them, too; he woke her at least once. He didn't know anyone on the *Evans* all that well, and certainly none of the seventy-four killed. When he looked at the list of the dead, he found out that Lyons and Kerr hadn't survived. He remembered their faces, vaguely.

Steve's four-year Navy career had him sailing on five different vessels. He got out shortly after the *Evans* disaster, though he made it to one final ship, the USS *John Paul Jones*. She was off the coast of California when a missile misfired during an exercise; it went up and straight down again. The incident terrified him, and there was no reenlistment thereafter.

Decades later he would discover that veterans from the *Evans*, the one ship he couldn't forget, were gathering annually. A few retired Korean War veterans in Texas who wanted to bring together old comrades created the USS *Frank E. Evans* Association in 1992. Soon the reunions drew not only sailors from the 1950s but also the older gentlemen of the 1940s, the younger ones of the 1960s, and eventually some who were there the night their ship was cut in two. By 2010 Steve had become a regular attendee and then vice president of the organization, and his wife, Donna, became the treasurer. The couple helped to plan the reunions, and it kept them busy well into retirement.

The annual gathering, held in cities coast to coast, had come to mean more than a reunion of old shipmates. Australian witnesses to the collision, full of the same melancholy and survivor guilt that haunted their American counterparts, started attending reunions in the late 1990s. It was at about this same time that a few former *Melbourne* sailors organized their own memorial to the seventy-four in Sydney on the thirtieth anniversary in 1999—hosting several *Evans* survivors as special guests at the service and even, in their homes. There would become a unique bond between the veterans of two navies, grieving men separated by thousands of miles of ocean; a friendship unlike any either nation had ever seen.

"Lest we forget," adopted from the Australian version of the *Ode of Remembrance*, an old British poem to the war dead, became the *Evans* association's slogan and driving theme.

38

A Fighting Crew

One by one, and in various forms that ranged from a simple phone call to a much more heartbreaking display in front of the nation's most visited memorial, the men of 1969 learned that their shipmates' names had been left off the Vietnam Veterans Memorial in Washington, D.C.. Some of the men wrote letters. In time, family members of the lost seventy-four had joined the USS *Frank E. Evans* Association and wrote their letters—or came to show the letters they had written years ago, and the responses from lawmakers, information passed down from the Pentagon. For some it was a matter of searching the Internet and stumbling upon the *Evans* association.

Some went to talk to their lawmakers straight away, or sought the assistance of anyone they thought could help. Over and over they received the same answer: that the seventy-four men of the *Evans* had died outside the official combat zone for Vietnam. Yet it was all a combat zone to them—especially to the families who received last letters home while the ship was anchored off Vietnam, on the gunline. The only reason they were in that part of the world was Vietnam: the ship had left Long Beach on March 29, 1969, to fight in the Vietnam War. To them, it was that simple.

Working with families, the veterans petitioned the government. In one decade alone a bill had gone to the U.S. Senate and Congress a total of five times without resolution. On June 3, 2003, a bill that would force the U.S. Department of Defense to review its policies toward the Vietnam combat zone went before a Senate Subcommittee on National Parks hearing. The *Evans* group got James Zumwalt, a retired U.S. Marine colonel and son of former Chief of Naval Operations Elmo Zumwalt, to speak on their behalf. James Zumwalt was a junior line officer in the Navy at the time of the collision and had seen the aft section of the *Evans* in Subic Bay that summer. In 1988 he had lost his own brother, the young Navy veteran Elmo Zumwalt III, to cancer related to Agent Orange exposure—another black mark on the Vietnam War. That very day in 2003, on the thirty-fourth anniversary of the collision, Zumwalt's editorial on behalf of the fallen *Evans* crew was published in *Washington Post*. At the hearing, he spoke eloquently and with determination:

> These eligibility standards have been given a broad interpretation over the years to in fact include others now whose names are on the wall, yet fail to meet the same criteria applied to the *Evans'* seventy-four. To avoid casting a shadow upon the entitlement of these other deserving heroes, I will only use generic categories to show the lack of uniformity exercised in applying the eligibility standards.

Zumwalt then provided details on 68 names added to the wall in 1983 that were the result of a plane crash in Hong Kong Bay in 1965--nearly 1,000 miles from the combat zone. This addition, according to the Vietnam Veterans Memorial Fund, came at the directive of then president Ronald Reagan.

Jan Scruggs, founder of the Vietnam Veterans Memorial, also spoke at that hearing. He told lawmakers that this proposed regulation would make way for up to a thousand more names on the Vietnam Wall, including those who were killed on the *Evans*. He said that new requests were becoming increasingly common, that one woman whose son died in an ordnance accident in Maryland thought his name belonged there because he was drafted, and he noted, "We only have four places on The Wall where names exceeding seventeen letters can now be placed. . . . Yet another issue is the financial cost—approximately $3,500 per name." A National Park Service official also testified, stating that the memorial only had room for twenty-four more names and that any addition would jeopardize the memorial's design. (In the ten years that followed the 2003 hearing, twenty-one names had been added, not including the six that were added the month prior to this hearing. To this day, more are being added. Fourteen names were added in 2014—one of a man who died in a hospital on the South Pacific island of Guam, the result of a heart attack. There is still, it appears, space on the memorial as of 2014.)

For the *Evans* crew and family theirs was fast becoming an uphill battle, and the issue was eventually lost in the Beltway bureaucracy. In 2010 the association went on to enlist the help of a California congressman whose constituents included the son of a man killed on the *Evans*. Congressman Adam Schiff of Pasadena thought the veterans and families had a case, and wrote a letter to President Barack Obama. There was a notion that this new president, one who promised hope and change, could do something. The issue was sent to Secretary of the Navy Ray Mabus for review; Mabus agreed with the *Evans* crew and families and passed the issue along to the Department of Defense, which in a year's time denied the request to add the seventy-four names to the wall. The final words stung, setting the group back at square one: the *Evans* had been outside the combat zone.

During the lulls, the patient waiting for letters with official letterheads from men in power, there were hopeful moments. There were notions that a person, a thing, or a political climate could reverse the decision to keep the seventy-four men off the Vietnam Memorial. There were strategies in all directions: enlisting the help of the Veterans of Foreign Wars, positive resolutions in statehouses, promising newspaper articles— anything brought a glimmer of hope. And then it all would come crashing down again. And they would pick up the pieces, regroup, and start over. As Steve Kraus told an ABC News reporter in 2014: "We're not quitting… We're going to keep pursuing it and pursuing it and pursuing it until someone realizes this is the right thing to do."

In addition to the Vietnam Wall issue, the *Evans* veterans have worked to place memorials in all the states where lost sailors had lived. They found family members in a mission they called Second Watch; they wanted loved ones to know their sons and husbands had not been forgotten, just as they wanted the families to help with the Vietnam Wall efforts. By 2006 the Missing Panel monument, which resembled the same granite and engraved typography as the Vietnam Wall, was erected in Mount Washington Forever Cemetery in Independence,

Missouri. It lists all seventy-four names and stands just a few feet from the grave site of Kenneth Glines, whose body was the only one recovered from the South China Sea that morning in 1969. The memorial was a solace for some veterans, but it also came with a new surge in resolve. Things were still not right. Steve Kraus, as determined and frustrated as the rest, knew what the group was facing. He and several others from the *Evans* crew had attended the unveiling of a memorial to the seventy-four crew members in a park in Long Beach, California, in 2004—a plaque in brick, surrounded by concrete, listing all seventy-four names. With the Long Beach waterfront in the background, Congressman Dana Rohrabacher knelt by the memorial, pointed to a name, and spoke passionately, with tears in his eyes, about his friend Henry Kenneth Frye, whom he remembered as a "peacenik" who had gone to Harbor Junior College with him. Steve saw opportunity and later approached the congressman. He told him about the Vietnam Wall and the exclusion. Rohrabacher indicated he would help, yet the congressman never returned his phone call. Later on, survivor Richard Burke would also send a letter and receive no response from Rohrabacher.

In 1999 Nebraska Senator Chuck Hagel spoke at the rededication of the Sage Brothers Memorial in Niobrara, Nebraska, an event attended by more than a dozen *Evans* survivors. He spoke of the sacrifice of the three brothers and a family that was shattered, acknowledging Eunice Sage in particular. The gray-haired woman, by then widowed, was revered by the town as the woman who had given all. Hagel was made aware of the issue of the seventy-four names missing on the Vietnam Wall by the very survivors seated before him.

When he was named secretary of defense in 2013 there was another glimmer of hope. But then nothing. In early 2014 Congressman Schiff met with Hagel, an unpromising meeting that led nowhere really. The past two secretaries of defense, aware of the *Evans* issue, hadn't moved on it, either.

Yet the group didn't give up; it has said it never will.

Steve Kraus, the letter writer and strategist, became the group's point man. At meetings he would provide updates to his fellow survivors and their families. When Hagel became secretary of defense in 2013, Steve had all the *Evans* veterans who had witnessed Hagel's 1999 speech in Niobrara sign affidavits proclaiming that Hagel had indicated he would assist them. That they would try to hold the politician to his word was just one strategy in the lineup of many. Among the former crew of the *Evans*, there is today an ever-present search for help in adding the seventy-four names missing from the Vietnam Wall. A signalman once and always, Steve continues to watch for signs.

On July 31, 2010, months after Congressman Schiff sent his letter to President Obama, Steve attended another memorial unveiling. This time it was for the Wall of Remembrance, a brick structure behind American Legion Post 149 in Escondido, California. The memorial is a twelve-foot, L-shaped wall, for which one can purchase a tile and have engraved on it a name, a branch of service, and dates of service—pretty much anything service related—for $100. Steve Kraus purchased a brick before the wall's construction. It was placed in the middle and reads, in all capitals,

LEST WE FORGET
LOST 74
6 3 1969
USS FRANK E EVANS

It stood out among the litany of names and dates, wars and military units. There was an air of mystery in the one word: *Lost*?

The unveiling was a busy gathering on a rather hot and sunny day, attended by a color guard, local politicians, firefighters, Eagle Scouts, police officers, and veterans. There were older gentlemen who walked with canes; there were biker types, men with beards and a lot to say. There were those in bright red caps and shirts—"killer tomatoes," the always-a-Marine sort with cropped hair and pride in their walk. There were others who wore navy-blue collared shirts and caps, a hull number and ship name embroidered on them. There were buttons and patches, the sort that told stories: where you were, what you did.

And there was a newspaper reporter there, a young woman in a sea of mostly older men, a slim notebook in one hand and a pen in the other. And she was looking at that one engraved tile, seemingly lost in the middle of the monument, yet distinguished. Steve spotted her; a journalist, it was obvious. He approached her and told her about that tile, about his ship, about Vietnam, and about the three Sage brothers among the dead, those lost at sea.

That reporter was me.

39

THE JOURNALIST

I considered myself as a history buff, but I had never heard of the USS *Frank E. Evans*. I had always thought the U.S. Navy didn't allow three brothers to serve together—surely, at least, not after the five Sullivan brothers perished at once in World War II. When I got home I started searching the Internet, and I found that Steve Kraus's story checked out. A few days later I contacted my editors and asked whether I could write an article about this local Navy veteran, about his old, sunken ship, about his seventy-four lost shipmates, and how their names had been kept off the Vietnam War Memorial in Washington, D.C..

It was going to be a brief article—newspapers were drastically thinning themselves, and space was limited. Later that summer I interviewed Steve and Donna in their home in Oceanside, and I conducted a few phone interviews with other survivors and family members of the seventy-four. I went to lunch with Pete Peters, another *Evans* survivor living in Redondo Beach, California—his voice cracking when he spoke of his fallen shipmates and that their names had been left off the memorial. Pete was one who had almost died in the collision and in some ways, as I would come to learn more and more as I went on to meet other survivors, had maybe wished he had. To help me along, Steve loaned me a large hardcover book that had been put together by USS *Frank E. Evans* Association historian Frank Jablonski. *The 278 Men of the USS Frank E. Evans* was heavy at 362 pages, a reference-style yearbook listing everybody who was on the ship on June 3, 1969, alphabetically, both the living and the dead. It contained their stories, as told by loved ones, their photographs, copies of telegrams and letters, and of those who survived, their reflections on the day that changed everything for them.

I read this book while caring for my two sons, both still in diapers. It was a breezy and warm August in California. My husband and I had just bought our boys a sandbox to play in—something to keep them from ruining the landscaping. While they played, I sat in a wicker lawn chair and read, running my finger across the pages. I took in the black-and-white images of callow eyes and baby faces, chiseled jawlines and shaved heads. Some families had submitted baby pictures for the book. I learned where these sailors lived and what their favorite songs were. One had been an inner city Philly kid—like myself, or rather, my brothers. I saw real people. I saw young men. I saw boys. Then I looked up from the heavy book in my lap to see my own.

I thought about how these boys had died so young. I thought about how terrible is war. I thought about how the cost of war far surpasses any estimation, anything numerical. I saw that theirs was a story largely left out of history.

And I realized that my article was too short.

40

THE MOTHER

The very same day the newspaper editors were preparing my article for print, I was on an airplane. My ticket was for Sioux Falls, South Dakota, but I was going to Niobrara, Nebraska, to meet the mother who had lost her three sons on the USS *Frank E. Evans*. It was a long way from California, yet I wanted to start there, with Eunice Sage.

The roads to Niobrara from Sioux Falls are long, flat, and straight, trees and pastures all around, cornfields in between. Before my trip I had spoken to Linda Vaa, Greg Sage's widow, who remarried in 1976 to a gentleman named Spencer Vaa, a Vietnam veteran who had been injured in early 1969 and whose unit had been nearly wiped out at Hamburger Hill. Linda was kind and helpful, telling me about the woman she considered a second mother. She said Eunice was a strong woman, and an honest one—brutally honest, if need be. She cussed sometimes, was the warning. "She tells it like it is," Linda explained, but added that Eunice was kind. "She's a very special woman," she continued, one who would help anybody out. She was full of love, and both tough and tender, as she always had been. "She had to be, because she held everyone together after that."

Eunice smoked cigarettes, Linda said, and it might bother me after a while. I mentioned that I used to smoke, and that no, it wouldn't bother me. Linda's words were in my mind as my little red rental car zoomed past the long stretches, the miles and miles of nothing but beautiful green, on the roads between South Dakota and Nebraska. Somewhere along the way I stopped for coffee and, on impulse, a pack of Marlboro Lights.

I arrived at Eunice's apartment by 10:00 a.m. on Saturday and politely, lightly knocked on her door. Eunice was living in a low-income apartment in a series of squat connected brick buildings with metal-framed windows on a cul-de-sac in what was called the new Niobrara. The old town had been moved in the mid-1970s; its original location was too close to the Missouri River, and flooding was fast becoming too common. The wide Main Street and checkered small-town layout was now a patchy nine-hole golf course and empty, flat lands. Razed and gone, it had been the Niobrara that Gary, Greg, and Kelly Jo Sage had grown up in. Its Main Street was memory lane for Eunice. That town was gone, replaced, higher up a hill, by a new string of buildings that resembled a government park, planned and built by the Army Corps of Engineers. A lot of folks hated it and had moved away; Niobrara's population had plummeted to just 420, almost half of what it once was.

The farmhouse was gone, too. Ernest, Eunice, and little Doug had stayed there about six more years before leaving. The old house had become too big, and too sad; nobody went upstairs, and Doug took to sleeping on the sofa. To move on, maybe they had to move out. Ernest couldn't farm anymore; he had lost his will and strength. They relocated to a smaller house with an apple orchard and a garage for Kelly Jo's motorcycle, and later on to yet smaller houses, until finally they moved to this apartment. Ernest died in 1996. I knew Eunice lived alone, and that she was eighty-seven years old. So I knocked again, a little harder. Maybe I should come back, I thought. And then I heard the click of a lock.

When Eunice opened the door, the first thing I noticed were her sky-blue eyes—they immediately breathed life into the scenery, up until that moment only a prosaically bleak wooden door on a quiet street in a town in the middle of nowhere. Her thin gray hair was cut in a pixie, her skin fair and wrinkled, and her clothing drab. She was wearing sweatpants and a sweatshirt—her pajamas, she would later say. Standing in the doorway, she was friendly yet reserved. She hadn't realized I would be coming so early, she said. The small tote bag on my shoulder felt heavier; I slumped a little. I can go away and come back later, I told her. "No," she said, "come on in."

The apartment had a simple, cozy feel. Standing in the doorway, I could see that it had one bedroom, a bathroom, a small eat-in kitchen, and an adjoining living room. The sofa was plaid, and felt rough to the touch. There was a little side chair with a blanket and a footrest. No photographs hung on the walls. And Linda was right: it smelled of cigarettes.

Eunice had been watching the news; Nebraska's Cornhuskers were playing that day, and she was waiting for the game to start. She invited me to sit down at the kitchen table and asked if I wanted coffee. I accepted, but insisted on getting it myself; I could see that she winced at every step. Her legs were swollen, she said, apologizing that she hadn't had time to clean, although there was no mess. That was the one frustrating thing about getting old, she said, your legs hurting so damn much. "I can't clean my own house," she told me, sitting across from me, looking down at the floor. Her accent was upper Midwest—Minnesotan—with long, exaggerated *o* sounds. And she said "damn" a lot.

We drank coffee out of milk-glass teacups, stained brown on the inside. It was the strongest coffee I had ever had, and Eunice drank hers pitch-black. The mood was just as concentrated, thick with silence. I saw an ashtray in the middle of the table and told her that I wouldn't mind her smoking. She didn't move, just drank her coffee.

"You're writing a book?"

I replied that I was.

And this woman who had lost three sons, a loss unfathomable to me, with two sons of my own, followed with an assessment born of old-age wisdom and the sort of experience that puts you in a league far from the rest of the world.

"Probably"—she paused, a smile peering through—"no one will read it."

I knew it wasn't personal. There had been many reporters over the years. By then I knew that a famous photographer from *Life* magazine had come for the memorial service in 1969, yet the magazine hadn't used the photographs. "They said it was too much death," Linda told me on the phone before my trip to Niobrara. Usually reporters came on anniversaries of the *Evans* disaster: ten years, twenty-five years, thirty. In 1989 one had come all the way from Philadelphia, working on a piece for the *Philadelphia Inquirer*. Ernest was still alive back then, and the mood, I later found out, was similar to this one. There was this same uncomfortable silence, and no easy place to begin. Journalist Michael Ruane left Niobrara thinking that it was a long way to come for the one sentence the trip added to the story. Other reporters had come along when the issue of Vietnam Wall exclusion came to the forefront. "Bastards" she would later call those who'd kept the names of her sons and the seventy-one others off the wall.

Sitting there in brown wedge sandals and a conservative navy blue dress—attire a woman in town would later dub as "fancy" when she saw me in a nearby café—I was just another in the long string of journalists. I kept my notebook and tape recorder in my bag and thought maybe I ought to leave. My coffee was lukewarm and Eunice remained silent. I looked at this woman and thought about how much she had been through. The tragedy violated the natural order of things: parents were not supposed to outlive their children, and certainly not losing three in one blow. A broken man, Ernest went to a state hospital for about a week sometime after the memorial service in 1969. Within a year Eunice found herself bleeding profusely into the toilet. Something painful and abdominal, she thought, and told Ernest to let her be, that she just wanted to die there in that white frame farmhouse on the hill. But there was Doug to care for. The little blond boy kept her alive, but her insides were torn. A hysterectomy, the removal of the very womb that had protected and nurtured her boys, followed.

The Sage family went to San Francisco later in 1970 to dedicate the new barracks at Naval Station Treasure Island. Eunice wept when she cut the ribbon in the foyer, her reflection in the immaculate floors of the new building showing a frail woman. Her legs were matchsticks, and her face was gaunt; she looked as if she was barely holding on. Sage Hall went on to house young Navy men for nearly two decades and would suffer the plagues of abandonment when the naval base was closed in the 1990s: graffiti, druggies, squatters, and small-time looters. The building, the entire base, the entire island, became a ghost town.

Ernest suffered a heart attack in the early 1990s and had to live in a retirement home. From that day in 1969 until the day he died, he never smiled again. Even in the couple's fiftieth wedding anniversary photo in 1996, Eunice had a smile on her face while Ernest stared into the camera, expressionless. A few months later he died. Finally, in that hospital bed a few towns away, Eunice saw him light up, as if the color was coming back in the sunlight through a window. It was a smile she hadn't seen in decades. That eighty-year-old Ernest died smiling because he was finally going to see his boys again became a part of family lore.

When Eunice was seventy-seven years old, the Veterans Administration took away her survivor benefits after discovering that she'd held a part-time job washing dishes and cooking small meals for an elderly neighbor—older than she was, at least. The $6.50-an-hour job sent her about $100 over the income eligibility guidelines for such benefits. Instead of the monthly check stemming from the untimely loss of her three sons, one day she got a letter. Because she had not reported her additional income earlier, she would receive $15 instead of $400. She took the hit in stride, telling an *Omaha World-Herald* reporter, "I don't have anything fancy to eat or nothing else . . . but I can get by." The issue was corrected within a year, long after she quit that meager-wage job. "I shouldn't have been working," she told that reporter. "I just can't hardly stand it when I don't have anything to do."

I knew some of these stories before I drove into town that day in September 2010. I didn't know where to begin; Eunice was still quiet. The noise from the television in the living room was a welcome distraction, giving me a few minutes to think. The uncomfortable silence continued as I drank the strong, cold coffee and wondered, What now? What should I say? What should I ask? I couldn't just leave—this was a different sort of interview, and I knew it right then. Eunice had been the strong one in the family, the one who held it together. I was desperate to know her, for others to know her. I wanted to write her story. So I looked down at my bag, pushed aside my tape recorder and notebooks, fumbled around for that small gold-and-white box of Marlboro Lights, and asked her if I could smoke a cigarette. "Then I will, too," she said.

Eunice had started smoking in 1969. It calmed her nerves. When the news cameras left that summer and the Sages were left with their thoughts, that's when it hit them. "The emptiest part of it all," the surviving son Doug would later confide in me. So over coffee and cigarettes, at a kitchen table in a small apartment it had taken me exactly one day to get to, I started to ask about her sons Gary, Greg, and Kelly Jo. What were they like? She told me that she didn't remember much; "it was a long time ago." Pictures? I continued, looking for a way in, a way to get Eunice to talk more. She said she had none; they'd lost a lot when the garage they used as storage flooded. "Damn water," she told me.

"Do you think of them?"

"Not much. You know, it was a long time ago," she repeated.

Oddly, she smiled a little. This woman was a sealed box, herself. I sat there and took a drag from my cigarette. True, it was an act for me, but I wanted Eunice to feel more comfortable. I hadn't smoked in years, and it was getting to me; I felt faint. Again I thought maybe I should leave. Then I thought about my boys and how profoundly motherhood had changed me. I often look at my boys and see them as part of me; they are physical parts of my body, but walking around outside it, discovering the world; living, laughing, and crying in it. They are separate creatures, but an invisible string holds me to them.

This powerful connection was beautiful and terrifying at the same time. This trip to Niobrara was my first time away from them, the farthest we had ever been from each other. I missed them, and I had cried a little the night before. I asked my husband over the phone in my hotel in South Dakota whether I was doing the right thing. "I want to be home," I said. I could hear them laughing and chattering in the background, sweet voices asking their father for milk. It was their bedtime. "Think of the moms who never got to see their kids again," he replied.

Right then, at the kitchen table in the new Niobrara—the old town having disappeared, and with it so many stories—I looked at Eunice. I was now who she had been a lifetime ago. I was a mother; she was a mother.

The words were still in the air—*Not much. You know, it was a long time ago*—as I watched her drink her coffee and smoke her cigarette.

And I didn't believe her.

So I started talking. I rambled on about growing up in a house with three brothers, how they seemed to eat all the food, about how I now felt like I was always feeding my own kids, how they always seem to be hungry and that they would someday—I knew it—be just like my brothers. They'd eat everything.

"They sure do eat a lot," Eunice interrupted, laughing. She was smiling again. "I want to show you something." She stood up, winced a little, steadied herself. I stood up and asked whether I could help her. "Oh no, I got it." She walked toward a small pantry in her kitchen, opened it up, and reached down. She pulled out a cornflower-blue Dutch oven, its enamel scorched, faded by time, chipped along the rim. "I used to cook their potatoes in this," she explained, the heavy pot shaking a little in her frail clench. "You know, I like to keep a few old things from back then."

The morning continued just like that. We were two mothers talking about raising boys. We went to lunch at the new café, which featured signs and black-and-white photographs from Green's, the old one. Across the street was the town museum where local volunteers helped preserve artifacts of farm and country life. There was an intimate tribute to the Sages on a long folding table. There were photographs, newspaper clippings, and more.

"You want to go to the cemetery next?" Eunice asked. At this point I wanted her to stay put. Her legs were hurting, and she couldn't—wouldn't—sit still at home. Before we left for the café, I offered to pick lunch up and bring it to her, and she declined. When she said she needed milk and a few other groceries, I offered to get them for her.

"I can do it," she said, so we went to the store and I carried the bag to the car. Now, back in the car, she could at least sit. I could drive, and she could talk.

The cemetery gate was scrolled, wrought iron marked 1874 and crowned with metal letters spelling out L'Eau Qui Court. This had been the town's original name in French, "the water that rushes," before it took on the name Niobrara, an Indian word meaning "running water." The government had given the Sages three headstones for the boys, and Ernest's headstone sat to the right of the three. But the place meant little to Eunice, as far as the boys were concerned; after all, it wasn't their resting place. And Greg's middle name was spelled wrong, she told me. "It doesn't matter," she told me. There was perhaps another place that mattered more.

We found ourselves driving several miles west of town,

making a left turn just after the bridge over the Niobrara River. We took a long gravel road that passed over some small hills, bending to the right, winding amidst trees and tall grasses to where the farmhouse had been.

"Right there," Eunice told me, and I slowed down at a swath of bald land, patches of grass, and some trees. It looked like a place where something had once been. With eyes as blue as the sky as she squinted in the sunlight, Eunice pointed to a long driveway and smiled as if seeing an old friend. "There, that's it."

The house had been burned to the ground decades earlier. It had become infested with bats and, at three-quarters of a century old, was condemned. But the land was there, and so were the trees and hills. The sky. Things that couldn't be taken away. This was the place where they had last been together as a family. About a month after the memorial service in Niobrara in 1969 the Navy came across some photos of the boys, taken by a Navy public affairs photographer on the *Evans* on May 24, ten days before the collision. The official white envelope arrived in the weathered white mailbox along that country road one day, as if out of nowhere. They were black and white and glossy—real. It was mail call on the ship and Kelly Jo was opening up his birthday card a few days early—on May 29 he turned 19. The photographs showed three young and tall men, in dingy dungarees, Greg's cap tilted to the side while Gary stood stoic and Kelly Jo smiled under his own brim. The photographs were a part of what was left, and this place, a beautiful spot. Eunice and I stayed there awhile and talked.

Then there was another place she wanted to show me.

At the center of the new Niobrara sits the Sage Brothers Memorial, an official historical marker made of bronze and stone, mentioned in State of Nebraska guidebooks. A plaque told the story of the *Evans* and the boys who had served on it. At its center was the photograph the boys had taken as a Mother's Day gift for Eunice. The area around the memorial was cordoned off and surrounded by benches, a semicircle crowned by tall flagpoles on which flapped the colors of Nebraska, the United States, and each branch of the armed forces. Eunice told me about the day in 1999 that they moved it to the center of town. Originally the monument had been near the high school, but there it had been lost in the tall brush and grasses. A few local veterans decided to raise funds to move it to this more prominent spot. Just before the rededication ceremony, Eunice had come here alone and wept; it was then that she felt something lifting from her shoulders. There was a release, she said. "Things changed after that."

About a dozen survivors of the shipwreck attended the ceremony in 1999. Sometime after that the members of the USS *Frank E. Evans* Association began pooling their money to pay for Eunice to attend their reunions. Over the years she became a special guest, the "mother of the association." When she arrived at the hotel for the reunion, however late, the wives of the veterans would inquire, "Can we help you, Mrs. Sage? Do you want to go to your room and rest awhile?" The answer was always the same: "I want a cigarette. I want a drink. And I want my boys."

People in Niobrara saw a change in Eunice. "When those boys started showing up," said a townsperson, "she really perked up." Survivor Bob Mason and his wife Dixie sent her a small, boxed Christmas tree every year, already decorated. Somebody—it was never known who—paid her tab at the grocery in town. The veterans called her on her birthday and sent her cards. I learned that the previous week one had "come through town and stopped along the way" to visit her. Dean Wyse lived in Arizona; it would have been a long way for him to come, to simply be passing through town on his way to somewhere else. Even an Australian sailor paid her a visit. "I lost three sons but gained a hundred," Eunice would say.

By nightfall on my first day in Niobrara, Eunice and I had gotten past the awkwardness. She told me stories about her boys, the fights they used to have, the quarrels that seemed to rattle the entire house. "Might have been okay with just two of them, but three, that made it a little hectic." She talked a lot about Doug, then forty-eight years old and about to remarry. Things were hard for Doug as a young child; it was years before he really understood that his brothers were never coming home. Whenever a newscaster mentioned Vietnam little Doug would run to the television set and wait. Cruel kids at school teased him, and he got into a lot of fights. He'd later admit that he always felt he needed to stand up for his brothers; throughout his life they'd been like ghosts, invisible but always present. Doug would grow to six foot three by his senior year in high school, and one of his high school football jerseys bore the number 74. He played in a small stadium named after his brothers, on the same grass where they had played. Doug, however, was a massive player; the *Niobrara Tribune*, in the caption accompanying a photograph of Doug knocking another player over, once called him the "monster man."

After high school Doug enlisted in the U.S. Navy. He

wanted to go where his brothers had gone, that exact spot in the South China Sea. He wanted to be with them. But he didn't stay in past boot camp. It was an honorable discharge, with various rationales attached—the Department of Defense's sole survivor policy being one of them.

In September 2010 Eunice was getting ready to attend a wedding in the fall. Doug was getting married again. "You want to see my dress?" I followed her into her small, modest bedroom, where there was a bed, a dresser, and, on the wall, four eight-by-ten pictures of her sons, their senior-year portraits. There were the three black-and-white portraits of handsome boys with side-combed hair, and then one portrait in orange-hued color off to the right, as if it had been taken in another lifetime. Doug was handsome and burly, with wispy, feathered hair.

"I have Doug's uniform here," she said, pulling out from her closet a heavy set of sailor dress blues, a fine layer of dust on the shoulders. I touched the uniform, feeling its rough wool. "Poor Doug," Eunice said, and told me of his struggles as the remaining brother. Ernest was not the same father to Doug that he had been to the other boys. He was less alive, not as funny, and he didn't take his youngest boy fishing much. Ernest was stuck on one subject; everything always came down to the boys. As Linda Vaa explained to me once, "Ernest would just sit there and cry and say, 'My boys, all my boys are gone,' and Doug would say, in an innocent assertion of a small child, 'I'm your boy. I'm here.'" Eunice told me Doug was going to the ship's annual reunion in San Diego in a week; she hoped it might help him the way the reunions had helped her. "I hope maybe Doug can get something out of it." There was tenderness in the way she spoke of Doug. A mother, I know, wants to make a child's wounds better. We want to fix things. And Doug was sad, she told me. Sad the way Ernie was. "They'd just go off and cry somewhere," she said.

Eunice put the uniform back in the closet, leaned in and pulled out a rose-colored woman's suit. Underneath she'd wear a floral button-down blouse, she told me. She didn't think she could wear any other shoes than the ones she had on now. She looked down and there was a pause, and then she looked back in the closet. She put the suit back. Leaning on the frame of the closet, she slid the hollow wood door shut, and reached over to slide open the other side. It was piled knee-high with boxes and an old sky-blue suitcase sat off to the side; on top of one box was a pair of old snow boots.

"You want to see something?" She pointed to the boxes and suitcase and took a seat on her bed, directing me to take them out of the closet. Layers of dust sat on the suitcase, as I knelt down and opened it. Papers and more spilled out. The boxes were small, yet also filled to the brim. These contents were all she had left of her three oldest sons; letters and photographs, high school memorabilia. I was hesitant but at Eunice's urging, I started pulling out musty albums, books, and loose photographs and took a seat on the floor. In that moment the three Sage brothers, to me photographs on a wall looking over us, had gone three-dimensional. There were a few letters and Kelly Jo's drawing books, some yellowing and marked by water. Kelly Jo owned a steel watchband bracelet with his name engraved on it. I held it in my hands as Eunice watched. I was taken aback by the baby pictures; at that moment, I thought of my own two sons. There was, I suddenly realized, about the same age difference between them as there had been between Gary and Greg.

The next morning I paid another visit, and there we were again, two mothers talking about life with children, a lifetime between us. It's how I got Eunice's story, by talking about my own.

"Where are your kids now?" she asked over lunch at the café in town.

"Home in California with my husband."

"You better get there soon. It's going to be a mess."

By late afternoon it was time for me to get on the road to make my flight out of Sioux Falls. Eunice had given me a few bundles of letters and photographs; I could try to have some stains removed from one of the photographs, I told her. It was a baby picture of Greg and Gary, with pudgy faces and old-fashioned white leather "walking" shoes. Of course I thought of my own boys when I saw that photograph. I still couldn't grasp how Eunice had gotten on with life after the wreck of the *Evans*.

As I was saying good-bye, I turned to her and asked, "Mrs. Sage, what was the one thing you want people to know about your sons?" It was a broad question, but one I felt inclined to ask after our two days of storytelling, laughter, and tears.

Eunice looked at me and said, "They were ordinary American boys."

Twelve days later Eunice died. A blood clot had broken loose in her pained legs and run up to her heart. And it was those surviving shipmates who helped carry her casket. Her boys.

41

THE PIECES

My research became two-pronged. I wanted to learn more about the people—the seventy-four men who died on the *Evans*, the families they left behind, and the men who survived the collision—but I also wanted to know why the survivors thought these names belonged on the Vietnam Veterans Memorial, why the names had thus far been excluded, and whether it was just. The people and the Vietnam Wall were my story.

At times it was just like that first morning in Niobrara, thinking I should leave. Often the research made me feel as if I was swimming to the bottom of the ocean, prying around a silt-covered, crushed, rusted shipwreck. These were final resting places, and sometimes I thought I should just leave things alone. At least one family member hung up on me. Some spoke curtly, telling me that they were busy and would call back, but they never did. One veteran told me he would talk to me and called back about an hour later in tears, choked-up syllables to cancel the interview. Maybe time had brought a sort of peace to these families and these men, allowing the terrible things to sink into the deepest abyss of memory. Maybe I was now bringing these back to the surface, and maybe, I worried, something would break along the way.

I didn't want to hurt anybody. But I wanted to tell this story and get it right. I told families how sorry I was. I told them that I knew they'd rather be here talking to their son, father, brother, or husband, not some journalist with a tape recorder. I almost dropped the project at least once. June 3, 1969, had been the last day of an old world for many of them, the day something had broken between the past and present. And I was bringing it all back.

In April 2012 I went to the town of Sebastopol in Northern California to meet Ron Stever, who had lost his twin Jon in the collision. Before I got there, Ron had already spread photographs and newspaper clippings out on the dining room table in his wine-country home. He had also just finished making copies of some of Jon's last letters. There were tapes, too, though he regretted to say that he had nothing to play them on. The family was from Altadena, California, and their house was so immaculate that, long after they left, it had been used in films and television shows.

Ron told me about when his parents received the telegram stating that Jon was among the lost, and about the day in the early 1980s when they found out his name would not be on the Vietnam Wall—before the memorial was finished. They wrote numerous letters to lawmakers, but the replies were not favorable; over and over again, they brought up what they saw as an unfamiliar term, *combat zone*. Yet the family had received several letters from Jon while the ship was on the gunline off Vietnam. As one of those last letters stated, they were going back—four more times, one letter revealed.

There were other things that bothered Ron in particular. Well into retirement from a career in computers, he had studied theology and become an ordained minister. He wondered often how his twin brother died; it consumed his thoughts at times. Was he killed right away? Did he suffer? Did he have time to pray? Ron was trying to put together the pieces, and so was I.

By that time I had already read all there was to read about the collision and had read, at least twice, the 611-page board of inquiry report. At the time I was indexing the massive document. I knew Jon had been a junior officer, and that his stateroom was at the front of the ship. It was the most terrible ordeal to imagine. The door had been blocked by a ladder that had come loose from the wall upon impact. I knew about the banging on this door leading to junior officer territory, and that all four of the men inside had died, trapped. At first I didn't want to say anything to Ron, but he kept talking about the collision—where Jon had slept, what he did on the ship. He spoke about a vision he had, things that he thought might have happened, and how it bothered him that he just didn't know.

I don't know when I crossed the line from objective journalist to something else, when I went from outside looking in to inside, their side. I found myself wanting to bring peace. I thought of the seventy-four nearly every day, it seemed. In my own silent way, I became a part of the Second Watch. I never joined the USS *Frank E. Evans* Association; I wanted—on paper, at least—to remain objective. Somewhere I had crossed a line and become part of the story, violating one of the first rules of Journalism 101, but where, and when? Was it when survivor Pete Peters introduced me once at a memorial service in 2013 as "one of them"? Or was it perhaps at that very moment, at Ron Stever's dining room table?

My lips trembled, and I looked away at a pretty picture on the wall. My eyes had welled up in tears, as had happened many times during these sorts of interviews. I looked at Ron sitting next to me at the dining room table and asked, "Do you really want to know?" He could see that I knew something. Ron had a kindness about him; he was the sort of person who would help anybody, and the sort of person I wanted to help.

I looked at him—I was crying—and he reached across the table for my hand. I tried forming the words. I took a deep breath, and I told him, in all likelihood, how his brother had been killed.

I drove across the fog-laden Golden Gate Bridge that night with tears in my eyes. Had I done the right thing? I received a letter about a week later from Ron. I had.

There were other instances like this. Sometime after that, I located an old United Press International photograph on the Internet auction site eBay. It was an obscure photograph that I am sure few knew was there: a picture of Linden Orpurt, standing in a small communications station deep in the belly of the *Evans*, dated 1969. Linden had big eyes and a rounded face with light brown hair and plump cheeks. In the photograph he was looking straight into the camera while standing on station, most likely where he was killed on June 3, 1969. I'd taken to searching for *Evans* photos periodically; collectors often listed old wire photographs. This one had likely been taken sometime before the collision but offered to the press as the face of an *Evans* casualty. I first phoned the Orpurt family in Chicago. I had spoken to a sister once, but I knew the family was not interested in an interview; it was just too much, and too long ago. Later on I read letters written by Mrs. Orpurt to Mrs. Botto, who had also lost her son. Mrs. Orpurt's letters were those of a broken woman, of one who had to endure the holidays and prepare for a daughter's wedding but could not move on. In one long letter written in January 1970, she confessed that she just couldn't seem to "function or participate in the activity of everyday life," she wrote. I hesitated to call the Orpurt family, but knew I just had to. The phone rang several times and then went to voicemail. My message was brief: *I am sorry to bother you again, and forgive this intrusion . . . There was a photograph of Linden on eBay . . .*

And then I called Dean Wyse in Arizona. Dean had been Linden's best friend and was supposed be on duty alongside him that night, but he'd been sent back to his rack in the aft section of the ship. It was going to be a quiet night, Wyse was told. The interior communications plot was a small compartment that sat low in the forward part of the ship; Linden didn't stand a chance. Dean Wyse had terrible nightmares about it; he saw Linden drowning, trapped in a whirlpool, screaming, dying. Dean went to his computer when

I called to tell him about the photograph, and I led him to the page on eBay. Dean was silent for a few minutes. "I have to go," he said, and hung up. Linden's sister phoned me later on, thanking me. But I couldn't get Dean out of my mind. I felt, in a word, terrible.

Some time later I saw Dean at a June 3 memorial service in Long Beach and felt uncomfortable. I felt as if I had disturbed something. When Dean approached me, I didn't know what to expect. It was a pleasant surprise when he let loose a smile and told me that after that night in front of the computer, his dreams got better. He didn't see Linden drowning anymore. He saw him alive. He saw him like he remembered him, his friend.

In 2011 I sat across from Marcus Rodriguez at a coffee shop in Fresno, California, as he relayed to me the long list of injuries he'd received when he was flung from the roof of the signal shack on the *Evans* to the steel flight deck of the *Melbourne*. In the 1960s he was tall and handsome, and had once been scouted by the Philadelphia Phillies. He now walks with a cane. His list of injuries sounded like something out of an autopsy report. Yet he was alive, sitting in front of me. Marcus had planned to attend the *Evans* reunion in 2010 as his first meeting with his old shipmates, but he'd changed his mind at the last minute.

Somewhat bitter, Marcus couldn't understand why no one had come looking for him as he lay battered and in a full body cast for months in an Air Force hospital. When he got back to his family's farm in Fresno, he was alone. A little girl from down the road came to bring him a cake, and he shooed her away. He cried when he told that story. "I owe that angel an apology." I later found out that many presumed he had been killed; a USS *Kearsarge* sailor would swear he'd heard over the public announcement system on the morning of June 3, 1969 that the injured man who had been airlifted to Vietnam had died.

Another thing bothered Marcus for years: he blamed himself. He thought he had missed something, overlooked some signal telling the *Evans* what to do. Not until some twenty years later, after his son had looked up the incident on the Internet, did Marcus get the relief he needed: "He told me, 'Dad, it wasn't your fault.'"

Marcus cried and laughed during our afternoon at the coffee shop. I brought along Frank Jablonski's book, and Marcus looked at all the names and faces. It was like going back in time, he told me, and followed with funny stories of the sorts of pranks they played on one another back then. He was sad about the friends he lost—he knew a lot of them. Yet he said he wasn't so sure the names of the seventy-four belonged on the Vietnam Wall. Looking at me squarely, he continued, "If you died in a car accident in Vietnam, should your name be there?"

Marcus was a decent man, yet a broken one. It wasn't just bones shattered that day in 1969. At first he didn't want to tell me anything, and said so just as I ordered the first of what would become four cups of coffee. But still, he had agreed to meet me, and I could tell he was all heart, telling funny stories about his shipmates. I knew as soon as he finished that last word about the Vietnam Wall question—*there*—that he had based his beliefs on a powerful misconception. As respectfully as I could, I told him that yes, if you died in an accident in Vietnam, your name would be on the wall. I'd repeated this often to doubters. I had to tell them that although Hollywood made people believe it, not everybody who died in Vietnam died in a firefight.

In reality, 25 percent of those whose names were on the Vietnam Wall died not as the direct result of combat but of other causes. Accidents were at the top of the list. The 134 sailors who died on the USS *Forrestal* in 1967 are listed on panel 24E. There were car accidents too numerous to list, and helicopter crashes. There was at least one death of natural causes: in 1966 David McLean Desilets, an officer on board the USS *Pyro* in the Gulf of Tonkin, contracted and died of meningitis. His daughter campaigned to have him included, and his name was added to the Vietnam Wall in 2012.

And not every name was of someone who died in Vietnam's combat zone, either. In one of the first major additions to the wall, the U.S. Department of Defense approved the inclusion of the names of sixty-eight men killed in a plane crash in Hong Kong in 1965—nearly a thousand miles from the combat zone—at the urging of then-President Ronald Reagan. I found out later that the wall included the name of U.S. Air Force captain Edward Brudno, who had taken his own life on American soil in 1973. After spending more than seven years as a prisoner of war, Brudno reportedly "shunned his own homecoming," news obituaries would reveal. He didn't want to celebrate—wanted no part in it, his father would tell reporters following his son's death at

33 years old. Had there been no Vietnam, the reasoning went, he would have never been shot down, never have endured the spirit-crushing life of a prisoner in an infamous North Vietnamese prison, and thus never have killed himself on June 3, 1973. His name was added in 2003.

But the *Evans* crew can employ that same rationale: if the Vietnam War had never happened, their seventy-four shipmates might still be alive. Ron would have his brother, and Eunice, her sons. And Marcus might have played baseball again.

My research took me to the National Archives in College Park, Maryland, to the Richard Nixon Presidential Library in Yorba Linda, California, and to the Naval History and Heritage Command in Washington, D.C.—more or less the last stop, since all trails led there. I was searching for connections between the *Evans* and the Vietnam War, the obvious and the more obscure. "The Navy still has all of that," an archivist in College Park told me one morning in the fall of 2011. I was told I could find it all in the U.S. Navy archives, housed in an old building at the Washington Navy Yard and, as I would soon find out, crumbling.

I made numerous unsuccessful Freedom of Information Act requests to the Naval History and Heritage Command. Long before my research trip to the Navy archives in 2012 I pleaded for more hours in which to search: the research room was only open on Mondays and Fridays and I knew I was looking for needles in a haystack. I needed uninterrupted days on end. Nothing worked to override the preset hours; e-mail requests went unanswered, as did phone calls. The archives were "relocating," I was told in 2011. (As of early 2014, it should be noted, they were still relocating.)

In person, I found the command to be disorganized. One historian urged me to check the Australian archives, claiming that they were better at organizing historical documents. I discovered that the Naval History and Heritage Command's previous director had resigned under pressure in 2012, that the archives were wasting away; an April 23, 2012, *Navy Times* article revealed that there was a "growing backlog of uncataloged holdings." When I arrived one sweltering summer day in July 2012, with only that one day to search, I found that the air conditioning wasn't working and overheard a hazardous-materials crew in the background speaking of rat droppings. Vermin were, as I understood it, literally eating naval history.

I saw other problems right away. The researchers pulled out boxes upon boxes of information, rolling them to me in carts. The file boxes, every single one of them, read VIETNAM. Southeast Asia Treaty Organization records were kept in the Vietnam archives—dozens of them. The scope wasn't the only problem; everything about the command seemed problematic. I had actually arrived at the archive a day ahead of my scheduled visit to see if I could make my request early, so I wouldn't need to spend an entire morning waiting for files; I was told no. I asked whether I needed cash for the copier, and was told I needed to pay by check. But when I arrived the next day, I was told that the copying machine had broken two days earlier. When I asked whether I could use a copier in another building, I was told I couldn't move the archives. "I have a camera on my phone," I said, to which I was told, "No phones allowed." After asking to see a supervisor, I waited an hour to talk to one. Finally I was allowed the use of my phone's camera; I had barely three hours left by then. I was, at that time, one of two researchers in the room. The other woman there worked for a defense contractor. Wishing me luck, she explained that she had been there a week earlier, examining a file; when she came to reexamine it, she was told that it was "classified."

Meanwhile, some materials listed on my request forms were still classified or had gone missing. And key items were simply not there. Mysteriously, the file that contained all the daily "ship locators"—maps that plotted the U.S. Navy ships in the South China Sea in 1969—was missing the dates May 30 to June 2. The Navy's Vietnam casualty file for May and June 1969 was also missing. By the late afternoon I was sweating. But I wasn't defeated.

Just two months before my 2012 trip to Washington, ten names were added to the Vietnam Wall. Four of these were the names of naval aircraft crewmen who died just off Cubi Point in the Philippines in May 1966, after their pilot ordered them to abandon the aircraft in severe turbulence. The four men, "the back end crew," jumped into the South China Sea; only one body was recovered. The men were left off the Vietnam Wall in 1982 because they had been lost outside the combat zone. It took the work of one former naval aviator, working with families and the surviving navigator, to produce the documents to prove that the flight's purpose was surveillance over South Vietnam—it was a military operation. In the words of the man who helped put the names on the wall, "Bureaucracy forgot but the families didn't." I was hoping for a similar outcome in my search for documents related to the *Evans* tragedy in the South China Sea. Before my trip I knew the ship had collected a Vietnam Service Medal dated "2 Jun 1969 to [blank]." Other warships there earned Vietnam Service Medals during this time period. I wanted to know how and why the *Evans*, and the others, qualified for this medal. According to the Department of Defense:

> To qualify for award of the [Vietnam Service Medal] an individual must meet one of the following qualifications:
>
> (1) Be attached to or regularly serve for 1 or more days with an organization participating in or directly supporting military operations.
>
> (2) Be attached to or regularly serve for 1 or more days aboard a Naval vessel directly supporting military operations.

It was a mystery. If the *Evans* hadn't been in the combat zone, then where was she? When I had a cartographer create a digital map for this book using coordinates provided by the U.S. Navy, the collision site was roughly 125 miles from the combat zone, 225 miles from Vietnam—off by 25 miles when compared to the U.S. Navy's original press statement that it occurred 200 miles from Vietnam. (Deck Logs from ships such as the USS *Larson* and USS *Kyes*—both present when she sunk—put her in the vicinity of the Navy's coordinates.) Other than the SEATO exercise, what else was the *Evans* doing? By then I knew, through communications among the USS

Frank E. Evans Association, lawmakers, and the Department of Defense, that the ship would have had to be returning to or leaving the combat zone for its fallen seventy-four to be included on the Vietnam Wall—a coming-and-going loophole that got the names of the sixty-eight men from the plane crash in Hong Kong on the wall in 1983. Given the Vietnam Service Medal, would that qualify the fallen *Evans* crewmen for inclusion on the Vietnam Wall? Or did I need to find a record of some sort of peripheral operation? A link that earned the *Evans* her final medal?

There were still a few research requests to make, and I knew I would have to come back. But within three months the naval archives were closed to researchers. Sequestration due to federal budget constraints was the official reason, in harsh red font on the Web site. E-mails to the new director went unanswered, and my research stalled. Some time later the history command stated on its Web site that it was limiting research requests to "official government inquiries only." This was the same Web site that, if you looked up the *Evans*'s ship history, the chronology stopped at the Korean War. (By 2014, photographs of the *Evans* were dead-linked: "Page cannot be found.") Bureaucracy had forgotten. The words, the attitude, incensed me; it wasn't fair. I couldn't wait, and neither could the survivors of the *Evans* collision. Already by 2013 two of those survivors—men I had interviewed and spent time with— had passed away.

Eventually I moved on with what I had, and what I had was enough. For now.

Although the *Evans* left U.S. Naval Base Subic Bay in late May 1969 to participate in the SEATO exercise, she was on call; she left with a full war complement of both men and ammunition. If she was needed in Vietnam that's where the Navy would send her. The SEATO exercise was secondary. I knew from letters that she was slated to go back to the gunline once the exercise was completed. Following the collision, deck logs confirmed that every ship in her destroyer squadron did indeed go back to the gunline or Yankee Station, otherwise known as the Gulf of Tonkin. I knew war planners wanted their ships in the South China Sea, close to Vietnam— memorandums all the way up the chain of command to the White House confirmed this. They wanted the world to know that they had the sea covered in America's battleship gray. I knew SEATO had much to do with Vietnam. These strings of connections meant little alone; but wound together, they created a rope. A transcript of the Senate Committee on Foreign Relations hearing of March 6, 1974, confirmed this: "As I recall, Secretary of State Dean Rusk in testimony before this committee did definitely tie the operations in Vietnam with SEATO," said Alabama Senator John Sparkman, the committee chairman. SEATO was no sideshow; it was part of the main event.

What I couldn't get past was that all the ships stationed there—not just the *Evans*—had been awarded the Vietnam Service Medal during and after the SEATO exercise. While these ships were anchored near the floating aft section of the *Evans*, their crewmen taking pictures and saying prayers, their vessels were collecting Vietnam Service Medal credit. I also discovered that other ships, during previous and subsequent SEATO exercises, had been awarded this same medal during strikingly similar maneuvers. Even a submarine had earned a Vietnam Service Medal during parts of a SEATO exercise.

But what had the *Evans* crew done to earn that one final unit medal? It was an answer worth fighting for. The evidence could be eleven hundred fathoms down in the South China Sea, or in an old building somewhere by the Potomac River, being eaten by rats, closed to researchers. This combat zone didn't mean much for the Seventh Fleet ships that cruised in and out of it weekly, I found—some intentionally cruised into the official war zone just for the slight bump in pay that its tax-free status offered. Ironically, a memorandum to President Richard Nixon dated June 3, 1969, noted that this sort of abuse was fast becoming a problem. The combat zone, created by President Johnson in 1965, was a vehicle through which the Internal Revenue Service could decide whose pay would be taxed and when. It had nothing to do with strategy, as is evidenced by the fact that Cambodia and Laos—roped into the war later on—were not originally part of this combat zone.

As I dug for information, I knew that the Vietnam Wall had become an incredible place of healing for many veterans. I knew that it had helped some out of a foxhole they swore they couldn't climb out of on their own. I knew how some of the *Evans* families had discovered that the names were not on the wall: they had saved money and cashed savings bonds for trips to Washington, D.C., to see names. And when they found no names, the pain was incredible. It didn't make sense, they said.

Frances Box, a mother in Alabama who lost her son,

Thomas Belue Box, on the *Evans* in 1969, went to Washington some two decades later to see his name etched in that granite. When I went to see her in Athens, Alabama, in 2011, Frances was living in the same house she had been in when she waddled three city blocks to the town hospital to deliver her firstborn son on a blustery day in late November 1947. She held that giant baby in her arms, and it was love, "as all I could see. Just love." It was in that same house that Tom learned to walk, weaned himself from the bottle, throwing it on the hardwood floor because the milk didn't pour out fast enough. She remembered their last family photo; it was Christmas in 1968, and towering, barrel-chested Tom, huddled in with his mother, father, and three little sisters, was bigger than the Christmas tree. Losing him had crushed her, and when she arrived home from her trip to Washington in the mid-1980s, she was brokenhearted again. "Did it mean he didn't die?" she wondered silently.

When I visited her, Frances insisted she, her daughters and I take a twenty-minute drive to the Vietnam Veterans Memorial in Ardmore, Alabama, near the Tennessee border. This wall, located off Interstate 65 and next to a massive Saturn 1B rocket left over from the space race, is dark and chevron-shaped. This memorial was built long after Frances's heartbreaking trip to Washington. Approaching her ninetieth birthday when I met her, Frances walked with a cane. She had a head of thick, curly gray hair and wore pink lipstick. In her friendly southern drawl, she told me that this wall here in Alabama with her son's name on it and a small headstone over an empty grave in the Athens City Cemetery was "all there was." That, the memories, and the terrible feeling that the country had forgotten that she had given her only son to that war.

I later found out that many smaller state, city, and school memorials to the Vietnam War dead have included the seventy-four casualties from the *Evans*. Columbia University in New York included *Evans* Ensign John Townsend Norton on its war memorial, under the heading VIETNAM CONFLICT. In Stockton, California, a Vietnam War memorial remembers Andrew Botto among its fallen. Not all memorials recognized the seventy-four at first, likely relying on the Pentagon's cropped list of casualties, but they later added them with little prodding. In 1968 Patrick M. Corcoran was a pizza-hustling, paper-delivering city kid from Philadelphia who enlisted in the Navy when the draft was breathing down his neck. By then several hundred Philly kids had already died over there, and his father, a Navy veteran, convinced him to go into the Navy. The Philadelphia Vietnam Veterans Memorial did not include Patrick's name when it was unveiled in 1987, but Tom Corcoran, a meat department manager at a local supermarket, wrote letters late at night. Within a year his son's name was added, making front-page news in Philadelphia on October 20, 1988. There was the poignant photograph of a man with a cane standing amid fallen leaves; he had just run his hands across a set of letters engraved in stone, much as one would stroke a child. "Beautiful," he said. Those who approved the addition of Patrick's name on the memorial echoed the sentiment once more: if there had been no war in Vietnam, he would not have been on that warship. That Tom never got to see his son's name on the wall in Washington was his second greatest heartbreak after losing his firstborn son. Tom died in 2006. Meanwhile, Patrick's alma mater, Father Judge Catholic High School in northeast Philadelphia, recognizes the young man as a Vietnam casualty.

In the years I spent gathering stories and documents, I knew the veterans and families were right. I knew that no matter how far the 74 were from the bulls-eye on the scope of an enemy's rifle that they did in fact die in the death march that was Vietnam, and that they had been overlooked in the carnage. I knew that some entity—the Nixon administration, the Department of Defense, the U.S. Navy—had worked to obscure the *Evans* connection to the unpopular war. They shrouded the *Evans* and her embarrassing fate for the sake of politics, sweeping seventy-four American boys out of the big story.

They put them in a footnote, eleven hundred fathoms down.

EPILOGUE

FRANCES'S DREAM

In September 2013 I flew into Norfolk, Virginia, to attend my fourth USS *Frank E. Evans* Association reunion. Arriving at the Virginia Beach Holiday Inn and Conference Center in the late afternoon, I walked into a lobby chock-full of familiar faces and well-traveled luggage; some had even come from Australia. Present were veterans from all over, their wives, and other family members—sons and daughters, brothers and sisters, and grandkids—of the seventy-four. I greeted the Chief, as I called Lawrence Reilly. Eighty-nine years old, he was sitting in a motorized scooter parked at a table at the lobby bar, his youngest son Jerry Reilly and grandson Jason Reilly having joined him. Others saw me and said hello, and asked about my children and, of course, this book. Greeting everyone in the lobby in Virginia was a banner, roughly fifteen feet wide and four feet high, of seventy-four names and photographs— the faces of the men I had come to learn so much about. The banner was tied up between two stone walls.

These reunions are jam-packed with events. There are the tour bus trips to museums, a bar crawl, catered dinners, a candlelight memorial service, and a survivors' meeting for those who made it off the ship and still struggle to understand: *Why them and not me?* The men tell their stories; with tears in their eyes, they talk of where they were when the ships collided. What happened next. Who they saw. What they saw. How they felt. Mothers, fathers, brothers, and sisters of the lost seventy-four attend this gathering, trying to understand what actually happened. Many of them were like Ron Stever that day in Sebastopol, California: they wanted to know where their son, father, or brother was when the ships hit. They wanted to know who they were with, and what they did, and how, really, fast it all happened. It's the only way they can find out; as I was told again and again, the U.S. Navy never told them anything. Attending a reunion got them answers they needed.

The reunions can be lighthearted, hilarious even. There's drinking at the bar, the telling of sea tales, and the remembrance of times past. Some of the men poke fun at each other as they did forty years ago, but instead of making fun of hairstyles or shoes, they're now making fun of the fact that many of them don't have much hair, and that they haven't seen their own feet over their protruding bellies for years. They tell jokes and buy each other drinks as if each will be their last. At a recent reunion, when a guest speaker—a Navy veteran of a more modern era—spoke too long, the Chief wheeled himself out of the ballroom and blurted, "Boy, somebody ought to write him up." Moments later another veteran, seeing a rush of people leave the ballroom to the thunder of applause, recalled the similar rush to emergency stations while a ship is in battle, followed with, "Did they just call general quarters?"

The annual gatherings are places of healing. John Stevenson, the former captain of the HMAS *Melbourne*, attended a reunion in 2000 with his wife. Survivor Jack O'Neil approached Stevenson and confessed, "I've hated you for thirty-one years." Stevenson put his arm on O'Neil's shoulder, O'Neil followed suit, and they looked at one another, their eyes moist. Stevenson urged him to say what he needed to say, to get it out. Survivors watching had a deep admiration for Stevenson for coming to the reunion and for accepting whatever they had to say to him, for helping them heal. (In late 2012 the Australian government would finally apologize to Stevenson for court martialing him and ruining his naval career in 1969; his wife Jo Stevenson, an author who documented his trials, died June 26, 2012, and had miss this absolution by a few months.)

In 2013 Australian Navy veteran Richard Cooke was seen in a long embrace with a tearful middle-aged woman wearing the black–and-white photograph of a sailor over her heart. Cooke had been battling post-traumatic stress disorder for years. Following the collision between his ship and the *Evans*, he was among those who jumped in the water to save Americans, but he hadn't saved many. It haunted him. He dealt with his survivor's guilt by attending reunions each year and by painting, putting the *Evans* back together with paint: faded battleship gray against cerulean waters, the sky blue and heavenly. That year he painted a portrait of John Norton that now hangs in Lena Norton's study.

The reunions are events at which someone who had lost a brother or father can gain another, or a hundred— like Eunice and "her boys." Ken Norton has been attending the reunions for years. He was seventeen years old when his family received the devastating blow, and he became lost in his grief; he never got over losing his eldest brother. Years later, Ken began standing in photographs alongside survivors at reunions. It was a gesture that meant something; he, too, had survived.

These reunions are where survivor Bill Thibeault, a passionate folksinger with long, gray hair, stands before a ballroom filled with survivors and sings a song he wrote for his fallen shipmates:

> *Those five-inch guns still echo in my mind*
> *Like the bell that tolled for the friends I left behind*
> *Where's the glory they deserve?*

The reunions are where guilt is put to rest, where one goes to hear "It wasn't your fault." It is where people get the answers they need. It is a place where people never forget, where it all comes back to them, and some know that that is a good thing. It is where new bonds are formed and old ones resuscitated. One morning at the 2013 reunion in Virginia Beach I sat with *Evans* veteran Joe Hoffman and his friend Tom Anthony. The two hadn't seen each other since a morning in November 1967 when Tom helped Joe carry his sea bag off the *Evans*. The trio of chairs sat on a terrace on the second floor of the main lobby, overlooking the walls where between the banner bearing the seventy-four names and faces hung. Tom, who I had come to know well, was one of the sixteen sailors who made that harrowing escape through the mess deck on June 3, 1969. He was, like many, haunted by the ordeal.

I first got to know Tom in February 2011 on a family-day cruise on the USS *Kidd,* a modern-day destroyer that had formed a "friendship alliance" with the *Evans* and her veterans. I was doing research. Tom, a balding man who wore wire-rimmed glasses over large, gentle eyes, was still dealing with old ghosts. He stood on the deck of the *Kidd* and talked with a Southern drawl about his struggles with life, and with sleep. He spoke candidly, looking out at the ocean curling and rippling, the way it does when iron slices through it. It was his first time on a cruising Navy ship since June 1969. He told me that he had been a mailman in Fort Worth, Texas and tried to live a normal life, but the *Evans* disaster had stuck with him. There were faces he couldn't forget, those last few moments when he thought he wouldn't get out of the ship, the moments before Robert Petty opened the hatch from the outside. He thought, what if we all just died there. And he thought about the ones who didn't make it. Every day.

As I talk with the veterans on the deck of a new ship, or on the phone, in their living rooms, at a table in a coffee shop, or in a hotel lobby, we almost always turn to the names not being on the Vietnam Wall. Some see it as a lost cause. Some say they will never stop trying. Some get drunk and say it pisses them the hell off. One veteran's official military service record doesn't even put him on the USS *Frank E. Evans*—ever—yet he testified at the Board of Inquiry in 1969; Andrew "Joe" Mulitch was the sailor trapped in the flooded bottom of the forward engine room on June 3, 1969. A small, agile young man then, he was the lucky one who was completely submerged, yet able to loosen one of the deck plates from the platform above and feel his way to the surface. "Somebody up there likes me," he told the admirals at the investigation when they asked why he survived. Wry yet passionate, he once said to me, "You know, Louise, it's like they just don't care."

It's how a lot of them feel. They want this resolved before they die. A few of them have already battled cancer and had been to their friends' funerals. They want the seventy-four names on the Vietnam Wall in Washington, but that seems impossible to some of them. There has been too much rejection and too much silence, long bouts of waiting and then nothing. Yet even as this book is published there are ongoing efforts; some are still optimistic. Every few months, it seems, the *Evans* issue makes a newspaper or newscast somewhere. In 2013 and 2014 the story saw its way into a half dozen news outlets. That very day of the reunion in Virginia in September 2013, a newspaper reporter with the *Virginian-Pilot* was on her way to the hotel to interview survivors and to learn about the Vietnam Wall exclusion. Many hearing about the issue for the first time are shocked that the names have not been included. Truth be told, it's hopeful and hopeless at the same time.

Joe Hoffman looked over the balcony railing in the balcony of the hotel lobby toward the large banner fastened to those stone walls. "You know," he said, "that right there might be the most important wall. That banner."

For now.

The Messier sisters attended every reunion I did. They came across the *Evans* Association in early 2010, when Joanne discovered the group on the Internet and phoned her sisters.

Within months they had purchased plane tickets to San Diego for the upcoming reunion. Steve Kraus, the man who first told me about the ship, put me in touch with Joanne beforehand, while I was still just a journalist working on a newspaper article. The day the Messier sisters arrived in San Diego for their first reunion, I met them for dessert and coffee in the Hilton restaurant overlooking San Diego Bay. White-haired Frances Cherry was the older sister, the matriarch; Anne White was a middle sister, and Joanne Messier-Derosiers was the baby. Blue-eyed, handsome Frederic "Dick" Messier had been their brother. He was twenty years old when he died.

The women told me about Dick, about how funny and sweet he was—which I later confirmed in the letters they let me borrow. He had been in the Navy for a year and a half and was supposed to get married to a girl named Joyce Cinieri when he got home. December 6, 1969 was the wedding date. In letters, he told his mother Anne Messier to get ready for the big day and that he missed home and his siblings, who took him bowling and waited on him "hand and foot, asking me if I wanted this and that" the last time he was home on leave. He called Joanne "Cook" and let Frances baby him a bit. The women told me how they had found out about the accident, and what it was like to wait to hear whether he had made it. They told me what happened when the family received the telegram. His mother had told a reporter that the two naval officers had told her to "presume he was dead but to keep on hoping." Joanne talked about Gilligan's Island and that hopefulness of the imaginative child she once was.

The women told me how much later they found out that

their brother was not on the Vietnam Wall, and how empty it made them feel. "To us he had died in Vietnam... it was like he didn't matter to anyone," Anne said. Then they came here, Frances said to me, to San Diego, and saw all these people and a banner in the lobby of the Hilton. They saw Dick's face there, lined up with the rest. They told me over dessert and coffee that they'd never imagined anyone thinking about their brother and this little ship that disappeared into the sea and then faded, as if it had never been. "We had no idea they got together like this," said Frances. "We didn't know anybody remembered him." By then, it had been forty-one years since the accident. But every memory was as fresh as yesterday, the women told me. "I can still hear his voice," Anne said.

Frances already had a husband and family of her own when Dick left for Vietnam in 1969. The last time she saw him, he was wearing a powder-blue sweater that matched his eyes; she remembers it vividly. He stood in the doorway and told Frances, "Don't worry. I'll be home for Christmas." Then he was gone. She thought about him every day, about those blue eyes and that sweater. And there was the one dream she kept having over the years. In the dream she was sitting at the back of a classroom. It was hazy—"like it is near the ocean," she told me. A sailor walked in—he was in crackerjack blues—and she knew it had to be him but couldn't see his face. He sat in the front and never turned around. She longed to see his face. Just once. But she always woke up too soon, her heart aching.

I called Frances after her first reunion to see how she was doing. It was Christmastime; the holidays were always tough on her, and I wanted to say hello. She told me at the reunion that the song "I'll Be Home for Christmas" was a painful tune, as those were Dick's last words to her. I wanted to call her and let her know that I hadn't forgotten anything she told me, and that I was thinking of her family.

But Frances seemed to be in high spirits. In breathy syllables and an endearing New England accent, she told me she was excited to hear me on the other line because she wanted to tell me about her dream. She had had another one about the sailor right after the reunion, after she had met all those wonderful people, she continued. It was the classroom again; hazy, as if near the ocean. The sailor walked in, and this time, instead of taking a seat, he walked toward her until he was right there, right where she could see him. It was her brother Dick. Blue eyes and all.

Afterword

As this book went to press in the summer of 2014 the United States House of Representatives passed an amendment in the 2015 Defense Authorization Act urging the secretary of defense—currently Chuck Hagel—to order that the 74 names of the men who perished on the *USS Frank E Evans* be added to the Vietnam Veterans Memorial in Washington, D.C. As of June 2014 that resolution, introduced by Congressman Adam Schiff, still needed the approval of the Senate and President Barack Obama.

The fight continues. It is through the steadfast efforts of the veterans, families, lawmakers, and now this book that we hope to be victorious.

In Memory of the Lost 74
of the USS *Frank E. Evans*
June 3, 1969

ALAN HERBERT ARMSTRONG
JAMES ROBERT BAKER
ANDREW JAMES BOTTO
THOMAS BELUE BOX
JAMES FRANKLIN BRADLEY
ROBERT GEORGE BRANDON
HARRIS MELVIN BROWN
WILLIAM DANIEL BROWN II
CHARLES WILLIAM CANNINGTON
CHRISTOPHER JOHN CARLSON
MICHAEL KALE CLAWSON
DANNY VICTOR CLUTE
JAMES RICHARD CMEYLA
LARRY WAYNE COOL
PATRICK MICHAEL CORCORAN
JOE EDDY CRAIG
JAMES WILBURN DAVIS
LEON LARRY DEAL
JAMES FRED DYKES III
RAYMOND JOSEPH EARLEY
STEVEN FRANK ESPINOSA

STEPHEN DONALD FAGAN
WILLIAM DONALD FIELDS
ALAN CARL FLUMMER
HENRY KENNETH FRYE
FRANCIS JOSEPH GARCIA
MELVIN HOLLMAN GARDNER
DONALD EUGENE GEARHART
PATRICK GENE GLENNON
KENNETH WAYNE GLINES
JOE LUIS GONZALES
LARRY ALLAN GRACELY
DEVERE RAY GRISSOM, JR.
STEVEN ALLEN GUYER
TERRY LEE HENDERSON
EDWARD PHILIP HESS
GARRY BRADBURY HODGSON
DENNIS RALPH JOHNSTON
JAMES WILLIAM KERR
WILLIE LEE KING
GEORGE JOSEPH LA LIBERTE
RAYMOND PATRICK LEBRUN
EUGENE FRANCIS LEHMAN
ISAAC LYONS, JR.
DOUGLAS ROY MEISTER
ANDREW MARTIN MELENDREZ
FREDERIC CONRAD MESSIER
TIMOTHY LYNN MILLER
JOHN TOWNSEND NORTON, JR.
GREGORY KOICHI OGAWA

MICHAEL ANTHONY ORLIKOWSKI
LINDEN RUSSELL ORPURT
DWIGHT SCOTT PATTEE
CRAIG ALLEN PENNELL
JEROME PICKETT
EARL FREDERICK PRESTON, JR.
LAWRENCE JOHN REILLY, JR.
VICTOR THOMAS RIKAL
GARY LOREN SAGE
GREGORY ALLAN SAGE
KELLY JO SAGE
JOHN ALAN SAUVEY
ROBERT JAMES SEARLE
GERALD WAYNE SMITH
THURSTON PERRY SMITH, JR.
JOHN RAYMOND SPRAY
JON KENNETH STEVER
THOMAS FRED TALLON
RONALD ARTHUR THIBODEAU
JON WAYNE THOMAS
JOHN THOMAS TOLAR
GARY JOSEPH VIGUE
CON WESLEY WARNOCK
HENRY DENNIS WEST III

ENDNOTES

To write this book I relied on dozens of interviews with USS *Frank E. Evans* veterans and their families, private letters, government and U.S. Navy documents collected at the National Archives, the Richard Nixon Presidential Library, the Library of Congress, the naval library at the Washington Navy Yard, and the Naval History and Heritage Command, stacks of newspaper and magazine clippings, in both microfiche and electronic form, videos, photographs, published books, unpublished materials, and more. The information occupies one filing cabinet, two bookshelves, three file boxes, an entire desk, and half of the floor in my home office in Temecula, California. As I write this, I am sitting at my dining room table.

I interviewed many people more than once and in some cases at least five times between 2010 and 2014. As an early introduction to who's who, I credit Frank Jablonski's *The 278 Men of the USS Frank E. Evans (DD 754) 3 June 1969*. Without that book and Frank's work—the compiling of stories and photographs from those who survived and families of the lost 74—I am not sure I could have written this one. I attended four USS *Frank E. Evans* Association reunions to further my research and to immerse myself in the life of former Navy men and their families.

To truly understand navy life as it was in the 1960s I relied on a number of personal interviews with those who did not serve on the USS *Frank E. Evans*, but served in the late 1960s. Various memoirs, detailed in my bibliography, and more informal sources, including Internet blog postings and online commentary by older Navy gentlemen who served in the era were tremendously helpful. I credit such groups as the engaging Tonkin Gulf Yacht Club Facebook group for giving me glimpses into their world.

For the chapters on the investigation of the collision I relied on interviews along with two main sources: the 611-page transcript of Board of Inquiry into the Collision Between the HMAS *Melbourne* and the USS *Frank E. Evans* and *In the Wake: The True Story of the Melbourne-Evans Collision, Conspiracy and Coverup* by Jo Stevenson, who wrote of the inquiry in vivid detail. Newspaper archives were also tremendously helpful in rounding out the story of what happened during those few weeks on U.S. Naval Base Subic Bay, Philippines. I also relied on the U.S. Navy's own public relations after report on the investigation, the original files and photographs provided to me by one of the men on the team, Brent Baker, a retired rear admiral and former senior public affairs advisor to Secretary of the Navy and Chief of Naval Operations (1989-1992).

I decided against traditional footnotes, as they interrupted the narrative writing style for this work. Furthermore, many sections were written based on a number of accounts and sources, with details woven together for the reader to gain a complete picture. The method is perhaps more time consuming—the manuscript started as a pile of index cards—but the finished product made it worthwhile. The following is a reader-friendly and detailed list of sources, organized by chapter. Informative asides on research have also been included.

Prologue

To write the prologue, I relied on numerous interviews with both Ann Armstrong-Dailey and Patricia Armstrong. Some material also came from e-mail exchanges, one that included the image at Patricia's wedding. The Armstrong family provided me the original of the old photograph, which unfortunately did not reproduce well enough to be printed in these pages but will be available for viewing on my Web site: www.louiseesola.com.

"It was if they were all drawn…" came from *To Heal a Nation: The Vietnam Veterans Memorial* by Jan C. Scruggs and Joel L.Swerdlow.

"Was there a point when the looming collision might have been averted?" came from *Choosing War: The Lost Chance for Peace and the Escalation of the War in Vietnam*, by Fredrik Logevall.

I relied on several materials to reconstruct Jan Scruggs' Vietnam experience and his steadfast efforts to create the memorial, included a *Washington Post Magazine* article, dated May 2012, and several books written by Scruggs, including *To Heal a Nation: The Vietnam Veterans Memorial* and *Why Vietnam Still Matters*. I also viewed the film "To Heal a Nation" (VHS 1993) to help recreate the scene and mood.

"By 3:00 a.m. Jan's…" and "I'm going to build a memorial…" came from *To Heal a Nation*.

"…black gash of shame…" was found in several newspaper articles and in *To Heal a Nation*, referencing Class of 1966 West Point graduate and Vietnam veteran Tom Carhart's testimony at a Fine Arts Commission meeting in Washington, D.C. on October 13, 1981.

"At the Binswanger…" was found in an Associated Press article dated November 13, 1982.

For information on the unveiling of the Vietnam Veterans Memorial and items left at the wall, I relied on several newspaper articles from both the

Washington Post and the *New York Times,* quoting specifically a November 10, 1982 *Times* piece by Francis X. Clines, "A Tribute to Vietnam Dead: Words, A Wall."

I also referred to a number of books, including *Carried to the Wall: American Memory and the Vietnam Veterans Memorial* by Kristin Ann Hass, *Letters on the Wall: Offerings and Remembrances from the Vietnam Veterans Memorial* by Michael Sofarelli, and *Shrapnel in the Heart: Letters and Remembrances from the Vietnam Veterans Memorial* by Laura Palmer. The letter to 'Smitty and the letter from a mother to her son are featured in Palmer's book.

Details on combat veteran Jeffery Davis's suicide came from a November 8, 2012 *USA Today* article by Chuck Raasch: "On Veterans' Day, a vet's suicide haunts those left behind."

To help add mood to the text, I used my own experiences at the Vietnam Wall—at least half a dozen visits including a newspaper assignment over Memorial Day weekend in Washington, D.C. in 2002, covering Rolling Thunder from the back of a motorcycle. I have also been to the traveling "Wall that Heals" exhibit at least four times, two of which I was on assignment to cover.

The Mess

To reconstruct the scene inside the mess deck of the *USS Frank E. Evans* at 3:15 a.m. on June 3, 1969 I relied solely on interviews with survivors, with two exceptions. What I referred to as a "crimson floor" was described by one survivor, Chris Dewey, during the official Board of Inquiry into the Collision between *HMAS Melbourne* and the *USS Frank E. Evans,* when asked about his escape route off the *Evans.*

Details about why red was selected as the color for the floor of *Sumner* Class destroyer mess decks came from Waring "Butch" Hills, who provided a tour of the USS *Laffey,* a museum ship in Charleston, South Carolina, in June 2011. My trip to study that ship, the only *Sumner* destroyer in existence today, also helped reconstruct the scene, as did a brief trip to the *USS Iowa*'s mess deck, a space only slightly similar, in 2013.

Lawrence Reilly, in an interview in 2010, recalled the last meal on board the *Evans.* Survivors who were in the bow at collision were interviewed between 2010 and 2013 and included: Del Francis, Tom Anthony, Tom Vargo, Dan Salisbury, Brian Crowson, and Jack Wimsett.

Chapter 1: Black Clouds

The introduction in this chapter was created through interviews with *Evans* survivors, including Steve Kraus, who enlisted two days before Christmas, and Joe Bob Mann, who lost a classmate in Vietnam the very week he left for U.S. Navy boot camp. Stories about boys playing war in their backyard came from interviews with Gerald Reilly in 2012 and 2013.

Details about Robert Hiltz came from interviews conducted over telephone and in his home in central California in 2011 and 2012. Further information was gleaned from letters he wrote home to his parents. Hiltz also provided me his scrapbooks and documents, including his draft notice. Slides of his first deployment in 1967-'68 on the *Evans* were also provided.

"Hiltz, you gonna watch..." was recalled by Hiltz in an interview in 2011.

"...some asshole sticking his finger in your stack of pancakes..." came from an interview with Richard Sawyer in 2012.

Details about Albert Sydney McLemore came from a telephone interview with his son, Albert McLemore Jr., in 2011 and the Class of 1949 California Maritime Academy yearbook—which described the parties he hosted at his parent's house in Vallejo, California. I also relied on other yearbooks to reconstruct life at that school in the late 1940s. Descriptions about his leadership style, often compared to the ship's previous captain Thor Hanson, came from interviews with Hiltz and Tom Bowler, who also served as a junior officer on the *Evans* from 1967 to 1969 and was interviewed in a series of phone conversations throughout 2011 and 2012.

Interviews with *Evans* survivors and newspaper and magazine clippings, including a piece in the *Los Angeles Times* in April 1969, helped provides details on the scenery in Oahu that spring.

"...California war protesters in speedboats baptized her gray hull with rotten fruit." came from a 2012 interview with Robert Suhr, who served as a junior officer on the *Evans* from 1968- '69.

"Bob, don't go. Make a stand." came from an interview with Hiltz in 2012.

"That they were all going over there," was deducted from various letters, interviews with family members, and hometown newspaper clippings—all of which planted the *Evans* in the Vietnam War. Anne White, who lost her brother Frederic Messier on the *Evans*, had told me once in 2010: "There was never a doubt he was going to Vietnam and that he died there." Surviving crewman Brian Crowson told me in 2011: "West Pac was code for Vietnam," referring to Western Pacific deployments for U.S. Navy vessels.

Special note: In the text I refer to the USS *Frank E. Evans* as a "she." According to the Naval History and Heritage Command:

"Why is a ship referred to as "she?"

It has always been customary to personify certain inanimate objects and attribute to them characteristics peculiar to living creatures. Thus, things without life are often spoken of as having a sex. Some objects are regarded as masculine. The sun, winter, and death are often personified in this way. Others are regarded as feminine, especially those things that are dear to us. The earth as mother Earth is regarded as the common maternal parent of all life. In languages that use gender for common nouns, boats, ships, and other vehicles almost invariably use a feminine form. Likewise, early seafarers spoke of their ships in the feminine gender for the close dependence they had on their ships for life and sustenance."

Chapter 2: The Chiefs

To recreate the scene in the chiefs' mess I relied on photographs from the 1967-'68 deployment provided by Robert Hiltz, and several interviews with Master Chief Lawrence Reilly, Ret., conducted between 2010 and 2013. To help paint a complete picture, I spent much time interviewing others who had served as chiefs in the Vietnam era. A Web site I found to be particularly helpful was *www.goatlocker.org.*

"Literally for one of the chiefs…" came from a 2010 interview with Lawrence Reilly, who recalled that Chief Edward Hess had often mentioned that he had been involved in two small collisions at sea. Hess would not survive his third.

"The wives and mothers had already packed…" came from several letters written home.

Details on holiday menus came from a review of archived ship menus, originals scanned and available at many ship Web sites—cigars and cigarettes were always on the menu. Robert Suhr, who served as the *Evans* supply officer, mentioned Baked Alaska more than once.

Information about Willie King came from Frank Jablonski's book *The 278 Men of the USS Frank E. Evans (DD 754) – 3 June 1969.* Naval historian John Sherwood, who wrote *Black Sailor, White Navy: Racial Unrest in the Fleet in the Vietnam War Era,* helped explain how difficult it would have been for King to make it to chief as a boatswain's mate. His words, in an e-mail exchange in 2011, were that King had to have been "exceptional." Details about Doris Miller came from the Naval History and Heritage Command: http://www.history.navy.mil/faqs/faq57-4.htm.

"We didn't have time for that junk," were Reilly's words regarding the question of racism on the *Evans.* Details about the chiefs being annoyed about having to dress up for the cameras came from several interviews, including one with survivor Jack Wimsett in 2012.

Details about the USS *Kearsarge* came from veterans from that ship and its 1969 cruise book, available at the Washington Navy Yard library.

A *United Press International* article from May 16, 1969, chronicling an episode of CBS's "60 Minutes," detailed the USS *Yorktown* incident.

Details regarding "admirals in meetings called 'leadership deficiencies' and 'a collision situation' came from a declassified document, "Seventh Fleet Fourth Quarter FY 1969 Scheduling and Planning Conference," dated February 2, 1969.

"Antiwar leaning press…" was taken from a 1999 Naval Institute Press oral history with Adm. Jerome King, Ret. in which the retired admiral criticizes the negative press coverage of the United States Navy during the Vietnam War.

"By its own admission…" came from the Naval History and Heritage Command, "Memorandum for Thomas H. Moorer," Records of the Immediate Office of the CNO.

Chapter 3: Chief Dad

I wrote this entire chapter based on interviews with Lawrence Reilly, his sons James and Gerald Reilly, and daughter Luanne Reilly.

Interviews were conducted, both formally and informally, between 2010 and 2013 over the phone and in person, in Reilly's Syracuse home, at restaurants, and at two USS *Frank E. Evans* Association reunions. The Reilly family would also answer questions over e-mail as needed. Details were also gleaned from family photographs.

Joyce Reilly provided Marion Reilly's colorful reference to the Amityville house in Long Island, New York.

Chapter 4: "Shooting on Whales"

Details for this chapter came from interviews with Lawrence Reilly, who spoke of his experience on the *Kearsarge* in August of 1964.

To recreate the scenes in the Tonkin Gulf I relied on newspaper clippings and *Truth is the First Casualty: The Gulf of Tonkin Affair—Illusion and Reality*, by Joseph C. Goulden. Also helpful was a February 2008 article in *Naval History Magazine*, "The Truth About Tonkin," by Pat Paterson.

"…a nice, fat blip" and "Turn on your lights…" came from *Truth is the First Casualty*.

Lyndon Johnson's remarks were taken from this report on Freedom of Information Act findings: http://www.pbs.org/now/politics/foia06.html. In summary: "The second attack on the *Maddox* has long been disputed, with Johnson saying to then press secretary, Bill Moyers, a year after the attacks, 'for all I know our Navy was shooting at whales out there.'"

Information and references to Johnson's famous "American boys" quote was found at University of Virginia's Miller Center as well as several books on the Vietnam War, including *Into the Quagmire: Lyndon Johnson and the Escalation of the Vietnam War* by Brian VanDemark.

Chapter 5: American Boys

I recreated the Sage farmhouse scene and upbringing through interviews with Eunice Sage, Greg's widow Linda Vaa, Doug Sage, and more than 100 letters written by the Sage brothers to their mother, father, and between Linda and Greg. Interviews took place between 2010 and 2014.

Linda Sage also provided photographs of the Sage's early life in Niobrara.

I visited Niobrara twice, spending days studying the contents of the town's museum—a hefty tribute to the farm-and-town life that so many residents lived.

The Niobrara Museum keeps files on every family and resident; volumes I found particularly helpful. I also studied *Niobrara Tribune* archives from the 1960s, kept on microfilm in the museum.

Interviews with several longtime residents helped recreate the story; sources included Michael Tichy, classmate and son of the town grocer, and Amy Barta, close friend of Gary's.

Ancestry.com was extremely helpful in pinning down dates, addresses, and family members.

For details on rural life, I relied on historical information available on the University of Nebraska's sprawling Web site on farming history.

The Village of Niobrara also created its own historical volume, a 482-page hardcover book entitled *Niobrara 1856-2006*, covering everything from the town's history to the people who continue to run it, including details on businesses, churches, and groups, including the extension club Eunice Sage was a founding member of.

For specifics on the Sage brothers, the school in Niobrara still keeps its files and I was able to glance at their growth charts (grades 5 to 12), their grades, and other records.

I also relied on photographs of the Sage farm, taken by *Life* magazine photographer Lynn Pelham, to recreate scenes in the farmhouse.

While venturing in and around Niobrara, I was able to explore a home in the neighboring town of Creighton, Nebraska that resembled the Sage 1960s farmhouse, which was torn down sometimes in the 1970s. The Nebraska towns of Valentine and Crofton were similar to Niobrara before it was relocated; spending time in those towns helped add color to this chapter and later chapters featuring the old Niobrara.

Photographs provided by Linda Vaa and Eunice Sage were tremendously helpful.

I also conducted telephone interviews with family members Gayle Pierce and Jim Johnson in 2011.

Chapter 6: All Three

Details about the early years of Lyndon Johnson's presidency were taken from archives, including the Lyndon Baines Johnson Presidential Library and University of Virginia's Miller Center, which keeps records of presidential speeches and phone conversations.

Details about Johnson's draft figures were taken from *Chance and Circumstance: The Draft, The War and the Vietnam Generation* by Lawrence M. Baskir and William A. Strauss.

A February 2011 article in *Air Force Magazine* entitled "Origins of the Total Force" also provided insight into the Vietnam War draft.

Newspaper archives and a number of books regarding the 1960s, listed in my bibliography, provided details on how Americans felt about the draft.

To provide information on brothers serving on U.S. Navy warships together, I relied on newspaper articles and archives, including information available at the USS *Arizona* Memorial in Pearl Harbor. The USS *Indianapolis* Association's Web site provided information and photos of the Koegler brothers. The Jones brothers on the *Evans* in 1967-'68 made headlines in an un-sourced newspaper clipping provided by Terry Vehr.

Details regarding Gary Sage's move to the *Evans* and subsequent order to the brown water forces came from letters between Greg Sage, Eunice Sage and Linda Vaa.

Details about Linda and Greg Sage's wedding and marriage came from their wedding book and photo albums, including a handwritten list of gifts received and a newspaper announcement. Details about the boys' last trip home in March 1969 came from interviews with Eunice Sage and Linda Vaa. Numerous photographs were also made available.

Chapter 7: Sailors

Linda Vaa provided details on the Sage's journey to the ship. Deck logs from the USS *Frank E. Evans*, available at the National Archives in College Park, Md., kept track of unauthorized absences and other disciplinary issues, including at least two courts martial just prior to the deployment. Out of respect I decided not to include details of such.

Lawrence Reilly and Robert Hiltz also provided insight into disciplinary problems just before deployment.

Information about where the Sage brothers slept came from interviews with shipmates and the *Evans* historian Frank Jablonski.

To create the scene inside the berthing compartments I relied on an official U.S. Navy video entitled "Shipboard Living Aboard Destroyers," produced in 1952.

I also read several books about destroyer men, including *A View from the Deckplates: Two Decades Aboard Destroyers During the Cold War* by George C. Chambers and two volumes of *Scurvy Dogs, Green Water, and Gunsmoke: Fifty Years in U.S. Navy Destroyers* edited by Bob Cohen and Terry Miller.

Specific stories about life in First Division on the *Evans* were hard to come by, as only six sailors survived out of the compartment. Interviews with Terry Vehr, Jack Wimsett, Tom Vargo, and Brian Crowson were of great assistance, as were letters written home by James Kerr (casualty). Richard Sawyer, who left the *Evans* before the collision, was also helpful when he met with me at the ship's 2012 reunion in Grapevine, Tex.

Chapter 8: The Incendiary

Nixon's campaign speeches are all available through a variety of sources both online and through the Richard Nixon Presidential Library in Yorba Linda, California. The account detailing his first night and morning in office, such as the song he played on the piano and his viewing of the casualty figures from Johnson's last day in office, came from *RN: The Memoirs of Richard Nixon* by Richard Nixon.

Newspaper articles and news footage from his inauguration helped create the scene in Washington, D.C. that day.

"What America didn't know..." came from Nixon Prolonged the Vietnam War for Political Gain—and Johnson Knew About It, Newly Unclassified Tape Suggest," by Colin Schultz, *Smithsonian.com*, March 18, 2013.

Details on Nixon's feelings about Eisenhower's death also came from his memoirs. Information on the relationship between the two men came form various newspaper articles and a recent book review—"Dwight Eisenhower and Richard Nixon: The Odd Couple"—in *The Economist*, dated February 2, 2013. "This togetherness bullshit..." came from that piece. The photograph of the two in March 1969 was published in several newspapers and taken by an *Associated Press* photographer.

"The schizophrenic nature" of Nixon's presidency, along with details regarding the first year, was described in the book *1969: The Year Everything Changed* by Rob Kirkpatrick. Dates and details on the completion of the Pentagon Papers came from *Secrets: A Memoir of Vietnam and the Pentagon Papers* by Daniel Ellsberg.

Details about the *Long Beach Telegram's* front page the day the *Evans* left Long Beach came from several sources, including Tom Bowler.

"Premonitions" was based on an April 2012 interview with Ron Stever and the private papers and letters of David Trupiano, who was pulled off the *Evans* just before she deployed. Trupiano sat down for an interview in May 2013.

The Jeanne Dixon connection was revealed in a number of letters, including one written by Terry Vehr to his sister in March 1969: "I forgot to tell ma and dad a big rumor..." Robert Suhr, who served as supply officer, also told the same story in an interview in 2011, stating that Jeanne Dixon had supposedly called Alleen Fisk Evans, the ship's sponsor, who phoned McLemore. Dixon's 1969 predictions came from an archived *Associated Press* column.

Reports on the Vietnam War casualty figures came from the *Associated Press* and *Stars and Stripes*.

Information on the RMS *Queen Mary* came from several newspaper articles and two chilling segments on two television documentary series: "Most Haunted" and "Deep Wreck Mysteries."

Chapter 9: The Graying Ghost

Information about the "superdestroyer" came from newspaper archives from 1945. Details about the ship and its new combat information center came from a number of books, including *Sumner-Gearing Class Destroyers: Their Design, Weapons, and Equipment* by Robert F. Sumrall and *U.S. Destroyers 1942-45: Wartime Classes* by Dave McComb and Paul Wright.

Further information regarding the *Evans* commissioning and namesake came from books produced by the *Evans* historian Frank Jablonski. The ship's history came from Jablonski and several USS *Frank E. Evans* cruisebooks, available at the Washington D.C. Navy Yard library.

"In 1966 with the Vietnam War in full swing..." was derived from the dissertation *Collision at Sea: The HMAS Melbourne-USS Frank E. Evans Collision June 3, 1969,* by Robert Tidwell, II, B.A., M.A., Texas Tech University, home of the Vietnam Archives.

"...the Navy was forcing it to leave for Vietnam unprepared..." came from a *Stars and Stripes, Associated Press* brief dated May 8, 1969, regarding the USS *Boston*, which reportedly had two boilers down and was slated to return to Vietnam regardless.

Information on Thomas Moorer's comments to congress were taken from a *Stars and Stripe* feature, entitled "The Fleet's in Trouble," dated May 18, 1969.

"Floating paint bucket" came from a letter written by James Kerr in May 1969 to his father.

Chapter 10: A Sinking Ship

McLemore's history was taken from the California Maritime Academy yearbook from 1949 and several cruisebooks from the USS *Bonhomme Richard.*

Details on the engineering crew on board the *Evans* that spring came from countless interviews, phone conversations, and time spent at four USS *Frank E. Evans* Association reunions between 2010 and 2013. Among the subjects: Jeff Covert, Duane Conely, Pete Peters, Jeffrey Hotter, Joseph Mulitch, John Gamber, and Joe Bob Mann—who told me he selected his rate from a "neat" photograph in the Bluejackets Manual. Information about snipes in general came from several books, including *Scurvy Dogs, Green Water, and Gunsmoke: Fifty Years in U.S. Navy Destroyers* edited by Bob Cohen and Terry Miller.

A *Popular Mechanics* article "Fighting Below the Water Line," August 1944, was also helpful in understanding engineering on warships.

Conely's confrontations with James Hopson and McLemore came from interviews with Conely in 2012 and 2013. Details about Hopson came from the Board of Inquiry transcript, his testimony providing his background. Information about Dennie Conely came from a DD214 military service record.

Information about the USS *Sperry*'s grounding appeared in several newspaper articles.

Numbers on who was qualified to serve as officer of the deck came from both the Board of Inquiry and Frank Jablonski. George McMichael was interviewed several times in 2011 and helped provide information about the officers on the Evans.

"...even if a rogue sailor decides to jump into the pilothouse..." came from a June 2011 interview with Tom Lettington, a U.S. Navy veteran and retired commander living in Rancho Bernardo, Calif. Lettington, who served from 1960 to 1982, helped me better understand what it was like to lead a ship during the Vietnam War.

"...the doldrums..." and information on surface warfare in the 1960s came from *Black Shoes and Blue Water: Surface Warfare in the United States Navy, 1945-1975* by Malcolm Muir, Jr.

Chapter 11: The Big Guns

Information about Ensign Gregory Ogawa coming aboard came from interviews with officers, including Tom Bowler and George McMichael. "...ship understaffed by a third..." came from Lawrence Reilly, and was confirmed by others.

Information about John McCain was found in several newspaper articles and in *Faith of my Fathers,* by John McCain, Jr. "The Wars of John McCain" by Jeffrey Goldberg, featured in the October 2008 issue of *The Atlantic* helped provide background.

"Among Abrams' concerns that spring..." was taken from *Vietnam Chronicles: The Abrams Tapes, 1968-1972,* a volume published by the Texas Tech University Press. It included the transcript of one conversation also documented in this chapter, with insights from several generals and Rear Adm. Elmo Zumwalt. Information about General Creighton W. Abrams was found in *The Fighting Pattons* by Brian M. Sobel.

"The ground troops asked for 56,000-ton battleships..." came from a February 1966 article in *Navy Magazine*: "Bring Back the Big Guns."

Headlines regarding the USS *New Jersey* were collected from the *Stars and Stripes* archives and *Saigon Daily News* archives.

"Decades later the Marine Corps calculated..." came from a *CNN.com* article dated December 6, 2005.

Headlines referenced were found in *Stars and Stripes* in 1968.

"In February of 1969 the Nixon administration was circulating a memorandum..." references a "Top Secret-Sensitive" memorandum for Col. Alexander Haig titled ""A scenario for Possible Military Actions Related to South Vietnam." It was drafted February 10, 1969 by Dean Moor and was found in the archives at the Richard Nixon Presidential Library in Yorba Linda.

"McCain, who had earned..." was found in *The Nightingale's Song* by Robert

Timberg.

"In 1966 when infantry commanders begged for the big guns of the battleships," came from the 1966 article in *Navy Magazine.*

Chapter 12: Presents for Charlie

"Early on, one prominent war proponent..." regards a well-publicized comment made by Ronald Reagan, before he was elected governor of California in 1967. (Ronald Reagan would be the first American president to see the cost in stone: the Vietnam Veterans Memorial.)

To understand naval gunfire support I relied on a number of sources, including *Life* magazine's August 6, 1965 feature "The Fleet Lashes Out."

To create the scene of the *Evans* on the gun line I relied on a number of sources, including interviews.

The information regarding Steve Espinosa's Navy Commendation Medal was found in a newspaper clipping, provided by the Clute family.

Letters written by Jon Stever and John Norton (both casualties) were particularly helpful, as were a series of audiotapes Stever sent home to his family regarding his experiences in Vietnam. Both the Stever and Norton families provided information about their sons and brothers. Ron Stever spoke of his experience at the Los Angeles County Draft Broad, providing the colorful "Alice's Restaurant" reference.

Details about the *Evans* on the gunline were also found in the ship's Family Gram, a newsletter sent home to crew members' families, and penned by Norton. A letter written by Danny Clute to his parents that month helped provide some information on the scenery and the ebb and flow of being on the gunline.

I also referred to the Seventh Fleet's daily record of "Naval Gunfire South Vietnam" activity, available through the Naval History and Heritage Command.

"By late May, the Navy reported..." came from a confidential memorandum dated 22 May 1969, found at the Naval History and Heritage Command, Vietnam Subject files.

Information about Operation Daring Rebel came from *America In Vietnam,* by Guenter Lewy and several *Stars and Stripes* articles between May 5 and May 17, 1969, including a front-page article headlined: "Allies Raid VC-Held Island."

"That damn Blackjack..." came from a May 20, 1969 *New York Times* article by *Associated Press* reporter Jay Sharbutt: " US Assault on Viet Mountain Continues, Despite Heavy Toll."

A summary of the Battle for Ap Bia and "Nixon ordered no more large-scale enemy engagements" came from *Hamburger Hill: The Brutal Battle for Dong Ap Bia, May 11-20, 1969* by Samuel Zaffiri.

Chapter 13: "Brave Men Still Die"

"Fighting continued light and scattered throughout most of the nation..." came from a *Stars and Stripes* piece dated January 3, 1969. Other *Associate Press* articles were also found in *Stars and Stripes*.

The text of Nixon's May, 14, 1969 speech is widely available: "Address to the Nation on Vietnam.," May 14, 1969. Online by Gerhard Peters and John T. Woolley, *The American Presidency Project*. http://www.presidency.ucsb.edu/ws/?pid=2047.

"...no serious response from Hanoi..." was found in newspaper archives and Nixon's memoirs.

Information regarding the future of Southeast Asia Treaty Organization was taken from articles in *Stars and Stripes* in May 1969, when SEATO delegates met in Bangkok that same month. *Associated Press* reports between May 10 and May 30 also helped provide details on that particular month in Southeast Asia and beyond.

"Nixon, in meeting with Australia's Prime Minister John Gorton..." came from a *United Press International* article dated May 8, 1969: "Nixon in Private Talks with Gorton."

Chapter 14: Relief

Details about the *Evans* hitting Subic Bay after the gunline came from at least a dozen interviews—too many to list—and detailed letters, including those by James Kerr and Jon Stever. Photographs of Olongapo City helped provide color. Books about sailors on Western Pacific Deployments helped fill in details. One such book *WestPac* by James Weldon Sadler was helpful. A subscription to the Tonkin Gulf Yacht Club's Facebook Page also helped me understand the era and what liberty entailed.

Information on pay for enlistees in 1969 is available at the Defense Finance and Accounting Service and can be accessed at http://www.dfas.mil.

Details about the U.S. Navy's role in Vietnam came from several books, including *The US Navy in the Vietnam War: An Illustrated History,* by Edward Marolda, who was also interviewed for this book. Several articles were helpful, including: "US Navy Guns Help Vietnam Ground War" in *The Baltimore Sun,* dated September 3, 1965; and "The Role of the Destroyer in Inshore Operations," by Anthony Harrigan, *Navy Magazine*, December 1965.

"...They were the chameleons of the fleet..." came from a confidential Naval Forces Vietnam (COMNAVFORV) memorandum dated February 1969 entitled "NGFS/Market Time Coordination."

"...75 percent of the enemy supplies in Vietnam..." came from a Department of the Navy, Office of Chief of Naval Operations memorandum dated August 2, 1965.

Chapter 15: Sea Spirit

Descriptions of Manila and its political makeup in the late 1960s came from a variety of sources, including photographs, books, and magazine articles.

"...told its ship commanders to use every opportunity to train..." came from "...including a few exercises over the past year..." came from the Board of Inquiry transcript.

"...admirals would find earlier in 1969 when discussing..." came from "Seventh Fleet Fourth Quarter FY 1969 Scheduling and Planning Conference" memorandum, dated February 2, 1969.

Information regarding Exercise Sea Spirit was found in Stars and Stripes articles as well as the Board of Inquiry transcript. I also referred to the declassified operations order for "Exercise Sea Spirit."

"In 1965, the ship took part in Operation Sea Horse..." was found in "Collision at Sea," by Tidwell.

"(Naval gunfire support) ships requirements have always exceeded..." came from a declassified Navy Department message to CINCPACFLT, dated March 1969.

"...the exercise was to take place in such proximity to Indochina.." came from U.S. Navy archives: the Commander in Chief Pacific, *Command History*, 1966.

Information about the *Evans* leaving Subic Bay with a full war allowance came from McLemore's testimony from the Board of Inquiry transcript. Information about the new recruits was garnered from that report and the *Evans* historian Frank Jablonski.

"These small relocations..." came from interviews with several *Evans* crewmen, including George Lare and Donald Murphy.

Information on the *Evans* summer schedule—four more visits to the gunline--came from letters, including one Jon Stever wrote to his family in May 1969 and one James Kerr wrote to his family in late May 1969. Letters written home by Frederic Messier also detailed plans for Christmas.

Details about the qualified officers of the deck on the *Evans* were found in the Board of Inquiry transcript, as were the details about communications readiness and the SEATO exercise.

"One subtle difference..." was explained in *Unsinkable Sailors: The Fall and Rise of the Last Crew of the USS Frank E. Evans* by Paul Sherbo.

"Sometime between reveille..." came from an informal interview with Joe Clark.

Chapter 16: Haunted History

Details and anecdotes about John Stevenson's naval career and expertise came from *In the Wake: The True Story of the Melbourne-Evans Collision, Conspiracy and Coverup* by Jo Stevenson and a June 7, 1969 *New York Times* piece by Robert Trumbull, "A Cool Hand at Sea: John Phillip Stevenson." I also interviewed Stevenson twice in 2011.

History of the *HMAS Melbourne*, including details of the *HMAS Voyager* incident, came from *HMAS Melbourne* by Timothy Hall.

To recreate the scene in the wardroom on the *Melbourne* I relied on the Board of Inquiry and *In the Wake*.

Information on the USS *Wasp*-USS *Hobson* collision is widely available. An April 22, 2012 *New Jersey Star-Ledger* article, "N.J. sailors who endured a naval catastrophe..." provided much information.

"...as one prominent officer on the *Evans*..." came from an interview with George McMichael, July 2011.

"McLemore took Stevenson's comments..." came from the Board of Inquiry, as did the whereabouts of the HMAS *Melbourne* Escort Handout, in which several *Evans* officers recalled seeing it at least once.

To recreate the scene of the opening ceremony for Operation Sea Spirit, including remarks in quotations, I relied solely on a *Stars and Stripes* piece dated May 28, 1969, "SEATO Very Much Alive."

Details on Soviet-Sino jamming were extracted from the Sea Spirit Operations Order, in which "enemy surveillance" was to be a peripheral part of the exercise. Plans for subsequent and previous SEATO exercises also called for enemy surveillance and jamming. After-reports on the exercise, including whether U.S. ships jammed enemy radio signal as instructed, were never made available or may not exist.

Regarding the transport of enemy supplies via sea routes, I relied on a number of sources available in the Vietnam Subject Files at the Naval History and Heritage Command, including official Naval Department memorandums: Naval Action in Vietnam, 20 February 1965 and Counter Sea Infiltration 9 August 1965.

Central Intelligence Bulletins between 1969 and 1971 reported communists moving enemy supplies into South Vietnam by sea.

"Russia and key supplier..." came from several sources, both books and online, that detailed the relationship between Hanoi and Moscow. In 1968, during Chinese-Russian border conflicts, the North Vietnamese began relying on Russia for supplies, supplies that had to go through China to get to Vietnam. See J. Llewellyn et al, "Chinese and Soviet involvement in Vietnam", Alpha History, http://alphahistory.com/vietnam/chinese-and-soviet-involvement/

Chapter 17: Ghastly

To recreate Stevenson's experience with the USS *Everett F. Larson* I relied on the Board of Inquiry transcript and *In the Wake*. I also referred to the Deck Logs for the USS *Larson* for details on the collision between the HMS *Tidereach* and HTMS *Tachin*.

The letter regarding Rear Adm. King admonishing the American escort ships was not addressed in the Board of Inquiry but revealed months later during the

Article 32 Investigation, The Record of Proceedings (dated 6-13 August 1969) made available to me by Frederick Tilton, Ronald Ramsey's attorney.

McLemore's comments regarding that letter were also addressed during the August hearings.

Rear Adm. Gordon's Crabb's testimony during the Board of Inquiry helped recreate his dealings with Commander J.J. Doak, who confirmed the meeting during his testimony.

Ronald Ramsey's statements on the *HMAS Melbourne* came from his unsworn statements, submitted to the Board of Inquiry.

"...'scared' of the carrier..." came from a 2011 interview with Jeff Covert.

"...Even the accents were difficult..." came from interviews with Covert, Tom Bowler, and George McMichael between 2011 and 2012.

"...*Evans* sonar man would write..." was revealed in *Los Angeles Times* article "Sailor's Letter Called Sea Exercise a Farce" by William J. Drummond, dated June 6, 1969. John Raymond Spray's letter was dated May 27, 1969.

"McLemore was exhausted..." was gleaned from the Oral History of Herbert Hetu (Naval Institute Press transcript) who told naval historian Paul Stillwell that McLemore had not slept in 36 hours before he retired to his sea cabin just after midnight on June 3, 1969.

Details on Sea Spirit on June 2-3 and *Evans* serving as plane guard destroyer was found in numerous testimonies during the Board of Inquiry. An October 2011 interview with Gerald Dunne revealed that he had seen the memorandum designating *Evans* as plane guard destroyer for that period.

"...mistakenly cruise..." was found in the Board of Inquiry.

Chapter 18: Darkened Ship

Details about McMichael monitoring the ship's loran and location of the *Evans* came from the Board of Inquiry transcript. Daily "Seventh Fleet Plotting Maps," available through the U.S. Naval History and Heritage Command, were only slightly helpful, as dates 29 May 1969 through 2 June 1969 are missing from the Vietnam Subject files. Deck logs for the USS *Larson* and USS *Kyes* helped complete the picture.

John Norton's last night on the *Evans* was recreated using letters home, written on other nights, his term paper dated November 1967, and interviews with Lena Norton, who recalled her son "had the sea in his eyes." Lena Norton also provided glimpse of Norton's life through his scrapbooks.

"The rumor was the new kids..." came from interviews with Lawrence Reilly, Jack Wimsett, Dan Salisbury, and Brian Crowson.

"...*what in the hell had I gotten myself into?*" was paraphrased from a letter James Kerr had written home to his father and brother.

Details about Sea Spirit on the night of June 2 and into June 3 came from the Board of Inquiry transcript. "Busy Circuits..."and details about McLemore's leadership style compared to Thor Hanson came from both Tom Bowler's testimony and an interview in 2011. Bowler, in that 2011 interview, provided details about his plebe year at the U.S. Naval Academy.

The text of John F. Kennedy's speech to midshipmen at the Naval Academy was found at the John F. Kennedy Presidential Library Web site: http://www.jfklibrary.org/Research/Research-Aids/JFK-Speeches/United-States-Naval-Academy_19630801.aspx.

Gerald Dunne provided details on "balancing" the watch teams during his testimony before the Board of Inquiry. Information on Dunne's family was found in the U.S. Naval Academy Class of 1964 yearbook.

Chapter 19: The Watch

Details on the relieving of the watch came from the Board of Inquiry transcript.

"It is among the most difficult tasks..." was taken from Thomas J. Quarton's testimony during the Article 32 investigation.

Descriptions of Ramsey were found in *In the Wake* and press photographs.

"One seaman would recall enjoying..." was a story told by Jack Wimsett in an interview in 2011, along with his quote "wasn't a pain in the..."

"Smart and capable, yet perhaps slightly egotistical and overconfident..." was deducted from interviews in 2011 with Tom Bowler, Gerald Dunne, Robert Hiltz, Robert Suhr, and Edwin Churchill.

Details about James Hopson were found in the Board of Inquiry transcript.

The story about Hopson and Hanson came from a 2011 interview with Bowler and a 1967 USS *Frank E. Evans* Family Gram.

Insights on the officers on watch that night were taken from McLemore's testimony during the Board of Inquiry.

"...be prepareds..." were Hopson's words during the Board of Inquiry.

"...was told to expect to maneuver as plane guard destroyer..." came from Ramsey's written statement and an 2011 interview with Tom Bowler.

"...consisted of mostly new guys." could be found in the Board of Inquiry. A 2011 e-mail from Robert Petty also provided details on the new men in the pilothouse that night. Robert Petty's e-mails also told of his path to the navy.

Details on who was on watch and where can be found in the Board of Inquiry and *Evans* historian Frank Jablonski's *The 278 Men of the USS Frank E. Evans (DD 754) – 3 June 1969.*

Details on the *Melbourne*'s watch team were found in the Board of Inquiry transcript and, in more concise form, in Stevenson's *In the Wake*.

Chapter 20: Juliet Seven

Details on the watch were found in the Board of Inquiry.

The editorial statement "Switching roles in the middle of a quiet night kept…" was gleaned from *Unsinkable Sailors*, written by experienced surface Navy officer Paul Sherbo.

To help explain how human error led to disaster on the *Evans*, without confusing the reader with highly technical details, I relied on the works of James Reason, the British psychologist who studied human error and created the "Swiss cheese model." His book *Human Error* was referenced for this explanation.

The entire sequence of events leading to the collision was recreated using several testimonies from the Board of Inquiry transcript, including that of James Hopson and John Stevenson. The unsworn statement submitted by Ramsey was also referred to in recreating this event. E-mails with Robert Petty also helped iron out specifics.

Chapter 21: Disaster

The description of the collision itself came from both Board of Inquiry testimonies and newspaper archives, particularly those provided in *Stars and Stripes*. CBS and ABC news segments featuring interviews with survivors also helped recreate this complicated scene.

Chapter 22: Three Minutes

The scene from the flight deck of the Melbourne was recreated using testimonies from the Board of Inquiry and interviews with Australian sailors, including Ron Baker, Richard Cooke, and Peter Varley. Several eyewitness accounts are also available in *The 278 Men of the USS Frank E. Evans*.

The scene inside the bow section of the *Evans* was reconstructed with Board of Inquiry testimonies and interviews between 2010 and 2012 with several survivors, including: Tom Anthony, Del Francis, Jack Wimsett, Brian Crowson, Dan Salisbury, and Tom Vargo. The account of Chris Dewey, another survivor, was taken from *Unsinkable Sailors* and his testimony during the Board of Inquiry.

In crafting this chapter I wanted the reader to understand the true horror and confusion of what took place in the middle of the night. For that I interviewed sleep expert Dr. Clete Kushida of Stanford University, who helped me understand trauma during sleep.

Interviews with Lawrence Reilly, Charles Wright, and George McMichael helped recreate the scene in the dark wardroom.

To recreate the scene in the forward engine room I relied on Board of Inquiry testimonies and interviews with Joe Mulitsch and Pete Peters.

For the scene on the aft deck I relied on Board of Inquiry testimonies and interviews with Chester Moneaux, Jeff Covert, Robert Hiltz, George Lare, Donald Murphy, Duane Conely, Joe Clark, Joe Bob Mann, Robert Berweger, Terry Vejr, Dean Wyse, Bill Thibeault, Richard Burke, and Jeffrey Hotter.

Chapter 23: Rescue

To recreate the scene in the water I relied on Board of Inquiry testimonies—particularly that of Albert McLemore—and interviews with Steve Kraus, Del Francis, Tom Anthony, Lawrence Reilly, and George McMichael.

The scene between McLemore and John Stevenson was found in the Board of Inquiry and newspaper articles following the collision.

Lawrence Reilly's account of finding out that his son did not survive came from interviews in 2010.

Chapter 24: Vietnam

To illustrate what happened in the Vietnam Office of Information I relied on a first draft of a press release sent to me via Freedom of Information Act Request to the Naval History and Heritage Command. It was subsequently reviewed by Brent Baker, then a public affairs officer and retired admiral, and James Reilly, also a public affairs officer who had served in that office the previous year.

The account of finding Marcus Rodriguez on the flight deck of the *Melbourne* came from statements made by Bob Winston, Royal Australian Navy, at a USS *Frank E. Evans* Association reunion in 2010. An interview with Marcus Rodriquez in March 2011 confirmed his injuries. Rodriguez also provided a statement to the Board of Inquiry from his hospital bed in Cam Ranh Bay, South Vietnam.

The analysis of the news reporting of the collision, as well as details on the organization of press pools to board the USS *Kearsarge* came from a post-action report created by the Seventh Fleet's public affairs office, Detachment Charlie (South Vietnam), and provided to me in its entirety by Brent Baker. It chronicles the public affairs team's response to the collision and includes several directives made by "higher authority."

I also relied on *The American Experience in Vietnam, A Reader*, edited by Grace Sevy to understand newsgathering during that war. Part Three, entitled "The Role of the Press," was particularly helpful.

Lastly, I used my experience as a daily newspaper reporter for over a decade, reporting on the military, to understand what likely happened to the press coverage of the Evans-Melbourne collision. Essentially, news outlets typically print what is provided in official press releases when handling breaking news.

Chapter 25: The Boys

I relied on a number of sources to recreate the scene in the Sage farmhouse that evening. Eunice's account was made available through several news sources, including the *Associated Press*, the *Niobrara Tribune*, and the *Omaha World-Herald*. Interviews with Eunice and Doug Sage helped tremendously, as did interviews with Linda Vaa.

I also viewed Walter Cronkite's CBS newscast, made available through the

Television News Archives at Vanderbilt University.

To recreate the scene between Ernest Sage and Rollie "Buck" Noyer I relied on an article in the *World-Herald*, dated June 3, 1969. Details on the police radio came from the *Niobrara Tribune* archives.

In 2011 I interview Rex Crowder, who remembered the scene at the farmhouse on the day he delivered the telegrams as a young Navy lieutenant based in Sioux City, Iowa. I also used newspaper archives and photographs to help recreate the scene on the porch outside of the farmhouse. CBS footage was also helpful.

Information about waiting for news about the Sages came from interviews with Eunice Sage, Linda Vaa, who explained the bandages on Eunice's legs, and Doug Sage. "The waiting was hell," were Eunice's words when I interviewed her in 2010. "You never think it's gonna happen to you," she followed.

Chapter 26: A Sea Like Glass

In 2011 I attended the USS *Frank E. Evans* Association reunion in Waterloo, Iowa. The event was held at the Five Sullivan Brothers Convention Center, which had on display several artifacts from the Sullivan brothers, who perished on the USS *Juneau* in 1942. Alleta Sullivan's letter written to the Navy department is also available there, as it is online: http://www.lettersofnote.com/2009/09/it-was-hard-to-give-five-sons-to-navy.html. It was then that I made the connection, as Mrs. Sullivan fulfilled her promise in February 1943.

The experience at 98 Adams Street in Waterloo, Iowa in January 1943 is documented in detail in the Epilogue of *Left to Die: The Tragedy of the USS Juneau* by Dan Kurzman. I relied on that book to recreate the scene at the Sullivan house in Waterloo, newspaper archives, and a 1944 film entitled "The Fighting Sullivans."

"Build ships faster..." was found in an Associated Press article dated February 22, 1943.

In 2011 I interviewed Dave Herndon, who was a corpsman on the USS *Tawasa* in 1969, who told of the journey to pick up the *Evans*. The *Tawasa*'s arrival on the scene at noon on June 3, 1969 is documented in the Board of Inquiry.

"But the order was changed..." came from the Seventh Fleet Charlie Detachment Charlie final report on the public affairs response to the collision.

Dave Herndon confirmed that the *Tawasa* almost lost what was left of the *Evans* twice.

"The exercise had already been cancelled..." came from the Board of Inquiry.

The ships' destinations following the exercise, collision, and rescue came from the Seventh Fleet's plotting maps for mid- to late June 1969, available through the Naval History and Heritage Command.

Information on the Vietnam Service Medals is available through queries at https://awards.navy.mil. I also found that ships participating in previous and subsequent Southeast Asia Treaty Organization exercises also received Vietnam Service Medals for parts of the operation. No explanation has ever been provided. The text for the *Evans'* final medal reads "2 Jan 1969" yet follows a medal earned during Operation Daring Rebel in May 1969. It is obviously a typographical error since the ship was in Long Beach in January 1969. Awards for the other ships are shown as "Jun."

Chapter 27: The Lost 74

"The number was fifty-seven..." was found in the earliest *Associated Press* reports on the collision. The original dateline on all articles was "Pearl Harbor," followed later on by "Manila."

"...would one day go missing..." was discovered during a July 2012 trip to the Naval History and Heritage Command. The Seventh Fleet casualty file for May-June 1969 is missing from the research box in the Vietnam Subject Files 660.

This highly descriptive chapter was written from a variety of sources including Jablonksi's *The 278 Men of the USS Frank E. Evans,* newspaper archives, interviews, letters, and telegrams.

A least a third of those killed were young fathers, with Thomas Tallon's son born a month following the collision.

Of the confirmed wedding engagements, Frederic Messier was going to marry his high school sweetheart in December, according to his sisters Frances Cherry, Joanne Messier-Derosiers, and Anne White.

The "pristine and handsome" house refers to what people in Altadena, Calif. call the "Rubio House," the childhood home of Jon Stever and the setting for a number of Hollywood films and television shows. (The current owners allowed me on the grounds in 2012.)

The fathers of Alan Armstrong and James Cmeyla were in the service in 1941 and were Pearl Harbor survivors. James Bradley's father helped build the USS *Frank E. Evans* at Bethlehem Steel on Staten Island, New York in 1944 and '45.

"The ships in the vicinity..." came from a number of recollections from sailors who served on the USS *Kearsarge,* the USS *Kyes,* and the USS *Larson.* Photos of the memorial service on the *Kearsarge* were made available.

"The Navy knew within hours..." came from the Seventh Fleet Charlie Detachment Charlie report on the public affairs response to the collision.

"...*the one who made me a mother*" is paraphrased from comments made in 2011 by Frances Box, who lost her firstborn and only son Thomas Belue Box, and in 2012 by Lena Norton, who lost her firstborn son John Norton.

Frances Box was recalled to have been washing dishes and broke one when the doorbell rang, according to her daughter Sara Box Green. Terry Lee Henderson's mother Mary Ann Buettner said in an interview in 2013 that she ran down the street when the Navy men showed up at her front door. Eunice Sage was said to have thrown her body on a truck when the news arrived. The father of James Kerr was recalled to have treasured his son's car, "all that was left of Jim," brother Fred Kerr would recall. That car was stolen later that year.

"Gilligan's Island" was referenced several times in interviews, including those with Mike Lehman, Luanne Reilly, and Sara Green.

"One wide-eyed little sister would go..." is Sara Green's story about searching for her brother Tom, revealed in an interview in 2011.

Survivor Joe Bob Mann answered the door of his home in Friona, Texas when his assuring telegram was delivered.

Survivor Chester Fontenot lived close to Lake Charles and posed with Alleen Fisk Evans for newspaper photographers.

In my research I gained access to a number of letters written to families by Mrs. Evans.

"In the mess deck on the *Kearsarge...*" came from an interview with Dudley Miller in August 2012.

Edward Melendrez provided some details on his family in an interview in 2010. Information on Robert Melendrez's death came from the Vietnam Veterans Memorial Web site.

Danny Salisbury was interviewed in 2011 and provided details about his letter, at the time reprinted in an Associated Press article.

Duane Conely recalled his father's reaction to his son surviving the *Evans* in an interview in 2012.

Chapter 28: Flags and Fathers

To recreate the scene in the Reilly home in Costa Mesa, California I relied on an article in the *Costa Mesa Daily Pilot,* dated June 4, 1969. All quotes, including "full of a sense...," "Everybody brings...," "He said don't hold out...," "I don't know how...," and "I don't think I want..." came from that article. Articles in both the *Los Angeles Times* and the *Long Beach Press Telegram*, annotated by James Reilly, also helped fill in the blanks for this chapter.

Lawrence Reilly's account of this flight home came from an interview in 2010.

In 2013 James Reilly provided an account of how he found out about the collision and that his brother had been lost. "He had been having lunch..." came from that interview.

Luanne Reilly was interviewed in 2011 and further helped recreate the scene at home in Costa Mesa. Gerald Reilly was interviewed in 2012 and 2013.

"He was the one Marion..." came from an interview with Luanne Reilly. "...Family lore..." came from an interview with Lawrence Reilly in 2010.

"In Costa Mesa, Marion..." came from an interview with Luanne Reilly in 2010.

CBS News video footage of Lawrence Reilly coming home was also instrumental, as were photos taken by the *Associated Press* and other news outlets. "Originally the press had thought..." came from a *Long Beach Press Telegram* article dated June 5, 1969.

"There was no time..." came from a CBS News report on June 5, 1969.

"...was already giving way to nightmares..." came from a 2011 interview with George Murphy, a *Kearsarge* sailor who helped Jack Wimsett when the *Evans* survivor was brought aboard the carrier. The account of the *Evans* sailors in Subic Bay and McLemore's tearful goodbye came from several interviews, including an interview with Terry Vejr in 2012, and newspaper articles. Associated Press photographs were also available.

The scene at the Long Beach Memorial was crafted using *Los Angeles Times* and *Long Beach Press Telegram* articles, along with photographs from other news outlets. Photographs of the base also helped recreate the scene. A 2011 interview with Dorothy Reilly helped provide details.

"They'd driven in silence..." came from a 2012 interview with Ron Stever.

"Sitting on Jimmy's lap..." came from a *Los Angeles Time* article dated June 6, 1969 and an account provided by Dorothy Reilly in an interview in 2011.

Mike Lehman provided his account of the memorial and his thoughts on why he joined the U.S. Navy at a USS *Frank E. Evans* Association reunion in Waterloo, Iowa in 2011. Lehman also provided photographs of himself during his early Navy career.

Chapter 29: The Inquiry

The scenes at the inquiry were crafted from a number of sources including the Seventh Fleet Detachment Charlie public affairs report, which kept records of reporters and the news of the day and more than a dozen newspaper articles. Jo Stevenson's *In the Wake* provided much of the color and description of the proceedings—everything from the weather to the mood.

Interviews with Brent Baker and Fred Tilton also helped recreate the scene.

"...virtually every man told me might be..." came from a number of interviews with survivors.

"... even a lowly officer..." came from an interview with Robert Hiltz in 2012.

"A young seaman..." came from an interview with Terry Vehr in 2012.

"The board would have..." came from the Board of Inquiry transcript.

Information on the HMAS Hobart attack is available in several news archives and *Pacific Partners: A History of Australian-American Naval Relations* by Tom Frame.

The description of the pressroom was found in Stevenson's *In the Wake*.

I also relied on photographs of George Dewey High School as well as news reels of the inquiry, including a scene in which all the board member convene for the first time.

Details on the board were found in numerous newspaper and wire articles as well as Stevenson's book. "The third Australian pick..." was gleaned from articles, including "Evans: The Politics of Poltroonery," found in *Can of Worms II* by Australian journalist Evan Whitton, and accessed at http://netk.net.au/Whitton/Worms23.asp. John Stevenson's quotes came from a 2012 interview.

Information on Rear Adm. Jerome King's career can be found his Oral History (1999) through the Naval Institute Press. In that interview King provided colorful details about his childhood and his years at Yale University.

Esquire Magazine's July 1969 issue was referenced by King in his 1999 interview. I purchased a copy on eBay in 2011.

Chapter 30: The Toll

Interviews with Lena, Robert, and Kenneth Norton between 2011 and 2013 helped recreate the scene in the Norton home in June 1969, as did the referenced article in the *New York Post,* dated June 4, 1969.

The "ambitious young reporter" was William "Woody" Woodward III, son of the infamous Ann Woodward, who killed her husband William Woodward, Jr. in 1955 in an accident-turned-scandal *Life* magazine called the "shooting of the century." The elder of two sons, William was two years out of Harvard University and working for the *New York Post* when he was sent on this assignment in Brooklyn—he was Johnny's age. Against the war in Vietnam and independently wealthy, William would eventually pay his travel costs to cover the war—his brother James had fought in the Army, lost a classmate, and became a heroin addict following his tour. Information on William Woodward was found in a May 8, 1999 obituary in the *New York Times* and Susan Braudy's 1992 book, *This Crazy Thing Called Love: The Golden World and Fatal Marriage of Ann and Billy Woodward.*

Lena Norton provided much background information on the family and her son John when I visited her apartment in Southbury, Connecticut in May 2012. I was granted access to John's scrapbooks and college papers. To help write this section I also visited the home on Narrows Avenue in Brooklyn, New York City in May 2013. Its current owners were helpful and hospitable and allowed me to see John's old bedroom.

The scene on the street in Queens was taken out of *Right Places Right Times* by Hedley Donovan, who wrote his memoirs in 1989. The description "immensely dignified black woman...is verbatim.

The scene inside the newsroom at *Life* was recreated using Hedley's book, *This was Life* by Ralph Graves, and *The Great American Magazine* by Loudoun Wainwright. *That was the Life* by Dora Jane Hamblin was also helpful. To help complete the scope, I viewed a photo essay compiled by *Time* magazine for details on the building interior: http://time.com/30406/time-life-building-60s-mad-men/.

In 2011 I interviewed Ralph Graves, whose insight was instrumental in crafting this scene. I was also provided a copy of the letter written by a *Life* secretary to the Sages that same month, telling them that the photographs by Lynn Pelham would not run in the issue. An interview with Linda Vaa helped explain further why the photo essay never ran: "Too much death."

Chapter 31: "We Share in Their Grief."

The scene in Niobrara in June 1969 and at the Sage memorial service was recreated using newspaper archives, memorial programs, and archived CBS and ABC news segments.

"...he had recently sent a girl..." came from a 2012 interview with Niobrara High School classmate Amy Barta.

Interviews with Eunice Sage, Linda Vaa, and Doug Sage helped add color to the scene. Photographs of the service helped complete the picture.

Chapter 32: The Hill

"The Pentagon caught wind that *Life* magazine..." came from the interview with Ralph Graves.

Details on Ap Bia were found in *Hamburger Hill: The Brutal Battle for Dong Ap Bia, May 11-20, 1969* and the controversy in *1969: The Year Everything Changed,* among other sources.

Headlines for late May and early June came out of the *New York Times,* the *Washington Post,* and *Stars and Stripes* archives, which I examined in chronological order to understand what Nixon was facing at that time.

I relied once again on Nixon's memoir for his sentiments and to craft the scene of the future president at Wake Island in 1944.

Letters signed by Nixon to the families of those lost on the *Evans* were made available to me.

In late June the administration, in a memorandum dated June 23, 1969 between the White House and the Department of State, issued new rules for military exercises "providing for a check against situations which could be politically embarrassing to the United States."

Details regarding Nixon's whereabouts, phone calls, and concerns are available in his daily diary, available here: http://www.nixonlibrary.gov/virtuallibrary/documents/dailydiary.php.

The thesis for this chapter came from an article by John Prados in *VVA Magazine* in January/February 2004 "A Forgotten Tragedy: Death on the Evans" and an interview with Prados in 2010. This statement from the article, "Desperate to reduce casualty reports from the Vietnam War Zone, the Nixon administration minimized any connection between the conflict and the *Frank E. Evans* loss," I found to be particularly true in my analysis of the news and timing. The entire feature is available at http://www.vva.org/archive/TheVeteran/2004_01/feature_ forgotten_tragedy.htm.

Chapter 33: A Collision of Truths

This chapter was written with information from the Board of Inquiry transcript, dozens of newspaper articles, and *In the Wake,* which provided a very descriptive view of the proceedings as well as John Stevenson's outlook during the ordeal.

An interview with Frederic Tilton and a preceding E-mail exchange in 2011 were also helpful in studying the board's proceedings and rules.

Brent Baker, in an interview in 2011, spoke of the controversy regarding Jo Stevenson's presence throughout the Board of Inquiry. Tilton confirmed this in a subsequent interview and E-mail.

Chapter 34: Key Witnesses

Sources for this chapter were the same as the previous, with the addition of King's insights, provided in his Oral History.

Chapter 35: Dereliction of Duty

To write this chapter I relied on the Board of Inquiry transcript, the Board of Inquiry's final report, newspaper articles, and *In the Wake.* A transcript of the Article 32 Investigation proceedings and newspaper archives were used to craft the latter part of the chapter.

An interview with Patricia Armstrong provided the final statement on the summer of 1969.

Chapter 36: Goodnight Saigon

Details for this chapter came from numerous interviews and letters written between family members of the lost, made available by both Lena Norton and Frances Camagna, sister of Andrew Botto.

To recreate the scene on the USS *John R. Craig,* I relied on information provided on the ship's alumni Web site: http://www.ussjohnrcraig.com/.

Information on the legacy of the *Evans* is found in *Black Shoes and Blue Water* and the training video entitled "I Relieve You Sir," now available on YouTube.

Newspaper archives helped create the mood of the end of 1969.

Chapter 37: Lest We Forget

The story of Steve Kraus came from a number of interviews with both Steve and Donna Kraus between 2010 and 2014. In November 2013 Steve and Donna took me on a "memory lane" tour of Pomona, which I found helpful in recreating the scenes in California in the 1960s.

Information about the USS *Forrestal* fire came from Gregory A. Freeman's *Sailors to the End: The Deadly Fire on the USS Forrestal and the Heroes Who Fought It* and video footage accessed on YouTube.

Chapter 38: A Fighting Crew

Information for this chapter came from Kraus and other association members, as well as the USS *Frank E. Evans* Association Web site. An interview with James Zumwalt in 2011 and his Op-Ed in the *Washington Post* in 2003 was useful. Details regarding the June 3, 2003 senate sub committee hearing came from the transcript: *Hearing before the Subcommittee o National Parks of the Committee on Energy and Natural Resources, United States Senate, 108th Congress, First Session on S. 268 and S. 296.*

It is important to note that in 2011 Congressman Dana Rohrabacher's office never adequately responded to inquiries for an interview with the congressman.

A *Long Beach Press Telegram* article dated July 11, 2004 confirmed the congressman's tears when speaking of his friend Henry Frye.

Video of Chuck Hagel speaking at the memorial in Niobrara in 1999 was made available to me, courtesy of Kathy Meier.

Chapter 39: The Journalist

Chapter is written in first-person. My article on the *Evans* ran in the *North County Times* on Sept. 13, 2010, but was available online the day prior. It can be accessed at: http://www.utsandiego.com/news/2010/Sep/12/oceanside-veteran-wages-battle-to-put-fallen/

Chapter 40: The Mother

Chapter is also written in first-person, with references to an October 8, 2000 *Omaha World-Herald* article. A brief history of Niobrara was gathered at the Niobrara Museum and in the *Niobrara Tribune* archives. I visited the area twice, once in 2010 and then again in 2012.

"...Ernest died smiling..." came from Eunice Sage in 2010.

Interviews with Linda Vaa and Doug Sage were conducted between 2010 and 2014. An e-mail exchange with Michael Ruane, now of the *Washington Post*, took place in December 2010.

"Can we help you, Mrs. Sage?..." came from Donna Kraus, in an interview in 2010.

Eunice's words, "I lost three sons but gained a hundred," came from Linda Vaa and confirmed, paraphrased, by several other townspeople and members of the USS *Frank E. Evans* Association.

Chapter 41: The Pieces

Chapter is also written in first person, with references to several interviews. I In 2011 I visited Frances Box in her home in Athens, Alabama. That same year I visited Marcus Rodriguez in Fresno, California. In 2012 and 2013 I visited Ron Stever in Sebastopol, California. I spoke with Del Francis several times between 2011 and 2013.

"...a USS *Kearsarge* sailor..." refers to a voice recording made on June 3, 1969 by Bob Pratt, who had been serving on the *Kearsarge*.

"shunned his own homecoming," came from several news obituaries on Edward Brudno, including one in the Global Jewish News Source on June 5, 1973: http://www.jta.org/1973/06/05/archive/capt-edward-brudno-pw-who-shunned-happy-homecoming-dead-at-33.

I visited the Naval History and Heritage Command in July 2012. As this book went to press the archives remained closed to researchers.

A transcript of a Senate Committee on Foreign Relations hearing on March 6, 1974 was available through Amazon.com.

References to the May 1966 loss of "the back end crew" came from a May 26, 2012 article in the *Independent Mail* of Anderson, South Carolina: http://www.independentmail.com/news/2012/may/26/to-honor-and-remember-one-mans-two-year-journey/?print=1

Information on the Vietnam Service Medals is available through queries at https://awards.navy.mil. I also found that ships participating in previous and subsequent Southeast Asia Treaty Organization exercises also received Vietnam Service Medals for parts of the operation. No explanation is available.

Information on Tom Corcoran was taken from an October 20, 1988 *Philadelphia Inquirer* article and a telephone interview with Tom Corcoran, Jr. in 2011.

Epilogue: Frances's Dream

This chapter was written based on my experiences at four USS *Frank E. Evans* Association reunions: 2010 in San Diego, California, 2011 in Waterloo, Iowa, 2012 in Grapevine, Texas, and 2013 in Virginia Beach in 2014. The USS *Frank E. Evans* Association also provided footage from the first reunion in Grapevine, Texas in 1992.

The image of Jack O'Neil and John Stevenson was found in Jablonski's book.

Photographs of Frederic Messier were made available to me, courtesy of the Messier family. I also received copies of his final letters home. Frances Cherry and I spoke several times, including the December 2010 conversation that took place a few days before Christmas.

BIBLIOGRAPHY

Archival, government, and university collections

The Bluejackets Manual. 18th Edition. United States Naval Institute, Annapolis, Maryland, 1968.

Commander in Chief Pacific, CINCPAC Command History, various volumes dated between 1960-1969.

Richard Nixon Presidential Library, Yorba Linda, California.

United States Navy Deck Logs, National Archives, College Park, Maryland.

United States Navy Judge Advocate General Corps, Washington, D.C. http://www.jag.navy.mil/library/jagman_investigations.htm

Vietnam Center and Archive, Texas Tech University, Lubbock, Texas. http://www.vietnam.ttu.edu

Vietnam Subject Files, Naval History and Heritage Command, Washington, D.C.

Accessed via third parties:

- Joint United States Navy/Royal Australian Naval Board of Inquiry transcript
- Record of Proceeding Article 32 Investigation (Ronald Ramsey, James Hopson, and Albert Sydney McLemore)
- Memorandums under subject "Public Affairs Aspects of the USS Frank E. Evans-HMAS Melbourne Collision and Combined Board of Investigation"
- USS *Frank E. Evans Cruise Book 1967-'68.*

Books and dissertations

Basker, Lawrence M. and William A. Strauss. *Chance and Circumstance: The Draft, the War, and the Vietnam Generation.* Alfred A. Knopf, New York, 1978.

Bodensteiner, Carol. Growing Up Country. Rising Sun Press, Pleasant Hill, Iowa, 2008.

Boss, Pauline. *Ambiguous Loss: Learning to Live with Unresolved Grief.* Harvard University Press, Cambridge, Massachusetts, 1999.

Brokaw, Tom. *BOOM! Voices of the Sixties.* Random House, New York, 2007.

Chambers, George C. *A View from the Deckplates: Two Decades Aboard Destroyers during the Cold War (1950-1970).* Authorhouse, 2003, 2004.

Cohen, Bob and Terry Miller. *Scurvy Dogs, Green Water and Gunsmoke: Fifty Years in U.S. Navy Destroyers, Volume One.* Oak Tree Press, Taylorville, Illinois, 2008.

Cohen, Bob and Terry Miller. *Scurvy Dogs, Green Water and Gunsmoke: Fifty Years in U.S. Navy Destroyers, Volume Two.* Oak Tree Press, Taylorville, Illinois, 2008.

Cook, Randall Gray. *Blue Water Brown Water: Stories of Life in the Navy and in Vietnam.* CreateSpace Independent Publishing Platform. 2011.

Daugherty, Leo. *The Vietnam War: Day by Day.* Lewis International, Miami, Florida, 2002.

Donovan, Hedley. *Right Places, Right Times.* Touchstone, New York, 1991.

Dupre, Judith. *Monuments: America's History in Art and Memory.* Random House, New York, 2007.

Dunn, Si. *Dark Signals: A Navy Operator in the Tonkin Gulf and South China Sea, 1964-1965.* Sagecreek Productions, Austin, 2012.

Ellsberg, Daniel. *Secrets: A Memoir of Vietnam and the Pentagon Papers.* Viking Pengion, New York, 2002.

Feldstein, Mark. *Poisoning the Press: Richard Nixon, Jack Anderson, and the Rise of Washington's Scandal Culture.* Farrar, Straus, and Giroux, New York, 2010.

Flamm, Michael W. and David Steigerwald. *Debating the 1960s.* Rowman & Littlefield, Lanham, Maryland, 2007.

Frame, Tom. *No Pleasure Cruise: The Story of the Royal Australian Navy.* Allen & Unwin, Crows Nest, Australia, 2004.

Frame, Tom. *Pacific Partners: The History of Australian-American Naval Relations.* Hodder & Stoughton, Sydney, 1992.

Freeman, Gregory A. *Sailors to the End: The Deadly Fire on the USS Forrestal and the Heroes Who Fought It.* William Morrow, New York, 2002.

Freeman, Gregory A. *Troubled Water: Race, Mutiny, and Bravery on the USS Kittyhawk.* Palgrave Macmillan, New York, 2009.

Goulden, Joseph C. *Truth is the First Casualty.* Rand McNally, New York, 1969.

Graves, Ralph. *The Life I Led.* Tiasquam Press, New York, 2010.

Halberstam, David. *The Best and the Brightest.* Random House, New York, 1969.

Hall, Timothy. *HMAS Melbourne.* Geoge Allen & Unwin, Sydney, 1982.

Hamblin, Dora Jane. *That Was the Life: The Upstairs Downstairs Behind-the-doors Story of America's Favorite Magazine.* W.W. Norton & Company, New York, 1977.

Hass, Kristin Ann. *Carried to the Wall: American Memory and the Vietnam Veterans Memorial.* University of California Press, Berkeley, California, 1998.

Jablonski, Frank. *Articles About Frank E. Evans –Melbourne Collision.* Lulu Press.

Jablonski, Frank. *USS Frank E. Evans (DD 754) 1944-1969, Volumes I and II.* Lulu Press.

Jablonski, Frank. *The 278 Men of the USS Frank E. Evans (DD 754) 3 June 1969.* 2nd Edition. Lulu Press.

Jernigan, E.J. *Tin Can Man.* Naval Institute Press. Annapolis, Maryland, 1993.

Johnson, Stephen. *Silent Steel: The Mysterious Death of the Nuclear Attack Sub USS Scorpion.* John Wiley & Sons, Hoboken, New Jersey, 2006.

Kelley, Michael P. *Where We Were in Vietnam.* Hellgate Press, Central Point, Oregon, 2002.

Kirkpatrick , Rob. *1969: The Year Everything Changed.* Skyhorse Publishing, New York, 2011.

Kovic, Ron. *Born on the Fourth of July.* Akashic Books, New York,1976.

Kubler-Ross, Elisabeth. *On Death and Dying.* Scribner, New York, 1969.

Lewy, Guenter. *America in Vietnam.* Oxford University Press, New York, 1978.

Logevall, Fredrik. *Choosing War.* University of California Press, Berkeley, California, 1999.

Logevall, Fredrik. *Embers of War.* Random House, New York, 2012.

Maddow, Rachel. *Drift: The Unmooring of American Military Power.* Broadway Books, New York, 2013.

Marolda, Edward J. *The U.S. Navy in the Vietnam War: An Illustrated History.* Brasseys, Washington, D.C., 2002.

McCain, John and Mark Salter. *Faith of My Fathers.* Random House, New York, 1999.

McComb, David. *U.S. Destroyers 1942-45.* Osprey Publishing, Oxford, UK, 2010.

McMaster, H.R. *Dereliction of Duty: Johnson, McNamara, the Joints Chief of Staff, and the Lies that Led to Vietnam.* Harper Perennial, New York, 1998.

Muir, Malcolm. *Black Shoes and Blue Water, Surface Warfare in the United States Navy, 1945-1975.* Naval History Center, Washington, D.C., 1996.

Nixon, Richard. *The Memoirs of Richard Nixon.* Touchstone, New York, 1978.

Obst, David. *Too Good to be Forgotten: Changing America in the '60s and '70s.* John Wiley & Sons, New York, 1998.

Olson, James S. *Historical Dictionary of the 1960s.* Greenwood Press, Westport, Connecticut, 1999.

Olson, Michael Keith. *Tales from a Tin Can: The USS Dale from Pearl Harbor to Tokyo Bay.* Zenith Press, Minneapolis, Minnesota, 2007.

Palmer, Laura. *Shrapnel in the Heart: Letters and Remembrances from the Vietnam Veterans Memorial.* Random House, New York, 1987.

Polmar, Norman. *The Death of the USS Thresher.* Lyons Press, Guilford, Connecticut, 2004.

Poyer, David. *The Circle.* St. Martin's Press, New York, 1992.

Sadler, James Weldon. *WestPac.* iUniverse, New York, 2006.

Schoenl, William. *New Perspectives on the Vietnam War.* University Press of America, Lanham, Maryland, 2002.

Scruggs, Jan and Joel L. Swerdlow. *To Heal a Nation.* Harper & Row, New York, 1985.

Scruggs, Jan. *Writings on the Wall: Reflections on the Vietnam Veterans Memorial.* The Vietnam Veterans Memorial Fund, Washington, D.C., 1994.

Scruggs, Jan. *Why Vietnam Still Matters.* The Vietnam Veterans Memorial Fund, Washington, D.C., 1996.

Sevy, Grace. *The American Experience in Vietnam: A Reader.* University of Oklahoma Press, Norman, Oklahoma, 1989.

Sheehan, Neil. *A Bright Shining Lie: John Paul Vann and America in Vietnam.* Vintage, New York, 1989.

Sheppard, Don. *Bluewater Sailor.* Presidio Press, Novato, California, 1996.

Sherbo, Paul. *Unsinkable Sailors: The fall and rise of the last crew of the USS Frank E. Evans.* Patriot Media Publishing, Niceville, Florida, 2007.

Sherwood, John Darrell. *Black Sailor, White Navy.* New York University Press, New York, 2007.

Sobel, Brian M. *The Fighting Pattons.* Praeger, Westport, Connecticut, 1997.

Sofarelli, Micheal. *Letters on the Wall.* HarperCollins, New York, 2006.

Stevenson, Jo. *In The Wake.* Hale & Ironmonger, Alexandria, New South Wales, 1999.

Stevenson, Jo. *No Case to Answer.* Alpha Books, Sydney, 1971.

Stillwell, Paul. *The Reminiscences of Captain Herbert E. Hetu.* Naval Institute Press, Annapolis, Maryland, 2003.

Stillwell, Paul. *The Reminiscences of Vice Admiral Jerome H. King, Jr.* Naval Institute Press, Annapolis, Maryland, 1999.

Tennant, Jean. *Knee High by the Fourth of July: More Stories of Growing up in and Around Small Towns in the Midwest.* Shapato Publishing, Everly, Iowa, 2009.

Tidwell, Robert. *Collision at Sea: The HMAS Melbourne-USS Frank E. Evans Collision, June 3, 1969, a Dissertation.* Texas Tech University, Lubbock, Texas, 2009.

Timberg, Robert. *The Nightingale's Song.* Touchstone, New York, 1996.

Unger, Irwin and Debi Unger. *The Times Were a'Changin: The Sixties Reader.* Three Rivers Press, New York, 1998.

VanDemark, Brian. *Into the Quagmire: Lyndon Johnson and the Escalation of the Vietnam War.* Oxford Universty Press, Oxford, 1991.

Wainwright, Loudon. *The Great American Magazine.* Alfred A. Knopf, New York, 1986.

Wetterhahn, Ralph. *The Last Battle: The Mayaguez Incident and the End of the Vietnam War.* Carroll & Graf, New York, 2001.

Windchy, Eugene G. *Tonkin Gulf.* Doubleday, New York, 1971.

Zhai, Qiang. *China & The Vietnam Wars, 1950-1975.* University of North Carolina Press, Chapel Hill, North Carolina, 2000.

Zumwalt, Elmo and Elmo Zumwalt, Jr. *My Father, My Son.* Macmillan, New York, 1986.

Zumwalt, Elmo R. *On Watch.* Quadrangle, New York, 1976.

Transcripts

Hearing Before the Subcommittee on National Parks of the Committees on Energy and Natural Resources, United States Senate, 108th Congress. June 3, 2003. Accessed at: https://bulk.resource.org/gpo.gov/hearings/108s/88261.txt

U.S. Commitment to SEATO: Hearing before the Committee on Foreign Relations,

United States Senate, Ninety-Third Congress, second session, on S. Res. 174, March 6. 1974. University of Michigan Library.

Videos

ABC and CBS News Archives, 1969, Vanderbilt University, Nashville, Tennessee.

Battle 360: The Bloody Battle of Guadalcanal. History Channel.

Destroyers in Vietnam. Traditions Military Videos.

The Fog of War. (DVD 2004)

I Relieve You, Sir. U.S. Navy. (Available on YouTube.com)

Letters to the Wall: A Documentary on the Vietnam Wall Experience. (VHS 2002)

Remembering Vietnam: The Wall at 25. Smithsonian Channel.

Shipboard Living Conditions Aboard Destroyers. Traditions Military Videos.

Standing Watch. Traditions Military Videos.

To Heal a Nation (VHS 1993)

The True Story of the Fighting Sullivans. History Channel video.

Victory at Sea. Mill Creek Entertainment.

Vietnam: Americas Conflict. Mill Creek Entertainment.

Author's Note: Videos accessed on YouTube provided imagery of the U.S. Navy's bootcamp in the 1960s.

ACKNOWLEDGMENTS

First, I owe immeasurable gratitude to the veterans and survivors of the USS *Frank E. Evans* and the families of the lost 74. This group embraced me from the very beginning and made this book possible. I cried and laughed with you all and I am forever grateful for your trust. There were 199 survivors from the collision and nearly 100 cassette tapes stacked on my desk at home—I could not have done this without all of you. Many of you went beyond the first interview and made yourselves available to me whenever I needed questions answered, even when the subject matter was deeply emotional, or the questions seemed repetitive. To the families, I will never forget your loss. I am so sorry you all had to endure this tragedy.

The USS *Frank E. Evans* Association was tremendously helpful. Special thanks to the leaders of the organization. I wish to especially thank ship historian Frank Jablonski: first, for putting together his own books on the ship's history and her men; and second, for providing me information and photographs whenever needed—this went on for years! Jablonski also reviewed a draft of this book. I cannot thank him enough. Endless gratitude goes to Steve and Donna Kraus, who always welcomed me into their home and were always available to answer questions; the couple in 2013 took me on an unforgettable trip down memory lane to Pomona to help retell their story. Steve, thank you for walking up to me on July 31, 2010 and for always being there. Knowing this group changed my life.

The association's communications director John Coffey, in addition to making me laugh on a regular basis, met me in Charleston, South Carolina to see the USS *Laffey* in 2012 and encouraged me from day one. Survivor Joe Clark also helped show me parts of the ship, the only *Sumner* Class destroyer in existence today. It was a trip that was, perhaps, difficult for him. Sylvia Campbell was also helpful in providing information about former crewmen, including a bound copy of the ship's final cruise book from 1967-'68. To survivor Pete Peters, thank you for always making me feel welcomed at the June 3 memorial service in Long Beach, California. As long as you have them, I'll be there.

Special thanks also goes to Duane "Butterball" Conely, an unforgettable survivor who not only brought my children cupcakes on a regular basis—we're practically neighbors—but shared with me stories with such candor that added color to these very pages. I am grateful for having befriended survivor Del Francis, who also helped me understand not only what he and others had been through, but also naval communications and other facets of work on a destroyer that I couldn't quite get just by reading about it. Thank you, Del, for answering all my "stupid questions." Special thanks to the other survivors who went above and beyond in helping me piece this story together: Terry Vehr, Richard Burke, Jack Wimsett, Joe Mulitch, Bill Thibeault, David Trupiano, Dean Wyse, Bob Mason, Robert Petty, Chester Moneaux, Joe Clark, John Gamber, Joe Bob Mann, Bob Hiltz, Tom Anthony, and Australian survivors Richard Cooke, Peter Varley, and Ron Baker. Thank you all for inviting me to listen to your stories at your survivor meetings. And over those hours-long phone conversations, you never cried alone. Survivor Tom Bowler, who sadly did not live to see this project completed, helped fill in a lot of the blanks on the ship and the leadership, and encouraged me time and again when he told me I was doing "God's work."

I owe much gratitude to the families of the lost 74 and the mothers in particular. Over my four years of researching this book

I was able to meet five of the women who raised some of these men who perished. I am forever grateful for their stories and trust. I will never forget you all. I love you and I learn from you. Marion Reilly, unfortunately, did not live to see this book. To the siblings, children, and other family members of the lost 74, thank you for embracing this project and helping me along the way. Your faith in me kept me going.

I don't know where to begin in thanking the Reilly family for all they have done to help me write their story. I first met retired Master Chief Lawrence Reilly in his home in Syracuse in late 2010. Instantly, I was grateful for the Chief's honesty, wealth of knowledge, funny personality, and strong character—that he never blamed anyone and acknowledged the collision as a terrible accident stuck with me from that day on. I am blessed to have been able to get to know him and his family. The children, James, Gerald, and Luanne Reilly were of great assistance in providing information and stories about growing up with Larry their brother, and dealing with his death later on. I never did get to meet Suzie but am sure I will someday.

The Sage family was also a tremendous help. Doug Sage, I cannot thank you enough for helping me piece together your family's life on the farm and the aftermath of such a terrible loss. (I will always be there to talk and, yes, I'll be your sister.) When I left Eunice that day in 2010, twelve days before she died, I told her I would do my best to tell her family's story. I hope that I have fulfilled that promise. I want to especially thank Linda Vaa, Greg Sage's young widow. From the beginning Linda provided me with everything I needed, even entrusting me with a huge box of letters and memorabilia of her life with Greg. Special thanks also goes to Spencer Vaa, Linda's husband who drove us chatty women around Niobrara in 2012. Spencer, I do believe you are Linda's knight in shining armor.

To help write about living and working on an old navy ship I visited three museum ships: the USS *Laffey*, the USS *Midway*, and the USS *Iowa*. Much thanks goes to the organizations that maintain these precious relics. (The maintenance man on the *Laffey*, whose name I couldn't believe was Evans Snipe, was helpful in allowing me to see compartments usually unavailable for public viewing.) In 2011 I spent a day aboard the modern-day destroyer USS *Kidd* and was grateful for the opportunity. Later that same year, the USS *McClusky* crew invited me to visit their ship for research. How lucky I have been to live near a navy town! Over the years I often sat down with several retired and former U.S. Navy officers who happened to live close by and helped me better understand the navy of the 1960s. Special thanks to Tom Lettington, Joe Quinn, and Gus Denecamp for answering all of my questions. Former Texas Tech Vietnam Archives researcher Robert Tidwell was very helpful in providing documents about the *Evans*. Over the years Tidwell, whose enlightening dissertation covered the *Melbourne-Evans* collision, has become a strong supporter of this project. Thank you Rob for all your assistance.

I want to extend thanks to the Village of Niobrara, which invited me to spend two days at their town museum and encouraged me along. To Niobrara Tribune editor Valerie Zach, thank you for your hospitality and feature article—how else would everybody know about this stranger in town?

In putting this book together I often had to leave my home and my children to concentrate on the work. I am grateful for friends Marine Lieutenant Colonel Chris Brewster, Esq., and Kimberly Primerano, who allowed me to stay in their homes for weekends at a time to write. Several people helped me care for my children while I worked on this book: my mother Zelmira Enriquez and our longtime babysitter and dear friend Mary Cline.

Several friends and colleagues helped contribute to the book. Janice Loll put her artistic know-how to work in helping with some of the more technical aspects of putting this project together. Photographer Lisa Gisczinski is another who deserves thanks and praise. Dora Vlassakis and Vincent Gragnani helped with research in Washington, D.C. and the New York City Public Library, respectively.

Several people read versions of the book and provided feedback. Thank you Kristy Mangan and, of course, my husband David Esola. My cousin Carlos Juarez, a newspaper copyeditor, not only encouraged me along, but also read through the earlier work and again, the final manuscript to catch those last-minute things that nobody else saw. My editor Miranda Ottewell saved me from a wealth of embarrassment—thank you for your hard work and eye for detail. Much thanks to Mill City Press for putting together this final project and putting up with me.

This book has been a labor of love for me and I could not have done it without the love and support of the ones I cherish. My family in Philadelphia and beyond was always supportive, believing in me, telling me how proud they were even though the book was just an idea, or merely a stack of index cards. To my children Salvatore and Santiago, thank you for all the hugs and kisses as I worked on what we all referred to as the book about "the 754 boat." To my husband, I don't know where to begin. In 2010 I came home from a newspaper assignment and told him I wanted to write a book and that I needed to go to Niobrara, Nebraska, to which he replied not "where?!" but "when do you want to go?" David, you encouraged me from day one and put up with me for four years of research, interviews, trips, writing, rewriting, editing, frustration, emotions, and more. I love you dearly and thank God everyday for you and our boys. Your love and steadfast support helped me see this book to its completion.

READING GROUP GUIDE

DISCUSSION QUESTIONS

1. The beginning of the book takes readers to the Vietnam Veterans Memorial in Washington, D.C. Today, the memorial is among the most visited in the capital. Why is the Vietnam Wall so important? Why was it so controversial? Why did it become so popular? Why would it be so painful to not see a name one expected to be engraved there?

2. One of themes in *American Boys* is the Army draft. How do you think the draft affected this generation? How do you think it helped bring protests that ultimately brought an end to the Vietnam War? Do you think the American military ought to reinstate a draft?

3. Is the statement "War was a boy's thing, a boy's dream" still true today? How have times changed? How did Vietnam shape America's view on the military?

4. Why do you think Master Chief Lawrence Reilly was so cynical about the Tonkin Gulf incident? Explain how World War II may have shaped the chief's views on the Navy and Vietnam War.

5. Eunice Sage was worried about her sons being together. Ernest Sage was happy they were not in the Army. The *Melbourne-Evans* collision was a freak accident. How do you feel about the Sages decision to serve together? Do you think the Navy should not allow this? Why do you think brothers want to serve together?

6. Regarding the premonitions, are you a believer in such foreboding sentiments? Do you think dread weighed heavy on the sailors as they set sail for Vietnam once again? Do you think the death toll from Vietnam, then between 200 and 300 dead a week, affected the mindsets of some?

7. There are two intimate scenes in the book involving President Richard Nixon. One is on the morning of his first day as president in 1969 looking at Vietnam casualties and another when he was leaving the Pacific Theater in 1944, overlooking an American cemetery at Wake Island. What did these moments say about Nixon?

8. What are your feelings about Captain Albert McLemore? Do you have sympathy for him? What about Captain John Stevenson? What did you think about their first encounter—mutual apologies—immediately after the collision?

9. Do you think it was right for Ronald Ramsey to not testify at the Board of Inquiry? What do you think this revealed about this individual? Ramsey disappeared from the radar after his court martial and has never been known to make contact with the relatives of the lost 74. Would you?

10. Admiral Jerome King likely knew the USS *Frank E. Evans* was at fault from the beginning since the destroyer turned into the path of the carrier. What did you think of King's actions during the inquiry? Did you agree with the way he

handled the proceedings? Do you think it was a conflict of interest for him?

11. Do you think *Life* magazine's decision to not run the photo essay on the Sages was a good decision? How did this foreshadow what would happen the to *Evans* story later on?

12. Many of the Australians and Americans who survived the collision have post-traumatic stress disorder and many suffer from survivor guilt. Some of them say talking about the ordeal helps tremendously. Why do you think that is?

13. The United States Navy was struggling throughout the late 1960s and Vietnam had a part in those struggles, from morale issues to the fleet's old, overworked warships. Do you think the collision was related to the Vietnam War? Do you believe the statement: had there been no Vietnam War, there would have not been a collision?

14. How do you think the Battle for Hamburger Hill and other events of May and June 1969 helped obscure the *Evans* disaster?

15. The USS *Frank E. Evans* was a warship that coasted in and out of the Vietnam War combat zone from 1965 until her sinking. She sank an estimated 125 miles outside of the zone. Why do you think the families and veterans thought the names of the 74 sailors killed on June 3, 1969 would be on the Vietnam Wall? Do you think they belong there?

16. What did you think of Louise Esola's experience with Eunice Sage? Would you have left Eunice's apartment given the woman's first assertions that she did not remember her sons, nor did she keep photographs around? What did you think about Eunice going into the pantry to retrieve

a cooking pot? What did that mean to her? What do you think about the author's decision to tell Ron Stever how his twin brother Jon was likely killed? Would you have done the same? Why do you think people need to know how a loved one died?

17. What do you think about Frances' dream? Why do you think the reunions have been so well attended by relatives of the lost 74?